NOLO *and* USA TODAY

NOLO
YOUR LEGAL COMPANION

For more than 35 years, Nolo has been helping ordinary folks who want to answer their legal questions, create their own documents, or work with a lawyer more efficiently. Nolo.com provides quick information about wills, house buying, credit repair, starting a business—and just about anything else that's affected by the law. It's packed with free articles, legal updates, resources, and a complete catalog of Nolo books and software.

To find out about any important legal or other changes to this book's contents, sign up for our free update service at nolo.com/legalupdater or go to nolo.com/updates. And to make sure that you've got the most recent edition of this book, check Nolo's website or give us a call at 800-728-3555.

USA TODAY
The Nation's Newspaper

USA TODAY, the nation's largest circulation newspaper, was founded in 1982. It has nearly 3.9 million readers daily, making it the most widely read newspaper in the country.

USATODAY.com adds blogs, interactive graphics, games, travel resources, and trailblazing network journalism, allowing readers to comment on every story.

1ST EDITION

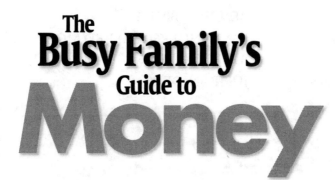

The
Busy Family's
Guide to
Money

by USA TODAY money experts
Sandra Block, Kathy Chu & John Waggoner

First Edition	FEBRUARY 2008
Editor	ILONA BRAY
Cover & Book Design	SUSAN PUTNEY
Proofreading	ROBERT WELLS
Index	JANET PERLMAN
Printing	DELTA PRINTING SOLUTIONS, INC.

USA TODAY CONTRIBUTORS

Book Editor	BEN NUSSBAUM
Contributing Editors	JIM HENDERSON, FRED MONYAK, AND GERI TUCKER
Special thanks to	JULIE SNIDER

Block, Sandra.
   The busy family's guide to money / by Sandra Block, Kathy Chu, and John Waggoner.
     p. cm.
   ISBN-13: 978-1-4133-0836-5 (pbk.)
   ISBN-10: 1-4133-0836-8 (pbk.)
   1. Finance, Personal. 2. Family--Economic aspects. I. Chu, Kathy. II. Waggoner, John M. III. Title.
HG179.B5547 2008
332.024--dc22

                     2007035638

For information on bulk purchases or corporate premium sales, please contact Nolo's Sales Department. For academic sales or textbook adoptions, ask for Academic Sales. Call 800-955-4775 or write to Nolo, 950 Parker Street, Berkeley, CA 94710.

About the Authors

Authors **Sandra Block, Kathy Chu,** and **John Waggoner** are highly regarded financial writers for USA TODAY. Together they have decades of experience in helping America's readers understand complex financial matters in order to make wise personal decisions.

Sandra Block is a personal finance columnist/reporter for USA TODAY's "Money" section. Her "Your Money" column appears every Tuesday in the newspaper and online at USATODAY.com. She joined USA TODAY as a markets reporter in 1995 and then moved to the personal finance team in 1996.

Prior to joining USA TODAY Block also worked as a personal finance reporter for the *Akron Beacon Journal* in Akron, Ohio; held a Knight-Bagehot Fellowship at Columbia University in New York; and was a reporter for Dow Jones News Service in Washington, DC.

Kathy Chu is a reporter for USA TODAY who has written about financial topics from credit card fees to Hurricane Katrina's economic toll on businesses and homeowners. Before working at the paper, she covered personal finance, corporate bankruptcy, and the aftermath of September 11 for Dow Jones News Service.

She has also written for *The Wall Street Journal, Asian Wall Street Journal,* and *Newsday,* and worked on LIFE Magazine's "Year in Pictures" and the European edition of a 1997 Fodor's travel guide. Kathy was a 2006 finalist for the Online Journalism Award and a 2004 recipient of a business-reporting award from the Newswomen's Club of New York.

John Waggoner is USA TODAY's investing columnist, and also covers personal finance, the stock market, and the economy. His investments column runs in a dozen newspapers via Gannett News Service. John writes an online question-and-answer column on USATODAY.com, and is a regular commentator for PBS's *Nightly Business Report.* He won the Strong/Medill Financial Writers and Editors Award for spot reporting in 2001.

Waggoner is author of *Money Madness: Strange Schemes and Extraordinary Manias On and Off Wall Street* (Business One Irwin), co-author of *The Parents' Guide to Money*, an interactive CD-ROM (Vertigo Development), and author of *The Fast Forward MBA in Investing* (John Wiley and Sons).

Before joining USA TODAY in September 1989, Waggoner was senior editor at *The Independent Investor*, an investment advisory newsletter. Prior to that, Waggoner was senior editor at The Donoghue Organization.

Table of Contents

Your Money Management Companion

Given everything parents have to do, it's no wonder that most of us feel both chronically anxious about money and chronically short of time to do anything about it. Who has time to make a detailed budget, read up on hot stocks, and figure out the smartest ways to save for retirement and the kids' college—when what we really need to do by tomorrow is write checks for the credit card and electric bills?

It's not that we lack for information or advice. In fact, the sheer volume of material on websites and in print, not to mention well-intentioned tips from relatives and friends, can be overwhelming.

But you do need good information if you're going to make smart financial decisions—decisions that can profoundly affect your family's future. That's where this book comes in. It contains a lot of nuts-and-bolts information about saving, spending, and investing. But not, we hope, too much information.

We've tried to concentrate on the things that every family needs to know, like:

- budgeting basics—just enough to get to know where your money's going
- socking away a reasonable fund for emergencies
- saving for retirement, including some ways you could easily overlook
- saving for college in a way that saves on taxes and gives you the most flexibility
- making smart decisions about your biggest purchase: your home

- investing with a simple strategy that will pay off in the long term, and
- protecting your family with insurance and some basic estate planning.

Sometimes, just getting started is the hardest part. So this book is organized as a series of steps. We'll let you know what steps are most important—and what can wait until you have more time, money, or both. You'll probably be pleasantly surprised to discover that you really can get a handle on your finances and start thinking about your financial future with confidence.

If you've tried before to tackle financial matters but given up, or you've just avoided the topic, you're certainly not alone. Most people haven't done much financial planning at all. Now's the time to stop worrying about what you haven't done and get to work. This book can help, with hands-on, practical advice. We hope it's a valuable companion along your path to a worry-free financial future. ●

Just You Two: Talk About Your Approach to Money

Here's a little experiment to try on your friends: Ask what words or thoughts come into their heads when they hear the word "money." Their answers are likely to range from "freedom" to "dirty word" to "something I need more of."

You'll soon realize that people's associations with money go far beyond the green stuff in their wallets. How people acquire, use, and spend money reflects a whole realm of deeply held values and habits. Different (and equally well-intentioned) people might believe, for example, that it's their duty to consume minimal resources and give lots to good causes, or to earn a lot to support a family, or to spend a lot to boost small businesses and the local economy.

What about you and your spouse or partner? Are you on the same wavelength when it comes to money? For many couples, financial matters are the number one source of conflict. As Kathy says, "Money is a touchy subject. It might mean financial freedom to one member of a couple—the one who runs out to put a down payment on that spiffy Porsche Boxster the moment the year-end bonus arrives. And it can mean security to the other partner—the one who pulls as much money as possible from each paycheck and directs it into a savings or investment account."

Whether or not money is a source of conflict in your house, sorting out your respective beliefs about it is an important first step to any financial planning. Your whole life and future are inextricably wrapped up in how you handle and approach money. This chapter will help the two of you by:

- providing a conversational structure to help you uncover and understand each of your beliefs
- suggesting a framework to arrive at your family's life goals related to money, and
- proposing a happy medium toward which you might work.

TIP

Single parent? Read this chapter anyway. The issues we raise are critical to think through, even if yu're doing the thinking on your own.

Compromise Is Key

According to Kathy's research about couples' approaches to money, if you have serious hopes of achieving financial peace with your partner, keep this in mind: Compromise is the most vital ingredient.

The first step toward compromise is simply to talk with each other about your finances. Trouble is, for reasons that baffle and confound financial planners, couples often spend more time planning their annual vacations than they do discussing their long-term financial goals.

Even couples who do talk tend to minimize their problems and exaggerate how well they're managing their finances. Major problems tend to include spending more than you earn and anointing one person the financial czar in the household, while the other person relinquishes all control.

What to do? First, acknowledge your problems. Not doing so can be an "absolute barrier to making progress on the road to financial security," says Greg McBride of Bankrate.com, a personal-finance site.

You also need a plan of action. A 2006 survey that the Financial Planning Association conducted for USA TODAY found that 60% of planners say the most valuable move couples can make to improve their financial lives is to set specific goals, such as socking away a set amount each month for retirement and the kids' college education.

That's critical, because, "How do you know you're on the right path unless you know what the destination is?" asks Dan Moisand, president of the FPA, whose members include about 27,000 planners.

 "Compromise vital to successful financial life; Couples must learn how to talk about money, goals," by Kathy Chu, April 28, 2006.

Conflict and Compromise:
How Each of You Behaves With Money

Below are a few questions for you to pose to one another. Each one concerns a different, common "money personality" type. Listen quietly to your spouse or partner's answers, and take note of where you are the same or different. There are no right or wrong answers. The point is to understand where the other person is coming from.

"The more couples discuss things and try to understand each other's perspective, the more they respect each other," said Bill Ramsay, a financial planner in Raleigh, North Carolina, in talking to Kathy. "The more they respect each other, the better their relationship works and the better their finances tend to go."

Eventually, your discussions and the exercises throughout this book may lead each of you to change some of your behavior around money. But don't expect overnight transformations or fundamental switches. For example, even if one of you knows you overspend on gifts for others, recognizing that fact isn't likely to change an underlying impulse to gift-give.

Any joint plan that you come up with will stand the greatest chance of success if it takes both of your beliefs and quirks into account, perhaps finding new ways to accomplish the same goals.

Question 1: Do you like thinking about money?

For some people, budgeting, saving, figuring out tax loopholes, and otherwise playing with money is actually fun. These folks are likely to study their bank statements for errors, scan the personal finance magazines, and follow the investment news. Other people couldn't care less. As long as the checks don't bounce, they'll choose to wash the windows and scrub the bathroom sink before opening a bank statement.

If neither of you really finds the subject of money interesting, give yourself big points for picking up this book. You're on your way to discovering that, dry as the subject may seem to you, it's intimately connected to things you care passionately about: your home, your leisure time, your children, and your future. And it's easier to learn the basics—just enough to make intelligent decisions with—than you think.

If one of you is more money-conscious than the other, that person is likely to feel like the sole occupant of the moral high ground. But before getting into an argument about it, try for a workaround. Assign the money-conscious half of the couple any relevant household tasks, such as balancing the checkbook and choosing investments, and give the other one some equally time-consuming jobs to do.

USA TODAY Snapshots®

Money and relationships

In a recent survey respondents said managing their finances is the biggest strain on their relationships. Complaints of respondents with financial issues:

Not being able to control partner's spending habits — 44%

Repeated questions about my spending habits — 21%

Partner not sticking to agreed-upon budget — 17%

Not agreeing on long-term savings goals — 14%

Partner is hiding money from me — 5%

Source: Quicken survey of 631 respondents. Margin of error ±4 percentage points.

By Darryl Haralson and Suzy Parker, USA TODAY 2005

Of course, we don't want to let the money-unconscious one of you off the hook entirely. If your behavior ends up hurting the very life goals and plans that you'll eventually agree on—for example, you can't be bothered to save credit card receipts, which drives your partner crazy and messes up your monthly spending goals—some changes are in order. Instead of punishing yourself, try to put some fun into the tasks that you hate, or even bribe yourself with a reward for every receipt you successfully bring home (chocolate kisses—or the real thing). Eventually, you'll get on board.

You also want to avoid giving too much control to one half of the couple. As Elizabeth Jetton, a financial planner in Atlanta, told Kathy, "You don't get to bow out of being involved. One of you may be better at handling the big picture, but you have to agree this is your goal."

Both of you should maintain a broad understanding of your combined assets and debts, and of how your money is being spent and invested. Knowledge at some point turns into control, so find some relatively painless way for the disinterested partner to stay clued in. Some couples schedule a regular candlelit dinner, then pull out the relevant financial statements and get down to serious discussion.

Five Tips for Talking About Money With Your Partner

Olivia Mellan, author of *Money Harmony: Resolving Money Conflicts in Your Life and Relationships* (www.moneyharmony.com) offered these tips to USA TODAY readers:

- Find a regular time to discuss money when both of you are relaxed and don't have pressing matters on your mind.
- Start the conversation with an expression of appreciation for your partner, whether about money or something else.
- Use nonjudgmental "I" messages, such as, "I feel scared that we're not saving enough for retirement." Don't say, "I feel you have a spending problem."
- Don't interrupt when the other person is speaking. Repeat what your partner says and acknowledge what he or she might be feeling.
- Reward yourselves for financial progress in a way that doesn't undermine your goals. Go to a museum, go on a bike ride, or devote a day to each other without phones or TV.

 "Compromise vital to successful financial life; Couples must learn how to talk about money, goals," by Kathy Chu, April 28, 2006.

TIP

Women, watch out for falling into old stereotypes. Kathy has found that, "In most relationships, men still oversee investments and take charge of most financial decisions. But there's a practical reason for women to get involved: They typically live longer than men. Divorce, too, tends to thrust financial responsibility suddenly onto women's shoulders."

Question 2: If you won $1,000, would you save or spend it?

This one is pretty simple. The world is divided into people who hoard money and those who eagerly spend it, varying only by degree. Whether you're more of a hoarder or a spender can sometimes be predicted by your childhood experience. People who grew up poor may be more careful about saving, as a hedge against later hard times. Then again, some of them are so happy when they finally get their hands on some money that they spend it right away. (We never said money psychology wasn't complicated stuff.)

The advantage to being part of a couple is that you can rescue each other from leaning toward extremes in spending or saving. One way is to keep

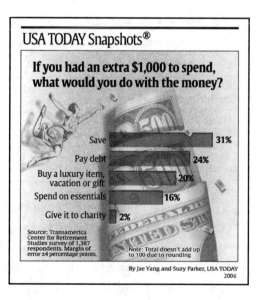

USA TODAY Snapshots®

If you had an extra $1,000 to spend, what would you do with the money?

Save — 31%
Pay debt — 24%
Buy a luxury item, vacation or gift — 20%
Spend on essentials — 16%
Give it to charity — 2%

Source: Transamerica Center for Retirement Studies survey of 1,387 respondents. Margin of error ±4 percentage points.

Note: Total doesn't add up to 100 due to rounding

By Jae Yang and Suzy Parker, USA TODAY 2006

your eyes on mutually held life goals. For example, a knee-jerk hoarder might admit that it's worth keeping your relationship strong with the occasional night out, and a profligate spender might nevertheless be willing to save for a retirement home on the beach. By creating a plan that encompasses your current, joint spending goals and your dreams of a good life now and later (which we'll show you how to do in Chapter 2), you can balance out conflicting tendencies.

Question 3:
Would you invest in my brother's "sure-fire" new business?

A big part of people's financial behavior comes from their willingness to take risks. And this, in turn, comes right from their internal levels of fear. These internal patterns are so fundamental, even physiological, that trying to talk someone into different behavior would probably be futile. Urging a non-risk-taker into high-rolling financial behavior, for example, would probably yield nothing more than sweaty palms and a speedy heart rate, even as it might be a source of grand excitement to a risk taker.

Mars and Venus again

The top areas where men tend to overspend are on high-tech gadgets, sports events, and equipment. Women tend to overspend on clothing and kids.

SOURCE: SURVEY THAT THE FINANCIAL PLANNING ASSOCIATION CONDUCTED FOR USA TODAY, SPRING 2006.

If you and your spouse or partner have different comfort levels when it comes to risk, try setting reasonable boundaries. For example, you might designate a limited portion of your income for the risk-taker to invest freely (short of taking it to the race tracks or Vegas). When things work out, the non-risk-taker is likely to be delighted, even impressed, by the other one's willingness to go out on a limb. When they don't, you'll at least both know that you planned for this possibility, and had set aside an amount you could afford to lose.

Question 4:
Does being part of a couple mean merging financial lives?

This question probably wasn't on anyone's mind a hundred years ago. Everyone-knows-who usually earned and managed all of the money. But now, you can throw all such assumptions out the window—or try to, if one of you has different beliefs than the other.

You've probably already noticed that living as a couple comes with many financial advantages. You need to buy only one house, one toaster, and maybe even one car. In April, you need to fill out only one tax return.

But that doesn't mean you need to merge all parts of your finances. Plenty of couples keep separate bank accounts for their separate incomes, or maintain their own credit cards. We know one couple that shares a credit card, but goes through the receipts to identify which purchases were purely personal, then pays for those separately, with checks from their separate bank accounts. Couples that take such measures often note that they reduce arguments, particularly if one tends to disapprove of the other's spending habits.

Merging all your financial matters is okay, too. But if one of you would rather merge your finances and the other one is opposed, look for ways to compromise. You might, for example, create a joint bank account into which each of you makes agreed-upon contributions from your separate accounts, then use this to pay joint and household expenses. Or if one of you wants to spend on the occasional luxury without the other one's judgment, that one could have a separate credit card, and agree to limit luxury purchases to a set amount. Some couples simply agree that you must consult the other before making any purchase greater than $500.

Separate Finances Doesn't Mean Secret Finances

Planning on keeping separate accounts? Don't go too far. In researching couples and money, Kathy discovered that nearly 55% of couples hide financial assets from one another, according to the FPA's survey of financial planners. This could mean, say, receiving an inheritance and failing to tell your spouse about it or opening a secret bank account in the Cayman Islands.

"If they have an account somewhere that they forgot about, then find it and come clean, then that's one thing," says Haran Levy, an accountant in Houston. "If they fraudulently do it, that's different."

Everyone needs some financial freedom. Agreeing to have separate bank accounts is one way to go about it. But hiding assets is not recommended.

"There's obviously a trust issue there that could go way beyond money," Moisand says.

 "Compromise vital to successful financial life; Couples must learn how to talk about money, goals," by Kathy Chu, April 28, 2006.

It's Not Just the Money: Agreeing on Your Life Goals

Think back to when you were first dating, and sat under a moonlit sky sharing your hopes and dreams for the future. (Violins, please.) Lately, however, you may have been too busy chauffeuring the kids to soccer practice or trying to catch up on sleep to follow up on those discussions. If so, now is a good time to bring them back. Every aspect of your life's plans—children, career, where you live, and when and where you retire—has a financial element to it. So let's make sure the two of you have your goals clear in your mind, and then we'll talk in later chapters about how you can meet these goals.

Here are some key areas to talk over:

- If you're thinking about having children, how many do you want?
- Are you happy with your current jobs or daily activities, or is it time for a career change?
- Would either of you like to increase or reduce your work hours?
- Are you settled on where you live, or might you move to a different city or buy your first house?
- If you already own a home, do you hope to buy a larger one later, or one in a better neighborhood?

- What changes can you reasonably predict in the coming years—for example, an elderly parent coming to live with you?
- What are your hopes for your children's education? Are you happy with the public schools, or is moving or sending your kids to private schools your best bet?
- Are there other significant expenses or purchases you'd like to plan for in the coming months and years, such as a vacation home?
- At what age would you like to retire? Do you want to move when you retire?
- When will enough be enough—that is, at what point can you declare your lives financially stable and materially sufficient, and perhaps cut back on work or financial worry?

After you've talked, slept on any new ideas, and talked again, write up a list or a short description of your key goals. For example, this might look like:

List of Goals

☐ Adopt a second child in two years.

☐ Terry cuts back to part-time work.

☐ Buy a home in a good school district.

☐ Take annual vacations in a warm place.

☐ Semiretire and open a B&B in Bali when we're both 55.

Don't be afraid of major changes. The first step toward doing the impossible is talking about it. And if your children are grown or nearly so, don't forget to talk about any big changes with them. You don't want to be like the family we know where the son assumed he'd take over the family farm—until he returned from college on vacation to discover that his family had sold it and was moving to a condo in Florida.

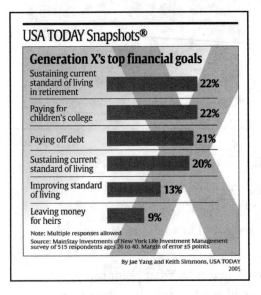

USA TODAY Snapshots®

Generation X's top financial goals

Sustaining current standard of living in retirement — 22%

Paying for children's college — 22%

Paying off debt — 21%

Sustaining current standard of living — 20%

Improving standard of living — 13%

Leaving money for heirs — 9%

Note: Multiple responses allowed
Source: MainStay Investments of New York Life Investment Management survey of 515 respondents ages 26 to 40. Margin of error ±5 points.

By Jae Yang and Keith Simmons, USA TODAY 2005

Depending on your children's ages, you might want to get them actively involved in some of your goal planning, perhaps after you've drafted an initial list yourselves. Their input, or at least a sense of having been heard, will be particularly important with goals that directly concern them—for example, if you plan to move to a different neighborhood in order to be in a better school district. And if they feel they've been made a part of the family's decision making, they'll be more likely to cooperate in your efforts, for example, to save up for a new car.

Does talking about retirement feel premature to you now? It shouldn't. You don't have to plan your retirement in detail, but knowing what you're aiming at—and making sure the two of you are aiming at the same target—will help guide your current financial decisions. It will also set you apart from the approximately one third of married couples surveyed by Fidelity (the mutual fund/financial services company) who gave completely different answers regarding what age they planned to retire at, their expected lifestyle in retirement, and whether they planned to keep working after retirement. If you're dreaming of retiring at age 62 and moving to a castle in Scotland, not knowing that your spouse plans to start a microbrewery in your garage at age 65 and never retire, some discussion is in order!

Isn't There a Right Way for Everyone?

Despite what some "experts" may try to tell you, there's no one-size-fits-all life plan, money philosophy, budget, or investment strategy. But there are certain themes you'll see throughout this book, which we've learned from financial experts and ordinary people over the years. Here's a summary:

Financial Wisdom Is:	Financial Wisdom Isn't:
• Realizing that money is a tool to realize your life goals. • Understanding that your time is too valuable to pinch every last penny. • Taking pleasure in parts of life that have nothing to do with money. • Putting off certain pleasures now if it will lead to greater, more meaningful happiness later. • Knowing when your life is materially rich enough.	• Losing your sense of generosity or charity. • Taking what isn't yours (like hotel bathrobes or your employer's stapler) in order to beef up your budget. • Chaining your life to a quest for an ever-rising standard of living. • Spending impulsively or with a sense of entitlement to daily rewards. • Clamping down on life's pleasures in order to squeeze out every dime.

Create a Family Spending Plan You Can Live With

For many families, spending money each month seems to just happen, as a byproduct of their usual storm of activity. A credit card payment here, an ice cream stop there, and by the end of the month you're either pleasantly surprised at what's left over or appalled at what's not—more often the latter.

It doesn't have to be this way. Nor do you need to become an accountant to take the reins of your family's spending. Simply take these four steps to remove the specter of financial uncertainty and bring you closer to meeting your life goals, big and small:

- find out how much money is currently coming in and where it's going
- zero in on the largest outflows and decide which can be changed
- get the family involved in setting specific financial goals, both sensible and fun, and
- track your success.

Although this may look like a numbers game, it's also psychological. You'll be evaluating what it truly takes to make each of you fulfilled and happy—and maybe even finding out that this doesn't take as much money as you thought. Almost everyone who goes through this exercise realizes that they'd like to reduce spending in some areas in order to support others. And as you make your new spending goals part of your life, you'll be developing new habits, which will soon remove any sense that you're on a deprivation diet.

USA TODAY Snapshots®

Home cooked
Average annual amount spent for groceries, per household:

Northeast	$6,049
South	$5,142
Midwest	$5,338
West	$6,051

Source: Census Bureau, 2003-04 data

By David Stuckey and Sam Ward, USA TODAY 2006

Just the Facts: Tracking Your Cash

The best way to understand your current spending and savings flow is to create a worksheet, something like the sample shown below, for a fictional family. Budgeting software (by Quicken, for example) or a spreadsheet like Excel can make this task easy. Another option is to upload your information to an online site like Wesabe.com or Geezeo. com (both free), which offer not only basic tracking programs, but a community of fellow users with whom you can share advice and support. But if you're a minimalist, you can create your own worksheet with a Word document and a calculator, or just by scribbling notes on a piece of paper. Do whatever is easiest for you.

RESOURCE
These websites have free budget worksheets to print and fill out, or budgeting software to purchase:
- www.personalfinancebudgeting.com
- www.planabudget.com
- www.quicken.com.

How much you bring in

Let's start on the plus side of your financial picture. Calculate your family's monthly net income—what comes home, not what you and your spouse or partner make before taxes and the rest. For most people this means a paycheck or income from self-employment. Some people's income also includes tips, royalties, rental income, dividends, regular gifts from family, disability payments, child support, or the like.

How much you spend

Start by listing all your categories of expenses, such as debt, food, rent or mortgage payments, entertainment, child care, and more. You might want to break some of these down into subcategories, like mortgage debt, student loan debt, and credit card debt. The greater the detail, the better, so as to remind you of easily forgotten items (like the camping equipment your child will need next summer).

Next, estimate approximately how much you must spend (or plan to spend) on each of these categories every month. It's a little artificial, because not all expenses will be monthly—some will occur weekly, irregularly, as a single lump sum, or even yearly. You'll have to play with the numbers to put them all into monthly terms, but doing so will help you picture your cash flow over a manageable time frame. For your spending information, look over old receipts, credit card statements, and if you use an ATM card or make electronic payments, your bank statement. Don't forget any automatic monthly withdrawals, such as for your DSL line, DVD rental service, or gym membership.

Receipts and bank statements won't tell the whole story, however. As Jean Chatzky, author of *Pay It Down! From Debt to Wealth on $10 a Day,* told USA TODAY, "Most people pull out $100 or $200 from the ATM and lump it as 'cash,' but they don't know where it goes." So search your brain and write down your regular and predictable outlays of cash, such as for parking meters, breakfast muffins, and vending machines.

Include on your chart any regular deposits you make into savings or retirement plans such as your 401(k).

For your outstanding credit card balance, enter the minimum payment as a monthly expense, but recognize that you'll want to work toward paying this off before too long.

(!) CAUTION
When dealing with weekly expenses, don't just multiply them by four. It may seem picky, but there are 52 weeks in a year, and some months have more than four weeks in them, so your calculations should take that into account. Let's say, for example, that you spend $50 each week to hire a housekeeper. You might think that you're spending $200 per month (4 x $50), or $2,400 per year (4 x $50 x 12). But wait: Your true annual spending is 52 x $50 = $2,600, a $200 difference. The accurate way to get your monthly spending on weekly activities is to calculate the annual figure and then divide it by 12 (52 x $50 = $2,600 / 12 = $217).

If possible, go through a full year's worth of receipts and records to figure out which expenses come up only once a year or irregularly over the course of a year. For example, you'll probably want to take an average of your spending on things like each family member's medical care or birthdays. Also look for significant one-time expenses like your car registration and insurance. If you're not using a software program to help you with this, simply take the total costs per year and divide by 12 to get a figure to add to your monthly budget.

Costs of children

Estimated average expenditures on a child from birth to age 18 by husband-and-wife families in the USA in 2005:

Total spent on raising a child
Low-income families
(less than $43,200 in pretax income)

$139,110

Middle-income families
($43,200 to $72,600 in pretax income)

$190,980

High-income familes
(more than $72,600 in pretax income)

$279,450

Source: Department of Agriculture

By Julie Snider, USA TODAY
2006

Sample Family Spending Worksheet	
Expense Type	Cost per Month
Household expenses	
Rent or mortgage, and any homeowners' association dues	$1,500
Insurance (homeowners', life)	$80
Property tax	$250
Utilities (water, garbage, gas, sewer, electric)	$160
Household furnishings (furniture, appliances, laundry and cleaning materials)	$90
Home office supplies (computer and printer, paper, file cabinets and folders, postage stamps)	$55
Household services (cleaning, lawn and garden care, pool maintenance)	$160
Phone and TV (including cell phone, cable, and DSL/Internet)	$145
Household repairs/decorating	$60
Food, beverages, and snacks (not including meals out)	$500
Personal expenses	
Health and dental expenses (insurance, prescriptions, glasses, co-pays, vitamins, therapy)	$80
Clothing and shoes	$100
Personal care (dry cleaning, haircuts, makeup, massage)	$50
Personal fitness and sports (yoga classes, children's activities and equipment)	$100
Pets (food, walking, grooming, and boarding services, veterinary care)	$85
Transportation expenses	
Gas and tolls	$100
Car registration and insurance (annual payment divided by 12), roadside assistance coverage (such as AAA)	$60
Maintenance/repairs	$160
Public transportation	$60
Entertainment	
Going/eating out (concerts, museums, restaurants)	$300
Books, DVD rentals, software and games	$25
Vacation	$250
Club dues or membership	$80
Gifts	$20
Hobbies such as photography or quilting	$40

Sample Family Spending Worksheet (cont'd.)	
Expense Type	**Cost per Month**
Other child-related expenses	
Preschool, private school, or college tuition	$2,000
Classes, activities, school expenses	$100
Day care	$0
Allowance	$70
Support payments	$0
Regular savings	
Elective retirement savings (IRA, 401(k))	$1,000
Rainy-day/special event savings	$20
Other savings	$0
Other expenses	
Legal or accounting fees	$30
Gifts to charity	$10
Other	$
Other monthly debts	
Car payment	$0
Credit card	$50
Student loans	$100
Unpaid bills on repayment plans	$0
Other	$0
Total of expenses and debts:	**$6,990**

What's left over

Now you're ready for the calculation that will reveal all: Subtract your monthly expenses from your income. Getting a positive number? Great, you're coming out ahead every month, and are ready to move forward with your goals, and possibly implement a savings and investment plan. But we're guessing you'll still want to make some intelligent changes regarding how and where you spend.

Or are you getting a negative number? Don't panic, you're not alone. Most Americans spend more than they earn each month—that is, they go into debt. But you've got some work to do. Keeping your spending levels within your income limits is a crucial first step to getting your family's finances on track.

Plugging the Leaks: Where Too Much Money Is Going

Almost everyone's completed Family Spending Worksheet turns up some surprises. As financial planner Elissa Buie, of Falls Church, Virginia, told USA TODAY, "This is where you'll find out if you have a Chinese takeout problem. People will say: 'Holy cow! I spent that much on takeout?'" Check your worksheet for patterns, starting with the highest dollar amounts. You'll start to notice:

- where you're paying too much for things you want or need
- where you're spending on things you don't really need or use, and
- where else you'd make cuts if you decided to shift priorities.

That just plain costs too much

Look for big dollar figures in your worksheet. The biggest one may very well be for housing, either in the form of rent or mortgage payments. Short of moving, you probably can't do much, if anything, to change this amount. And rather than resent these payments, remember that they're helping you keep a roof over your children's heads. But you might be surprised at which of your other major expenses could be reduced. See "Must-Have Expenses Can Be Cut," below, for advice.

Must-Have Expenses Can Be Cut

USA TODAY's Mindy Fetterman says it's not coffee or ATM fees that bust your budget. It's the cost of health, home, life, and auto insurance, your mortgage, your car loan.

In their book *All Your Worth: The Ultimate Lifetime Money Plan*, Elizabeth Warren and Amelia Warren Tyagi argue that Americans should "forget about the pennies and worry about the dollars" Says Warren: "I'm a bigger fan of cutting insurance costs over cutting cable TV. I'd miss it too much."

"People get their home insurance from their mortgage broker or realtor when they bought the house, or they shopped for it once ten or 20 years ago and haven't looked at it since," says Tyagi. "With a little bit of shopping, you can cut a lot of money."

Their tips for what you do need:

- **Health insurance.** You must have this, even if you think you can't afford it. Get a plan that doesn't cover routine costs, such as doctor's visits or immunizations, but covers catastrophic illness and at least some hospitalization costs. A high-deductible policy will cost you less.

- **Re-shop home and auto insurance.** If you haven't shopped around for a while, get on the phone. Try to "bundle" both policies with one company; they'll likely give you a discount. Ask about other discounts. Some homeowner policies offer discounts for nonsmokers. As with health insurance, get a high-deductible policy.

- **Term life insurance.** "This is one of those places where renting is better than buying," says Tyagi. Don't get whole life insurance, which combines savings with insurance, she says.

- **Disability insurance.** "Everybody needs disability, and getting it through your company is best," says Warren.

Must-Have Expenses Can Be Cut (cont'd.)

Here's what you do not need:

- **Specialty disease insurance.** Policies that claim to cover cancer or emphysema, for instance, are "almost always a bad idea," says Tyagi. Plus, "if you're already known to be at high risk for the disease (like being a smoker), they cut you out."

- **Credit card insurance.** "Ack! Ack! Ack! These schemes are scams, pure and simple," says Warren. People think that if they get sick or laid off, their credit cards will be paid off. No. The minimum payments will just be suspended for a time, and "you won't get any new credit when you're ill and you need it," says Warren.

- **Mortgage insurance.** Just as bad. "On average, mortgage insurance costs three times more than ordinary term life with the same amount of benefits," says Tyagi. Just get life insurance, and if you die, it'll pay for your mortgage.

USA TODAY usatoday.com "Must-have expenses can be cut with a little effort," by Mindy Fetterman, April 22, 2005.

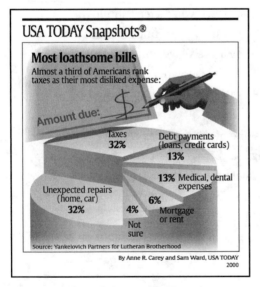

USA TODAY Snapshots®

Most loathsome bills
Almost a third of Americans rank taxes as their most disliked expense:

Amount due:

- Taxes 32%
- Debt payments (loans, credit cards) 13%
- 13% Medical, dental expenses
- Unexpected repairs (home, car) 32%
- 4% Not sure
- 6% Mortgage or rent

Source: Yankelovich Partners for Lutheran Brotherhood

By Anne R. Carey and Sam Ward, USA TODAY 2000

Perhaps some simple research will help you reduce how much you're paying for regular or major expenses. If so, you win. It's the most painless way to bring down your spending. Sure, the research can be a bit dull—no one likes reading over an insurance policy—but it gets a lot more interesting if you think of your return in terms of hourly pay. Let's say that with 20 minutes' reading and 40 minutes of phoning you were able to reduce your homeowners' insurance premium by $150—that's $150 an hour you'd have earned, or roughly 25 times the federal minimum wage.

That costs money, and no one's using it

A second revelation that might come to you while scanning your spending worksheet is that you're spending money on things you're not really using. A second car isn't a bad thing by itself, but if you use it only on weekends because one of you now works at home, you could live without it (it's okay to call a cab sometimes). And DVD rentals, museum memberships, and magazine subscriptions are fine unless your family's gotten too busy with other activities to make use of them. Eliminating some of these items will be relatively painless and will free up your money for other things.

While we're at it, have you trained everyone to turn off lights when no one's in the room? Energy costs can feel like a sneak attack on your budget, but you can take steps to control them. Other steps include replacing your bulbs with compact fluorescents, plugging drafts, replacing air filters on your heating/

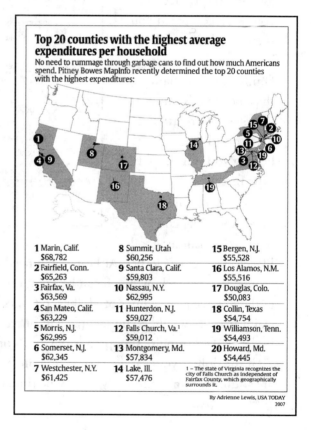

Top 20 counties with the highest average expenditures per household

No need to rummage through garbage cans to find out how much Americans spend. Pitney Bowes MapInfo recently determined the top 20 counties with the highest expenditures:

1 Marin, Calif. $68,782	8 Summit, Utah $60,256	15 Bergen, N.J. $55,528
2 Fairfield, Conn. $65,263	9 Santa Clara, Calif. $59,803	16 Los Alamos, N.M. $55,516
3 Fairfax, Va. $63,569	10 Nassau, N.Y. $62,995	17 Douglas, Colo. $50,083
4 San Mateo, Calif. $63,229	11 Hunterdon, N.J. $59,027	18 Collin, Texas $54,754
5 Morris, N.J. $62,995	12 Falls Church, Va.[1] $59,012	19 Williamson, Tenn. $54,493
6 Somerset, N.J. $62,345	13 Montgomery, Md. $57,834	20 Howard, Md. $54,445
7 Westchester, N.Y. $61,425	14 Lake, Ill. $57,476	1 – The state of Virginia recognizes the city of Falls Church as independent of Fairfax County, which geographically surrounds it.

By Adrienne Lewis, USA TODAY
2007

cooling system every three months, and insulating ductwork, hot water pipes, walls, and your attic. Also check the temperature on your water heater; a "low" setting, or 120°F, will usually provide all the hot water a family needs.

Maybe that could go, too

Want to free up some additional money? Then it's time for a talk with your family. Ask which expense items each of you would willingly cut first if you had to—for example, if your family's main wage earner lost a job. Maybe you feel like you've already pared your spending down to the bone. But even wealthy families tend to claim that they live "simply," so unless you're driving a horse and buggy, we're betting you can simplify a little further.

For a lot of families, excess spending comes down to consumer goods, like electronics or clothes. Although you need some clothes and toys, there's no limit to how much can be spent on such things (just look at the divorce proceedings of Hollywood stars, one of whom is sure to claim that life would be impossible without a $5,000 a month clothing budget). And impulse shopping is the death of many a spending plan. So if the dollars your family is spending on late-evening Internet orders are adding up uncomfortably, it may be time to assign everyone a limit.

Survey asks: What can you cut?

What financial planners say are the two monthly expenses easiest to cut back on.

Expense	Percent
Eating one less dinner out	81%
Buying one less takeout dinner	27%
Cable TV costs	22%
Cellphone use	18%
Gifts	17%
Other[1]	14%
Buying CDs, books	9%
Movie rentals	5%
Computer and software	4%
Health club membership	4%

1 – Includes buying a less expensive car, taking less extravagant vacations, impulse buying on clothes.

Source: March 24-31 non-scientific survey for USA TODAY sent to 5,000 members of the Financial Planning Association. It was completed by 260 people.

By Julie Snider, USA TODAY
2005

But before you start picturing yourself wearing the same old T-shirt every day, remember that just about anything you need (or really, really want) can be found at a discount, or used, with a little online research or by calling around. We like the idea of buying local—and sometimes if you call a local merchant and explain the deal that's available online, they'll negotiate a discount with you.

RESOURCE
Plug into good deals. Websites that can help you shop wisely include:
- www.consumerworld.org (particularly for electronics, but with links to all manner of information on shopping and discounts)
- pricegrabber.com (with price comparisons from different merchants, and consumer ratings), and
- shopping.com (with similar features).

After deciding which major expenditures you could eliminate or reduce, you might also want to tackle some minor ones. Whole books have been written on creative ways to save. The key is to choose methods that don't take more time than they're worth, and ideally are fun for you and your family. Examples include checking out books, music, and DVDs from your local library, trading hair-dye jobs with friends, cooking more at home, keeping track of free-admission days at your local museum or zoo, and much

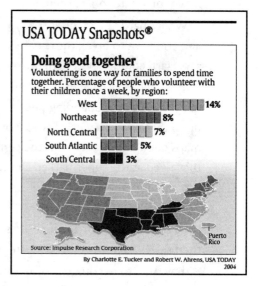

USA TODAY Snapshots®

Doing good together
Volunteering is one way for families to spend time together. Percentage of people who volunteer with their children once a week, by region:

West 14%
Northeast 8%
North Central 7%
South Atlantic 5%
South Central 3%

Source: Impulse Research Corporation

By Charlotte E. Tucker and Robert W. Ahrens, USA TODAY 2004

more. Doing family volunteer work is a great way to get out without spending money. Also see Chapter 4 for more tips on saving.

One Couple's Path to Controlling a $400,000 Debt

In a USA TODAY "Money Makeover," Kathy profiled Tim and Caren Mayberry. While the couple's combined income was $165,000, their spending—on gifts, dinners out, and home fixups—was exceeding their income, and their debt had risen to over $400,000 (including $285,000 in mortgage debt, and $125,000 in credit card and loan debt). But they were hoping to retire in ten to 15 years, sell the house, buy a boat, and do missionary work in the Caribbean. Here's what Kathy found, and what a financial planner recommended:

One thing they're not worried about is the cost of Caren's son Edson's college education. They've decided that college expenses shouldn't derail their retirement savings. "We basically told him that he can work his way through college," Caren says. "He can get loans; he can get a job."

Bill Hart, a financial planner in Jacksonville, is calling for a "lock-down" on discretionary spending by the Mayberrys for at least a year.

"What's hard about this is that you guys have developed habits, and you have to break those habits," such as eating out regularly, says Hart, cofounder of Retirement Strategies.

The Mayberrys have made a leap off the starting line. They've cut out most impulse spending, such as eating lunch and dinner out up to three times a week. Instead, on weekends, Caren Mayberry maps out a dinner menu for the coming week and buys everything they need at the supermarket. During the week, they try to bring leftovers for lunch.

"We spend $100 on groceries (for the week), instead of spending $100 on dinner for one night," she says. They've also resigned themselves to putting off home improvements.

They tried to negotiate a lower rate on a credit card that charged 16% interest. Their card issuer turned them down. So they transferred the balance to a card with a 1.9% rate.

One Couple's Path to Controlling a $400,000 Debt (cont'd.)

Hart says that if the couple can reduce their spending target in retirement to $65,000 a year from $100,000, they may both be able to stop working in 2021, when he'll be 65 and she 57. But this assumes they pay off debt by the end of next year and then save at least an additional $500 each month for the next 15 years.

The Mayberrys know they'll need to make some big sacrifices. Still, "There's a light at the end of the tunnel, and the tunnel is not that long," Caren Mayberry says.

 "Spending contributes to inability to save," and "It's time to break some expensive habits," both by Kathy Chu, May 22, 2006.

We Could Do That With Our Money? Changing Goals and Spending Habits

Almost no one is completely content with where their money is going. We're not here to lecture you, but to remind you that, with some trimming and shifting in your spending, you yourself could be happier with the outcome. It's partly a matter of will. If you want something badly enough, you'll make it happen. But first, let's figure out what you and your family really want.

After discussing with your family where you're now spending money and how that could be changed, draw up a new, draft Family Spending Worksheet. This won't be a final version yet—no one says you have to make every possible cut. And new priorities will no doubt occur to you as you read this book. Think of your Family Spending Worksheet as a tool, allowing you to see where shifts can be made.

Now, go back to those life goals that you discussed in Chapter 1. Will your revised Family Spending Worksheet start you down the road toward meeting them? For example, will it allow you to meet certain goals right away, such as paying down your credit card and buying an outdoor grill? And will it allow you to start saving, making larger life goals seem possible? (We'll talk in later chapters about how to actually save up for these larger goals.)

You probably won't be able to meet all your goals right away. But when you look at the possibilities side by side with your prospective spending changes—selling the second car versus getting out of debt, for example—you may decide to finalize pieces of your draft Family Spending Worksheet. Keep comparing and running the numbers until you come up with a spending plan that you and your family can happily stick to—for a while at least. Again, this will be a work in progress.

Don't forget to keep the kids involved. Otherwise, they may worry about why Mom and Dad are talking about money or are planning to cut out things they're accustomed to. Involve your kids in some of your goal shifting, just as you did in the original goal setting. Explain what you're working toward (a new house with separate rooms for each child?), and how the new family habits will help you all get there.

Kids over age nine may even be ready to take over their own, mini-portion of the Family Spending Worksheet, perhaps by being allotted a certain amount with which to plan Friday night's family entertainment. It may sound insignificant, but some kids get a kick out of assuming this kind of responsibility, and it helps them understand your struggles in stretching money to fit everyone's wishes.

Holiday Spending Need Not Eat Up Your Budget

When do most people seek credit counseling services? In January, after holiday spending sprees. Kathy suggests the following ways to avoid seasonal budget troubles:

- Sit down and figure out how much you can spend without going into debt. Do this before you hit the shops.
- Make a list, check it often. Once you know how much you can spend overall, set a specific dollar limit for each person's gift.
- If the perfect item for your spouse costs a little more than you planned for, pare back on someone else's gift.
- Compare prices at websites such as PriceGrabber.com and Shopping.com.
- Shop early. This will prevent that panic attack on December 24 that leads you to grab the first acceptable gift you find—possibly blowing the budget.
- Gift cards can keep your spending in check because they are available in various amounts. Before you buy, however, ask about restrictions. Some expire after a year or two, while others lose value if you wait to use them.
- If you've finished your holiday shopping, congratulations. Just don't undo that good work by hanging around the mall.

 "A holiday spending budget can help avoid debt hangover," by Kathy Chu, November 25, 2005.

Making It Happen: Living by Your Chosen Plan

Okay, so now you've got a draft Family Spending Worksheet. How do you implement it? Some changes can be made in one fell swoop, for example, if you refinance your mortgage or end a subscription. Others you may want to make automatic, for example by setting up a bill payment account that deducts your credit card or mortgage payments directly from your bank account. (How does this work with credit cards, where you don't know in advance how much you'll owe? You can normally tell your bank to pay either the minimum payment every month, your balance in full, or a fixed amount. And you'll get a message on your credit card statement telling you the amount of your payment and the date it will be deducted.)

In a nonscientific survey USA TODAY sent to 5,000 members of the Financial Planning Association (www.fpanet.org/public), the 260 who responded ranked "sticking to a budget" as the third most valuable step people can take to improve their financial lives, after "establishing goals" and "paying yourself first."

But what if you've sworn to cut back on irregular expenses, like restaurant costs or your garage-sale habit? And what if your kids said they wouldn't mind spending less on clothing if they could save toward a special goal? You'll all need to track your spending patterns, so that you know how far you've come.

Tracking day-to-day spending

Only the most diligent of budgeters will run home after shopping to enter all expenditures into a software program and print out neat reports. (But if you can, great.) Your more likely method is to keep a separate pad of paper with you, and tally up every expense you make in a certain category over the month. For the kids, you might want to create a separate tally sheet and show it to them, or for the more independent ones, dole out cash week by week. When you hit the limit, stop spending. If the pen and paper method doesn't work for you, you might have to switch to cash for a while. Draw out your cash limit in a certain spending category from the bank, put it in a separate wallet or envelope, and use that to pay for items until the cash is gone.

> **TIP**
>
> **Find ways to have fun other than shopping.** Planners say the Number 1 way people waste money is impulse spending on clothing, shoes, and technical gadgets. As financial planner Alice Bullwinkle of North Star Financial Direction in Lakewood, Colorado, told USA TODAY, "The spontaneous purchases really hurt. People shop for fun, and they don't want to go home without something."

Track your success over time. Take out your Family Spending Worksheet every few months, and rerun the numbers on your income and expenditures. If money is still mysteriously slipping away, try to figure out why. Is there an expense category you hadn't really noticed before? Were your goals too ambitious for the moment? Or have old habits simply set in? Whatever the issue, try to turn your and your family's focus toward the larger goals that you set.

Some people find that they basically have to trick themselves into cutting their spending and setting aside money. For example, they'll have Uncle Sam take the maximum out of their paycheck (not the best idea, since you're losing interest on that money), or put a portion of their salary into a separate bank account that's hard to access. Only you know what tricks will work to change your and your family's spending behavior. Just remember, the idea is to use the more extreme tricks temporarily, until you develop new habits that you naturally and willingly live by.

> **TIP**
>
> **Do you spend more around certain friends or relatives?** A study in the *New England Journal of Medicine* found that 19% of people who overspend chalk it up to peer pressure—while 65% of rich people say networking helped them get where they are. (Weight gain was shown to be similarly contagious among friends and family.) Don't dump your friends, but do examine whether or not they're helping you reach your financial goals—and don't go shopping or dining with the ones who inspire you to overspend!

At the other end of the spectrum are families who realize they've gone too far—their savings efforts are turning into straitjackets, and no one is having any fun. There will usually be at least one family member who feels seriously deprived and is making noise about it. In that case, you might want to adjust the spending worksheet, or simply create a new line item for "spontaneous fun." Then make sure everyone knows about it. Plenty of fun family activities don't cost a lot of money.

Government cheese

Urban legend, or real? It's true: During the Reagan era, this blended, processed, orange-yellow food-surplus cheese mix was provided to needy U.S. families. But no need to mourn its departure. No one seems to have good memories of its effect on digestion.

Once you've met your goals for a few months, celebrate! Don't blow the entire wad, of course, but plan a family outing that will remind you all of the benefits of your newfound planning.

Organizing your records for long-term success

Scribbled notes can take you only so far. Eventually, you'll need an organized system for keeping track of your family's spending—and, while we're on the topic, to manage other financial matters.

You may have noticed that our sample Family Spending Worksheet included a line item for office supplies. That's because every household that plans to be financially responsible needs to invest in setting up a basic home office. Good intentions will get you nowhere if you can't find the receipts that let you claim a rebate or a tax deduction.

Here's a basic system that works: Buy a filing cabinet (preferably one that locks) and manila folders. Then create folders with relevant titles such as "Bank Statements," "Car Insurance," "Car Maintenance and Repairs," "Credit Card Statements," "Home Repair and Improvement Receipts," "Product Manuals," "Homeowners' Insurance," "Tax Deductions [year]," and more. Keep them in alphabetical order. When new documents or receipts come in, file them right away—or at least put them in a special "to be filed" in-box.

In addition, a fireproof safe can be a worthwhile investment, allowing you to protect not only key documents but jewelry and other valuables from fire and theft.

Also find a location outside your house where you can keep copies of critical records, such as your house deed, loan, and insurance papers. Add a few blank checks to the mix. A safe deposit box is good, as is a secure place at a trusted friend's house (for weekend access).

USA TODAY Snapshots®

Holiday spending pushes the limit

What people say about their holiday spending habits:

I exceed my spending limit
40%
I do not set a limit
39%
I stick to my spending limit
19%
I spend less than my limit
2%

Source: eToys   By April Umminger and Julie Snider, USA TODAY
2005

When you receive your monthly bank and credit card statements, take the time to look at them before putting them in the appropriate file. With any luck, you'll get to watch the numbers on your bank statement go up while the numbers on your credit card statement go down. If not, that's another good time to find out what's up.

Adjusting Your Family Spending Worksheet

Over time, of course, your income and your needs will change. Major changes, such as a new job or your child's entry into private school, are a good time to revisit your worksheet. Go through the same exercise as you did initially, thinking about whether your goals and needs have changed, or whether certain goals can be met sooner or must wait until later.

If your income goes up, however, don't make the mistake that many families do and simply adjust all your spending to dispose of it. This can easily spiral into a situation where you're working harder and harder just to maintain your everyday standard of living. Keep your eye on those fundamental life goals that you identified at the beginning. Perhaps retiring early was one of them, in which case your pay raise shouldn't go straight to new clothes and redecorating.

Teenagers: More Independent, But More Expensive

Raising a teenager can put unexpected pressure on the household budget—so if your child is approaching the teen years, get ready! Here's what Kathy found:

Week after week, Eleanor and Todd Hugus of La Jolla, California, are reminded of the price of raising an active teenager. In April, their 13-year-old daughter, Brooke, went on a whirlwind eight-day East Coast tour with her history class to, as Eleanor Hugus puts it, "walk in the paths of our Founding Fathers." The cost: $1,800, broken into four payments.

"This was something we weren't anticipating," says Hugus, 49. "But you kind of have to think that she's going to be the only kid left at school; how is she going to feel?"

The Huguses have been saving for retirement and for Brooke's college education. But, like other middle-class parents, they've been caught off guard by something they hadn't planned for: the rush of expenses that envelops parents in the preteen and teenage years.

School trips. Clothes and shoes for rapidly growing bodies. Refrigerators to fill, and refill, for ravenous children and their friends. Prom dresses. Piano and guitar lessons. Football uniforms and cheerleading outfits. And, yes, iPods.

Planners, parents, share four important strategies to help manage the expenses that go with raising a teenager:

- **Budget, budget, budget.** Sit down at the start of the year and talk to your kids about what expenses are coming down the pipeline. If you know ahead of time about that pricey school trip, you can start saving for it—as can your teenager.
- **Educate children.** When young children are old enough to count, give them a piggy bank. Explain that if they save money for later—instead of spending it now on candy—they can get the remote-control car they really want. As your kids enter the preteen years, you can open a bank account for them and teach the value of using debit cards. (You can't spend money you don't have.)

Teenagers: More Independent, But More Expensive (cont'd.)

- **Give allowances.** You can help prevent teens from overspending by giving them a set weekly allowance—and not caving in to their pleas if they use all their money and want another $10 to go to the movies. Giving teens a regular stipend for clothing can also teach fiscal restraint.

- **Manage expectations.** Parents should be clear about exactly what expenses they're willing to cover, such as sports uniforms and athletic contest fees, and what expenses teens will be responsible for paying themselves, such as cell phone bills and car insurance.

 "Parents of teens ride waves of expenses," by Kathy Chu, May 15, 2006.

Draw the Line:
Take Control of Your Debt

ractically every U.S. adult is in some sort of debt, whether from a student loan, home mortgage, or credit card bill. Debt is such a normal feature of modern life that you can actually hurt your credit rating by not carrying enough of it. But there's a reason they call debt a "burden"—get in too deep, and it starts to take over your life, closing the doors to other financial options. Any expert will tell you that the first step toward family financial stability is to get your debt down to manageable levels, difficult or impossible though that might now sound.

This chapter will help you shed your debt burden intelligently and successfully, by showing you:

- how much debt is reasonable
- how your use of debt gets turned into a credit score, and why you want to keep your score high
- how to begin paying down your debts
- how to control your credit card debt
- how to manage your remaining student loan debt, and
- ways to stay on top of future debt.

RESOURCE
We're assuming you're not on the brink of bankruptcy. If your debt situation is this bad, please turn to other resources like *Solve Your Money Troubles: Get Debt Collectors off Your Back & Regain Financial Freedom*, by Robin Leonard (Nolo).

In Over Your Head?
How Much Debt Is Too Much

Handled responsibly, debt can be a sensible part of your family's financial strategy. It allows you to afford things you otherwise couldn't, by spreading out your repayments over time. In fact, a home mortgage—one of the most common and largest family debts—offers other benefits as well, by allowing you to not only buy a place to live, but to simultaneously build equity and avoid throwing money away on rent.

The key to making debt your friend, however, is to be sure your various monthly payments can be managed within your household budget. Before we talk actual numbers, check in with what you know already. Are you having trouble making payments on time, waiting desperately for payday, approaching the limits on your credit cards, or charging purchases because you have no other way to pay for them? While we're at it, are your financial anxieties affecting you physically? If so, the lights on your debt dashboard are already flashing red.

Different people, of course, feel comfortable with different debt levels. However, lenders have developed certain guidelines that help them decide whether to lend you money, and you can use these, too.

The lenders use a percentage called your "debt-to-income ratio." This simply means the percentage of your gross (pretax) income that goes toward paying off your monthly debts. For example, if your salary were $50,000 a year, but your debt obligations totaled $20,000 a year, you'd have a debt-to-income ratio of 40%—too high for comfort. (See "Is Your Debt-to-Income Ratio Too High?" below.) Not only would 40% of your income be tied up in promised repayments, but income taxes would eat up an additional $7,500 or so, leaving you with only around $22,500 a year with which to deal with new expenses and everyday life.

You can easily check your debt-to-income ratio using your Family Spending Worksheet from Chapter 2. (Divide your total debt by your total, pretax income, move the decimal sign two digits to the right, and put a percent sign on the end.) Or use calculators on websites such as www.bankrate.com.

Is Your Debt-to-Income Ratio Too High?

If your debt-to-income ratio is:

- **30% or below:** You're doing great—keep it up.
- **30% to 36%:** Good job; lenders may even offer to lend you more money. But you'd be better off focusing on bringing your ratio down below 30%.
- **36% to 40%:** You're skating on thin ice. If an emergency arises, you may have trouble making your payments.
- **40% or higher:** Uh oh. You're stretched to near breaking, and should look for ways to bring down your debt burden.

Aim for the Stars— Or at Least a 700+ Credit Score

Ever get the feeling you're being watched? When it comes to your use of debt—that is, your ability to juggle loans, make your payments on time, and take on an amount of debt that you can handle—you're right. Your track record, or "credit history," is constantly being monitored by three consumer reporting companies: Equifax (www.equifax.com), Experian (www.experian.com), and TransUnion (www.transunion.com).

This isn't like other consumer monitoring, which might, at worst, result in your mailbox filling up with baby clothing catalogues rather than surfing supply catalogues. Your credit history and a resulting number called your credit score (or "credit rating" or "FICO score," discussed below under "Get and interpret your credit score"), have become the means by which you'll be judged by almost everyone except your mom. Your prospective landlord, employer, lender, credit card issuer, car and home insurer, and others may all check your credit history and score before giving your application a thumbs up or thumbs down. (Thank goodness they still need to get your signature before running these checks.) They're all intent on learning whether you behave responsibly with money, and by implication, with everything else—or whether you're a bigger risk than they're willing to take on.

If your credit score is unimpressive, you'll pay for it—literally. For example, all types of insurers, whether for homeowners', auto, or individual medical policies, normally charge higher premiums to people with low credit scores. Similarly, lenders or credit card issuers jack up interest rates for people with low scores—and not only when you first apply for the card. Your credit card company will routinely check your credit score, and can raise your interest rate if it doesn't like what it sees.

> **TIP**
> **Why should your credit score affect, for example, your car insurance rates?** Joseph Annotti, a spokesman for the Property Casualty Insurers Association of America, told Sandra that a credit report "is a solid predictor of risk. People can get tickets taken off their record, DUIs get changed into running a stop sign—there are lots of ways to play with your motor vehicle record. It's less likely for a person who is inherently financially irresponsible to, all of a sudden overnight, change their behavior."

Think paying slightly higher interest is no big deal? Think again. Kathy explains that lower rates could save you hundreds of dollars over the term of your loan. For instance, if you have $10,000 in credit card debt with interest accruing at a 20% rate, it'll take you 33 months to pay it off, according to Bankrate.com. (This assumes you pay $400 each month. Most issuers set the minimum payment at 4% of the balance, so the minimum would start at $400 and drop as your balance does.) At a 14% interest rate, though, that debt would take 30 months to get rid of, assuming the same monthly payment. That's three more $400 payments, or $1,200, entirely due to your credit score.

Also check out the varying interest rates that Fair Isaac (the company that created the FICO score) reported people with different credit scores would pay on a $216,000 30-year, fixed-rate home mortgage in mid-2007, below.

How your credit score affects your interest rate		
If your credit score is:	Your interest rate will be:	Bringing your monthly payment to:
760 - 850	6.26%	$1,331
700 - 759	6.48%	$1,363
680 - 699	6.66%	$1,388
660 - 679	6.87%	$1,419
640 - 659	7.3%	$1,481
620 - 639	7.85%	$1,562

Source: www.myfico.com, August 2007.

Even if you think your credit history is pretty clean, you should find out what information is actually in your file. Do so now using the instructions below, and resolve to check again every year or so. Mistakes and mixed-up identities are frighteningly common—and there's little point in cleaning up your own act if someone who shares your name is messing things up. Kathy reiterates that, "Because negative information typically stays on credit reports for seven years, one mistake can lead to higher rates for everything from credit cards to mortgages and car loans." And if you've made some mistakes, such as paying bills late or defaulting, now is a good time to face them and turn over a new leaf.

Get your credit report and fix any errors

Federal law requires the big three credit reporting companies (mentioned above) to provide you with a free copy of your credit report—that is, a written summary of your credit history—once every 12 months. You can get a separate report from each company by going to a central website, www.annualcreditreport.com, or by calling 877-322-8228. It's worth getting all three reports, because they're rarely identical. Stay away from other websites and services, which may advertise a "free report" but try to sell you something in the process.

Get ready: Your credit report may go on for pages and pages. Focus on making sure the critical information is mistake-free, including:

- your name
- your Social Security number
- your addresses over the past several years
- a list of your creditors and the amounts you borrowed
- the results of any collections actions or judgments against you, and
- a list of your late payments.

All manner of mistakes are possible, from bits of credit history that aren't yours to a false claim that you paid a bill late. You may even discover that someone else is using your name to borrow money fraudulently, in other words committing identity theft.

What if your report says you were late paying a bill, but you're sure you paid on time? This isn't one to let slide. Creditors don't normally report late payments until 30 days or more have gone by. In fact, your record of paying on time accounts for approximately one third of your credit score, so fixing any errors is well worth your time.

> **Managing your money is so easy!**
>
> *You just use your credit cards! You pay your American Express with your Discover, your Discover with your Visa, your Visa with your MasterCard. Before they catch up with you, you're buried in a glorious crypt in Bel-Air!*
> — CAMILLA, CHARACTER ON TV SERIES
>   *THE NAKED TRUTH*

To dispute errors and get your report amended, contact the appropriate reporting agency using the procedure and forms it provides. You'll be fighting a bureaucracy, but hang in there. You do have rights under the federal Fair Credit Reporting Act ("FCRA"), including the right to see what's in your file and have any inaccurate, incomplete, or unverifiable information deleted.

If all three agencies misreported the information, you'll have to contact all three. Each agency's dispute instructions are available on its website, accessible through www.annualcreditreport.com. All three agencies offer (and encourage you to use) an online dispute process, but you may eventually need to talk to someone in person or mail in receipts or other documents to back up your claim. For phone calls, make sure to take notes on the conversation, including the date and name of the person you spoke with.

The credit reporting agency has 30 days, in most cases, to investigate your complaint and give you its written findings. If it can't verify that its version of events is correct, the agency is supposed to remove the information from your file at that time. If it won't, you have the right to place a statement in your file giving your version of what happened.

Also contact the creditor directly, to see whether it will help you solve the problem and advise the credit reporting company. Perhaps you can settle with the creditor for a lesser total amount, to be paid immediately. Likewise if you have proof of an error, it may be faster to go directly through the creditor than to correct it through the reporting bureau.

Get and interpret your credit score

The big three credit reporting agencies do more than compile your history. They also feed this information into a software program created by the Fair Isaac Corporation. The program gives numerical weight to factors like your outstanding debt, late payments, and delinquencies, then cranks out a number that we'll call your "credit score" (also called a FICO score or credit rating). See the pie chart below, "What Makes Up Your Credit Score," for details. Just as each company may have different information in your file, each may give you a different credit score.

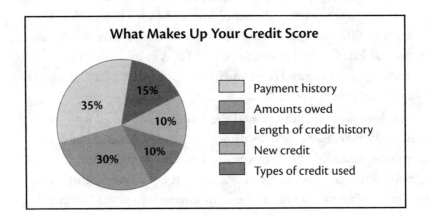

What Makes Up Your Credit Score

- 35%
- 15%
- 10%
- 10%
- 30%

- Payment history
- Amounts owed
- Length of credit history
- New credit
- Types of credit used

Credit Counseling Services Available, But Not All Reputable

Getting out of debt is hard. But Sandra found that if you sign up with an unscrupulous credit-counseling agency, your problems could get worse.

Reputable agencies make a sincere effort to help consumers get out of debt. But distinguishing between legitimate agencies and shoddy outfits that gouge and mislead vulnerable consumers is difficult, consumer advocates say.

Although a few states have cracked down on agencies for engaging in allegedly unethical practices, the industry is largely unregulated. There are, however, steps you can take to protect yourself. Beware of counseling agencies that:

- **Push you into a debt-management program.** In a typical debt-management program, the credit-counseling agency contacts your creditors and tries to negotiate a lower interest rate. You make a single monthly payment to the agency, which pays your creditors. In return, creditors pay the agency a fee based on the amount of your debt the agency recovers. Some agencies, eager to collect on payments from creditors, pressure clients into signing up for debt-management plans, even when that may not be in the individual's best interest, the CFA (Credit Foundation of America) says.

- **Dodge questions about their fees.** Be wary of an agency that says its services are free or that payment is voluntary, says Deanne Loonin, staff attorney for the NCLC (National Consumer Law Center). Some agencies claim payments are voluntary, then pressure customers to pay, she says.

- **Skimp on customer service.** Consumer advocates recommend using the "20-minute test" to evaluate a counseling agency. An agency that offers you a debt-management plan in less than 20 minutes hasn't spent enough time reviewing your finances, the CFA says. A good counseling session takes at least 30 to 90 minutes.

Credit Counseling Services Available, But Not All Reputable (cont'd.)

- **Promise the moon.** In an effort to distinguish themselves from competitors, some counseling agencies have launched extensive marketing campaigns. Many reputable agencies advertise their services. But be leery of ads that claim an agency can help anyone get out of debt, Loonin says. "For some people, the causes of the problem are much more complex than counseling or a debt-management program" will solve, she says.
- **Have a history of complaints.** You can check out a company at the Better Business Bureau website, www.bbb.org.

 "Debtors, beware: Not all credit-counseling agencies honest," by Sandra Block, April 15, 2003.

Are you one of the few remaining Americans who hasn't used much credit, with the result that your credit history is relatively thin? Fear not, Fair Isaac will find a way to score you. They'll do so based on nontraditional credit data such as your deposit account records, payday loan cashing, and purchase payment plan performance. This produces what's called a "FICO expansion score."

Unfortunately, you probably won't find your credit score in your free report. You'll have to pay extra to get it (unless you live in California or your state follows California's lead and requires that consumers be given their scores for free in certain circumstances, like when getting a mortgage). You can purchase your credit score either from the individual consumer-reporting websites or by going to www.myfico. com (about $16 for each company's score, or more if you want regular updates). Alternately, if you're willing to register at e-Loan.com, they'll give you your score for free (you can opt out of receiving their marketing emails).

Your credit score will be a number somewhere between 300 and 850—the higher the better. If your score is in the 700s, it's considered pretty strong. Most people are in the 600s or 700s.

Raise your credit score

A low credit score isn't set in stone. You can, with some effort, push your number up again. Take a quick look at the pie chart, and you'll see that the most important steps are the most obvious: Pay down your debts (to deal with "amounts owed") and make all your payments on time (to deal with "payment history").

By paying down your debts, you improve your score under "amounts owed" in more than one way. You not only reduce your overall burden, but you also reduce your "credit-utilization ratio." That's a credit concept meaning the amount of your actual debt compared to the amount of loan money you have access to on revolving accounts such as credit cards. (So if your total revolving debt is $2,500 owed on a credit card with a $10,000 limit, your ratio would be 25%.) The higher the ratio, the worse your credit score. Creditors like to see a credit-utilization ratio of 30% to 35% or less. Another way to bring the ratio down is to ask your credit card companies to raise your credit limits— but if you're struggling with a low credit score, they may say no.

If you have trouble getting payments in on time, see the tips under "Dig Out From Under Credit Card Debt," below. The later you pay, the lower your score goes. But why be so much as a day late?

> **TIP**
> **"You can make your financial lives easier by automating bill payments,"** advises Kathy. "The mortgage, student loans, and credit card bills will automatically come out of your account every month. You won't miss money you don't see. And you won't have to whimper about that $39 late charge you got hit with for sending in your credit card payment one hour past the deadline."

Ready to move on to the other slices of the credit score pie chart? That 10% slice devoted to "new credit" counts new loans or credit accounts as a bad thing, so your next step is to avoid taking them on. And to protect the 15% that represents the length of your credit history, avoid canceling credit cards that you've had for a long time. That length measurement includes the age of your oldest existing account and the average age of all your existing accounts—and if you cancel the account, it won't be factored in. Besides, cancelling accounts doesn't wipe out the negative parts of their history.

The last 10% pie slice, for "types of credit used," is the one you can do the least to improve on short notice. The scorers are looking for variety here—but if you don't already have a home mortgage or car loan, improving your score isn't a reason to go out and get one. In the unlikely event that you have no credit card at all, getting one would help. But in general, it's best not to open new accounts just to change this aspect of your scoring.

Let's end with a bit of good news. The longer you show good credit behavior, the better. Your old transgressions will, over time, be given less and less weight.

> **RESOURCE**
> **Need help patching up your credit?** See *Credit Repair*, by Robin Leonard and John Lamb (Nolo). It offers plain-English explanations and over 30 forms and letters to help you negotiate with creditors, get positive information added to your credit record, and build a financial cushion.

Pay the Worst First: Prioritize Your Debts

Now, back to your current debt situation. Take out the Family Spending Worksheet you prepared in Chapter 2, and look at your list of debts. If the only debt that remains unpaid each month is some portion of your credit card bill, skip to "Dig Out From Under From Credit Card Debt," below.

If, however, your repayment troubles are bigger than that, and you've been missing some debt payments, keep reading. You first task will be to divide your debts into "essential" and "nonessential" ones, so you can prioritize them for repayment.

Crisis management:
Identify essential and nonessential debts

Although repaying all debts is important, when you're in a financial crisis, you'll have no choice but to prioritize them in terms of which are absolutely essential to repay and which can wait. Essential debts are those that carry severe consequences if you fail to repay them on time. Examples of severe consequences include landing in jail (for nonpayment of child support or taxes), having your gas and electricity turned off (for nonpayment of utility bills), or losing your apartment (for nonpayment of rent). Also, any "secured" debt should be considered essential—meaning a debt for which you guaranteed

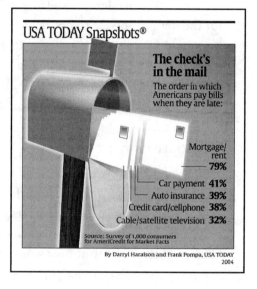

USA TODAY Snapshots®

The check's in the mail

The order in which Americans pay bills when they are late:

Mortgage/rent **79%**
Car payment **41%**
Auto insurance **39%**
Credit card/cellphone **38%**
Cable/satellite television **32%**

Source: Survey of 1,000 consumers for AmeriCredit for Market Facts

By Darryl Haralson and Frank Pompa, USA TODAY 2004

repayment by promising an item of property as collateral. A home mortgage is the classic secured debt: If you don't make your payments, the lender can foreclose on and sell your house, and claim the proceeds to pay what's left of your debt. Car loans are another example (beware the repo man).

Nonessential debts can't be ignored, but they can at least be put off momentarily while you deal with the rest. Your nonessential debts may include credit card bills, department store and gasoline charges, loans from friends and family, newspaper and magazine subscriptions, legal, medical, and accounting bills, and other unsecured loans. This doesn't mean not paying them won't produce any consequences. For example, you should at least try to make the minimum payments on your credit card bill, or you'll probably be hit with a late fee, not to mention damage your credit rating. Nevertheless, we're assuming your situation is difficult enough that you'll have to make some difficult choices.

A few types of debts or obligations may straddle the line between essential and nonessential. The consequences of not paying these on time may be painful, but not usually drastic. You'll need to do your research and consider your relationship with the creditor and your need for the item or service to decide whether to put these on your essential or nonessential list: medical insurance, car payments, court judgments, and federal student loans (See "Manage Your Student Loan Debt," below). In some cases, you may be able to negotiate with creditors to reduce your debt or stretch out your repayment period.

Negotiate with creditors

Hiding under a rock is the least effective way to deal with debts—but many people's fear or shame lead them to try it. A surprising number of creditors are, however, willing to reduce payments, extend the time to pay, drop late fees, and make other adjustments (such as reducing your insurance coverage). But they won't if you don't ask.

For example, if you've been a good tenant otherwise and your place will be difficult to rerent, your landlord might actually prefer lowering the rent (at least temporarily) to losing you. Even mortgage lenders are becoming increasingly willing to negotiate, to avoid the hassles and potential monetary losses of foreclosure (as discussed in Chapter 8). The key, of course, is to show that you're making an honest effort to pay your bills.

Writing a letter is usually the best way to start, preferably as soon as you know you'll have trouble paying. The letter should explain the problem. Perhaps you or a family member have had recent medical troubles or an accident, you've been laid off, or you've been faced with another emergency expense or tax bill. Explain what you're asking for and why you'll be able to handle your proposed new payment schedule or other requested accommodation—for example, because you've got a new job on the horizon and have reduced your other expenses.

Unfortunately, you may encounter small-minded creditors who insist you default (fail to pay) before they'll so much as negotiate with you. Still, that doesn't mean you can't open the lines of communication and ask for help in keeping the default out of your credit report.

A few creditors won't give you the time of day, no matter how strong your case for an amended payment plan. Don't take it personally, that's just the way they operate.

Plan and implement your payment strategy

Your next step is to add up how much you owe each month on your essential debts, then consult your Family Spending Worksheet. Can you set aside enough money each month to pay off this amount—preferably before having to face any dire consequences? Make this your top financial priority.

You'll probably need to go on an extreme financial diet. That's right, let your hair grow long, cancel subscriptions, drink only water with dinner, and use all the other tips you'll find in Chapters 2 and 4 of this book. Incorporate a month-by-month repayment plan into your Family Spending Worksheet.

USA TODAY Snapshots®

Spending habits women find hardest to break

Eating out or getting takeout **49%**

Shopping for clothes **28%**

Daily coffee fix **17%**

Personal beauty products **14%**

Note: Respondents could select multiple answers.
Source: Harris Interactive QuickQuery of 1,202 women, Nov. 21-23. Margin of error ±4 percentage points.

By Mary Cadden and Julie Snider, USA TODAY 2006

In curtailing your spending like this, you'll have to simply close your eyes to the levels of consumption around you. As Stuart Vyse, professor of psychology at Connecticut College and author of the book *Going Broke: Why Americans Can't Hold on to Their Money*, told USA TODAY, "Never have Americans, who have always liked their toys, been faced with a situation where their impulses are so hard to control. If you want a new widescreen TV in your house in one day, you can do it. The effort involved in shopping has been reduced to nothing, and everyone is made to believe they can afford anything." But you've already learned the hard way that this is a mass delusion—everything must be paid for eventually.

USA TODAY Snapshots®

States where fewest people pay bills late

States that have the lowest percentages of people paying late bills (percentage of people who were late on a credit card or loan payment at least once in the past six months):

South Dakota	16.0%
Minnesota	16.6%
Montana	16.6%
North Dakota	16.7%
Vermont	17.3%
Iowa	17.8%

Note: Data are for February 2005

Source: Experian (www.NationalScore Index.com)

By Shannon Reilly and Marcy E. Mullins, USA TODAY 2005

Pay off items on the essential list until you can start dealing with the nonessential debts as well. (See the next section, "Dig Out From Under Credit Card Debt," for help with that.) Eventually, you'll work your way through the backlog of debt, and can graduate to a stable balance of earning and spending. Then the main danger will be backsliding: See "Avoid a Relapse: Be a Smart Borrower," below.

If, however, you don't have enough to pay even your minimum, essential debt obligations each month, you'll have to move some to the nonessential list for now. But get in touch with those creditors, as described above, to see whether you can negotiate your way around the consequences of nonpayment.

Dig Out From Under Credit Card Debt

Most Americans carry six or seven credit cards and an average debt of nearly $10,000. And 13% of respondents to an online poll reported balances higher than $25,000, according to CardTrack.com. "Unfortunately," notes Kathy, "credit card debt has become a way of life for many couples who use plastic to spend more than they earn." And, as Greg McBride of Bankrate.com told Kathy, this "disconnect between spending and income" leaves "little room for saving or flexibility."

But that doesn't mean you have to follow the herd. Follow these strategies to reduce and control your existing credit card debt:

- **Pay the highest-interest debt first.** With average interest rates around 19%, but some venturing as high as 29%, credit cards are among the most expensive borrowing methods to be found. And some card companies have found sneaky ways to charge you high interest, like calculating interest based on your average daily balance from previous months, regardless of how much you currently owe. So if you use more than one card, figure out which ones are charging you the most, and start paying those off immediately.

- **Arrange to lower your interest rates.** As your credit score improves, you can try negotiating with each credit card company to lower your interest rate. Tell them you've been offered a better deal elsewhere! A less desirable option is to close the account and transfer your balances to a new card with a different company. But this may lower your credit score, because you're reducing the length of your credit history and taking on new credit. Besides, transferring balances isn't always as good a deal as the advertising pretends—many companies offer the favorable interest rate only on the transferred balance, not on new debt, and charge you a setup fee as well.

- **Close accounts with high rates and fees.** Interest payments aren't the only way the card companies make their profits. Some charge high annual fees, which you may not have even noticed, since they sometimes kick in after a no-fee first year. Some companies also pile on other fees—for example, $39 for a late payment or exceeding your credit limit. If you've got a card with lousy terms like these, you might be better off just closing the account. And we don't just mean cutting up the card; that may lead to yet another fee, for account inactivity. The only reason to keep a credit card with high interest and fees would be if it's crucial to maintaining your credit score because of its long history or high credit limit. But that's unlikely, especially since a high-cost card isn't helping you pay down your debt, which is also highly relevant to your credit score. To close an account, you'll need to send a letter to the customer service department and destroy the cards. If you can't yet pay off the outstanding balance, fear not, they'll keep sending you monthly bills.

- **Own a home?** You could, in theory, use a lower-interest home-equity line of credit to pay off credit card debt. It's tempting, because the difference in interest rates could save you thousands of dollars, and home equity interest might also be deductible on your taxes. But we don't advise using this strategy unless you're 100%, positively sure you can make the payments: You're turning your house into collateral, and you could face foreclosure if you fail to repay.

- **Close any account that you're delinquent on.** If you don't, the issuer may close it for you anyway. As described above, you'll need to write a letter, and expect to receive bills for what's left owing.

- **Always, always pay on time.** We've already discussed the serious damage that late bill payment can inflict on your credit score. Paying on time also helps avoid being whopped with penalty fees. If you've had trouble making timely payments in the past, try paying the bill the absolute minute it arrives, or setting up an automatic payment plan. If you don't like either of those options, and are paying by snail mail, at least give yourself a buffer of several days. Ever noticed how the U.S. mail seems to slow down mysteriously when it comes to bill payments? And it's no fun trying to convince the customer service rep that "I put the check in the mail a week ago, honest!" What if your paycheck regularly arrives later than your monthly payment due date? Ask your lender to change that date. For example, if you get paid on the 15th and your due date is the 14th, ask that it be changed to the 21st.

- **Don't be tempted to pay only the minimum balance.** As you reduce your credit card debt, your minimum balances will go down too (since they're normally calculated as a percentage of the amount you owe). But you're not being offered any big favors here. The less you pay, the longer you'll owe the credit card company money, and the more interest you'll eventually pay.

  Decide how much you can put toward each credit card every month (again, starting with the highest-interest cards), and then stick with that figure.

- **Get to where you can pay your cards off in full each month.** "Ha!" many people would respond, "What's the point of a credit card if you pay off the debt within a few weeks?" Actually, this is the perfect way to use

USA TODAY Snapshots®

Spending tax refunds

How Americans who expect or already received a tax refund say they plan to use it:

Pay off debt
26.4%

Save or invest it
25.8%

Other
7.3%

Buy products (cars, electronics, furniture)
18.7%

Give to charity
1%

Mortgage, education
3.4%

Vacation, entertainment
6%

Make home improvements
11.4%

Source: FreeTaxPrep.com Inc.

By Quin Tian, USA TODAY 2006

your card. You don't need to carry around much cash, you create an automatic record of your purchases, you qualify for any rebates or perks, and you build your credit score. Except in rare instances, no one should be using credit cards to buy things they can't pay for within the short term.

Get a Tax Refund? Pay Down Credit Cards

If you happen to get a tax refund this year, Sandra suggests investing it in something that will provide a guaranteed return of 14% or more: your credit card balance.

Applying your refund to your credit card balance can save thousands of dollars in interest. For example, if you invest $1,743 in an $8,488 credit card balance, you'll save more than $2,000 in interest over the life of the loan.

But why are you getting a sizable refund, anyway? A better idea would be to increase your withholding and put the money toward your debt. Everybody loves a refund. But if you're carrying a credit card balance, you're giving the government an interest-free loan at the same time you're paying 15% or more on your debt.

 "Don't blow that tax refund: Pay off your credit card debt," by Sandra Block, March 19, 2002.

Manage Your Student Loan Debt

Kathy observes that, "Getting through college and earning a degree is hard enough. For many, an even bigger challenge arrives later: paying for all that education." So what should you do if you're struggling to pay your student loans?

It depends on the type and source of your loan. You're likely to have a range of options, including reducing or deferring your monthly payments. Federally backed loans offer the most flexible repayment terms. By contrast, loans not federally guaranteed, called private loans, offer the least favorable rules: They often carry higher interest rates, which usually aren't capped, and fewer borrower protections.

"If you're having trouble making your payments, don't wait until it becomes a problem," says Mark Kantrowitz of FinAid.org, a financial aid site. "Call the lender early."

What you don't want to do is default. If you fail to pay for 270 days on a federal loan or 180 days on a private loan you're generally considered in default (unless the lender granted you a deferral). Your loans will be turned over to a collection agency, and you'll have a black mark on your credit record.

If it's a federal loan, the government can sue you, garnish your wages, withhold Social Security payments—yes, some people are still paying down student loans after they retire—and take your tax refunds.

Kathy offers the following options to keep on top of your student loan payments:

Repayment plans. Generally, you have ten to 15 years to pay off your federal and private loans. You can seek an extended-payment plan—of up to 30 years—if you need more time. Don't do that unless absolutely necessary, though, because you'll end up paying more interest over the life of the loan.

Your payment is based on your total debt, the life of the loan, and the interest rate; you can usually change your repayment plan once a year. Some lenders, such as Sallie Mae, will let you change your plan more often.

With private loans, you typically can make an identical payment each month, though that payment can rise or fall slightly with interest rates. Or you could have your payments rise over time under a graduated plan. Many lenders also let you extend the repayment period for up to 30 years. That will trim your monthly payments, but you'll pay more interest in the long run.

Most federal loans offer all those options. They also provide a payment plan pegged to your income; if your pay rises, so will your payments.

Deferrals and forbearance. With federally subsidized loans, your loans can be deferred for six months after you graduate; the government pays your interest during this time. Unsubsidized federal loans—such as Stafford loans that any student qualifies for—also let you defer payments, but interest will accrue.

Even after you've begun repaying, you have the right to defer payments for up to three years if you lose your job or suffer some other hardship. (If you have a Stafford subsidized loan, based on need, the government will pay your interest for up to three years.)

Borrowers with the highest debt loads and those with the lowest salaries are most likely to defer paying on their federal loans, the Education Department says.

You don't have such flexibility with private loans. You'll often get a six-month grace period after graduation. But you'll be charged interest—typically, at far higher rates than with federal loans—until repayment begins. And if you fall on hard times, it's up to the lender to decide whether to let you postpone payments.

Consolidation. This strategy involves combining all your student loans into one with the same interest rate (fixed or variable). The beauty of consolidation is you can lock in a fixed rate on federal loans issued before July 1, 2006. (Loans issued after that already have a fixed rate of 6.8%, so consolidation won't affect the rate these borrowers pay.)

You can opt to extend the term of your loan with consolidation, lowering your monthly payment, but you'll pay more interest overall. Be careful not to consolidate federal loans with private loans; if you do, you'll lose the borrower protections and flexibility of federal loans.

Lenders often let you consolidate all your private debt into one loan. Most of them, including Sallie Mae, the largest private student-loan provider, give you a variable rate that adjusts with the market. Citigroup is one of the few lenders that offer a fixed rate on a consolidation loan, based on your credit record.

Private-loan consolidation often isn't wise because of fees and high rates. "Generally, unless your income changes substantially, and the APR (annual percentage rate) on the new loan is better than the average of the loans you have, it doesn't make a lot of sense for most people," says Willis Hulings of the Education Resources Institute.

> ⓘ **CAUTION**
> **Married couples shouldn't plan on jointly consolidating their loans.** For one thing, it's a bad idea, leaving you both on the hook for each other's debt. For another, federal loans no longer (as of 2006) allow consolidation with a spouse.

Default. If you're in default on your federal loan, you can redeem yourself. Contact your lender and work out a payment plan. Once you've made at least nine to 12 timely payments—depending on the loan—you can apply for "rehabilitation." This means the default will be taken off your credit record.

If you default on private loans, you can emerge from default by making three consecutive on-time payments, according to the education institute. But this default will not be taken off your credit record.

Cancellation. It's nearly impossible to discharge federal and private loan debt through bankruptcy. But you can have your federal loan debt forgiven if you die, become totally and permanently disabled, or if your college closed before you earned a degree. (You can't cancel private loan debt this way.) Also, if you teach in a low-income school, you may be able to have part of your federal debt discharged.

Another option for chipping away at your debt—albeit an extreme one—is to join the military or AmeriCorps. The Army and Navy will repay up to $65,000 of your loans if you enlist. AmeriCorps will give you up to $4,725 after you've finished your service, to put toward tuition or student loan payments.

In high-demand career fields, such as health care, employers may also pay off

> *You know you've made it when:*
> *You're offered an AMEX Centurion card, widely touted as the most exclusive in the world. Membership is by invitation only, and it promises "highly customized personal services and access to elite travel benefits." But don't fret if your invitation is slow to arrive—annual fees are $2,500.*

your student loan debt as a recruiting tool. "Some hospitals in rural areas, to get talented people, will do this," says Howard Dvorkin of Consolidated Credit Counseling Services, based in Fort Lauderdale. "It's a very good deal."

RESOURCE
For more information on handling your student loans, check out:
- www.finaid.org
- www.projectonstudentdebt.org
- http://studentaid.ed.gov (an Education Department site containing details about qualifying for loan cancellation)
- www.studentdebtalert.org (by the U.S. Public Interest Research Group), and
- www.studentloanborrowerassistance.org (by The National Consumer Law Center).

Avoid a Relapse: Be a Smart Borrower

Having paid off your major debts, reduced your debt load, and cleaned up your credit file, you'll probably feel a halo is in order. And you definitely deserve congratulations, at the least. But don't use that as an excuse for a new spending and borrowing binge. Here are some tips for staying on top of future debt:

- **Consult your Family Spending Worksheet before taking on new loans.** Don't listen to what lenders say about what you can afford. They're more interested in their chances of profiting from you than in whether you can repay them without selling your engagement ring. Stick with the plan you created in Chapter 2.

- **Keep no more than one or two credit cards.** That's all anyone really needs. And if a card comes with rebates, frequent flyer miles, or other perks, use that card for all your purchases—but, of course, no more purchases than you can pay off each month.

- **Choose any new credit cards wisely.** Look for ones with low interest rates and fees (preferably no annual fee). Avoid retail and store cards, which usually charge high interest. If you're particularly cash strapped, look for cards with low minimum monthly payments (but realize that, because you're borrowing more money each month, you'll end up paying even more in interest than with a card that forces you to repay your debt faster). And what about those perks? Cards that offer direct cash back for your purchases are usually the best value. But don't pay high annual fees just to get a card with perks like frequent flier miles—the tradeoff isn't usually worth it.

USA TODAY Snapshots®

Staying on track

Which is more challenging to stick to?

55% A diet

45% A budget

Source: Kelton Research for Medifast. Jan. 25–29 survey of 1,000 adults ages 18 and over; margin of error is ±3 percentage points.

By Cindy Clark and Julie Snider, USA TODAY 2006

RESOURCE

Find a card that matches your needs: Comparative information and related advice is available at www.cardtrack.com, www.bankrate.com, and www.federalreserve.gov/pubs/shop.

- **Treat plastic like real money.** People tend to spend more when using credit cards instead of cash. As a result, you'll hear countless tips designed to reduce your access to your own plastic money: freeze a card in a block of ice, leave it in a can at home and sign it out before buying anything, wrap it in hard-to-remove tape or rubber bands, and more. But they all boil down to the same basic idea: Until you realize that credit card purchases are as real as any other, and act mindfully before whipping out the card, you'll never get your spending in check.

- **Don't make impulse purchases.** Not even if you find something at a 99% discount. If you didn't think you needed it before you walked into the store, don't buy it.

RESOURCE
Is there a compulsive spender in the house? Shopping produces endorphins for some people, and can be as addictive as drinking or gambling. Debtors Anonymous can help; go to www. debtorsanonymous.org.

Set Aside a Rainy-Day Fund

Ask any financial planner: One of the first and most important steps you should take to safeguard your family's financial stability is to set aside an emergency reserve fund. The idea is that the fund can be used either for a major unexpected cost (such as medical expenses) or to cover your family's basic living expenses if you or your spouse is temporarily out of work.

How Much Is Enough?

Exactly how much money you should keep in your emergency fund is open to debate. At an absolute minimum, however, it should cover your family's daily living expenses for three months. Six months would be wiser. Some planners recommend a full year, which is impractical for many folks.

Just how cautious you want to be depends on your personal circumstances and what it takes to give you peace of mind. If, for example, you have well-to-do parents who've always been willing to back you up in a financial jam, a three-month emergency fund might be just fine. If, on the other hand, you'd reach for your credit cards in an emergency, and would then wind up paying 15% interest on the debt, you'd be better off saving at least six months' worth. And if your income fluctuates—perhaps you're self-employed or make some of your money from commissions—you'd do well to have a bigger cash cushion.

USA TODAY Snapshots®

Many Americans unprepared
How long could you cover household living expenses with your current liquid savings?

24%
17%
14%
10%
19%
17%

Less than one week
One week to less than one month
One month to less than three months
Three months to less than six months
Six months or more
Declined to answer

Note: Total doesn't add up to 100 due to rounding
Source: LexisNexis Martindale-Hubbell's Lawyers.com survey of 2,318 adults 18 and older. Margin of error ±3 percentage points.

By Jae Yang and Marcy E. Mullins, USA TODAY 2006

TIP

Choosing between putting money into your emergency fund, your credit card debt, or your 401(k)? Start with the credit card debt. There's no point in having your own money sit in a bank earning 2% interest while you're simultaneously paying 15% interest to use someone else's money. Contribute to the 401(k) next. This is especially true if your employer offers a match—not taking advantage of it would be turning down free money. In the worst-case scenario, you can later borrow from your 401(k) (as described in "If All Else Fails: Drawing from Your IRA or 401(k)," below). But as soon as you can, return to the project of setting up an easily accessible, separate emergency fund.

Don't feel like you have to create your entire fund this week. Most couples start by setting aside a monthly amount—for example, 5% of their paychecks, or another amount that lets them build up one month's worth of living expenses over the course of a year.

If you're not in the habit of saving, how do you even begin? Hopefully, you've already begun to find the answer yourself, as you monitor your monthly spending, and look for areas you can trim. You'll find more tips below.

Now, for the logistics of setting up such a fund. John advises, "Don't count on yourself to write a check each week to your savings account. Set up an automatic deduction program, from your checking account to your savings. Even better, see if you can arrange to have money shifted directly from your paycheck to a savings account." This will probably go by the name

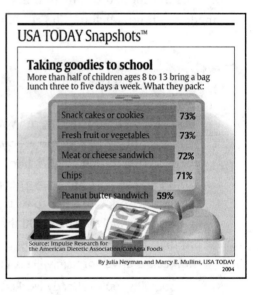

USA TODAY Snapshots™

Taking goodies to school
More than half of children ages 8 to 13 bring a bag lunch three to five days a week. What they pack:

Snack cakes or cookies	73%
Fresh fruit or vegetables	73%
Meat or cheese sandwich	72%
Chips	71%
Peanut butter sandwich	59%

Source: Impulse Research for the American Dietetic Association/ConAgra Foods

By Julia Neyman and Marcy E. Mullins, USA TODAY 2004

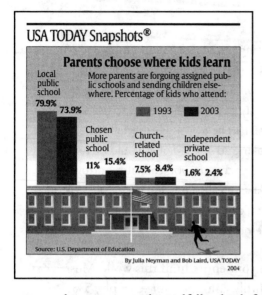

USA TODAY Snapshots®

Parents choose where kids learn

More parents are forgoing assigned public schools and sending children elsewhere. Percentage of kids who attend:

■ 1993 ■ 2003

Local public school
79.9% 73.9%

Chosen public school
11% 15.4%

Church-related school
7.5% 8.4%

Independent private school
1.6% 2.4%

Source: U.S. Department of Education

By Julia Neyman and Bob Laird, USA TODAY 2004

"automated payroll deduction." It's similar to direct deposit, but means your employer agrees to put part of your paycheck, rather than the whole thing, into a savings or checking account. (Check with your employer to find out what it can offer you.)

If you can save even faster than the 5% or whatever amount you've chosen, by all means do so. And if you receive any promotions, work bonuses, or other unexpected windfalls, think first about adding them to your emergency fund—before you get used to spending the extra money.

What's the Worst It Could Be? Talking Dollars

Let's see: Braces will usually run you around $5,000. Full-time day care costs over $600 per month on average. Private schooling for kindergarten through high-school graduation can cost anywhere from $3,000 to $27,000 a year (depending partly on where you live—New York City tends to be the highest). The median price of a house was well over $200,000 the last time we looked. A new roof on that house will probably cost at least $12,000. And an "average" new car to drive home in will set you back around $27,000.

Hopefully, you've already worked some of these items into your family spending plan, in Chapter 2. But no matter how carefully you budget, inevitably some surprises or changed plans will come along and threaten to eat up your cash on hand.

USA TODAY's Financial Diet Tips

To help families cut spending and improve their savings, USA TODAY developed a set of "fiscal exercises" with the help of Elissa Buie, a Falls Church, Virginia, financial planner. The idea is that whatever money you don't spend as a result of these tips, you'll put into a savings account. Here are some of our favorites:

- Pick one luxury item that you pay for each month and eliminate or reduce it. Skip a massage/facial/manicure/car wash/maid service.

- Look for some service you can trade. Join a babysitting co-op or cat/dog/house sit for a neighbor in exchange for the same.

- Take your lunch to work for a week instead of buying it out.

- If you're not using all your cell phone minutes each month (putting you among the 40% of people who pay for minutes they don't use), renegotiate your cell phone contract or switch providers.

- Cable TV, satellite TV, TiVo, on-demand movies—you might not be using all these services enough to justify what you're spending for them. "The average American spends $90 a month on cable for hundreds of channels, but they really only watch ten," says Bach, author of *Start Late, Finish Rich*. "There's a basic cable plan for $29.95. Just making that one switch would save you $60 a month, or over $720 a year."

- Have the house cleaned every three weeks instead of every two.

- Cut your own grass for a few months.

 "Kids college fund can wait, but your future security can't," by Sandra Block, May 13, 2005; "Financial diet tip #1: Carve up your expenses," and "Must-have expenses can be cut with a little effort," both by Mindy Fetterman, April 22, 2005.

Couple's First Step: Get Emergency Fund Going

USA TODAY reporter Christine Dugas profiled Tony Lai and Sunisa Chanyaputhipong, a couple married since 2004. He's a family therapist and she's a doctor, giving them a combined annual income of $151,190. Their long-term goals include having two children and saving enough to both send the kids to college and retire at age 55.

"In many ways, Tony Lai and Sunisa Chanyaputhipong are model individuals," says Barbara Steinmetz, a financial planner in Burlingame, California. They're trying to pay down their mortgages. They have no credit card debt. And even though they don't have a huge investment portfolio, they are maximizing their contributions to Roth IRAs and Chanyaputhipong's 403(b) plan.

But while the couple have set several worthy financial goals, Steinmetz feels they lack a thoughtful strategy to reach them. And despite all their objectives, they have no emergency cash fund.

So now is an excellent time to get organized. Steinmetz's advice:

They should stop making extra payments on their second mortgage until they establish an emergency cash fund. "This should be in a liquid investment with check-writing privileges and should equal between three and six months of living expenses," Steinmetz says.

The couple wonder if Lai should stay at home once they have children. Steinmetz's response is to suggest that the couple sock away all of Lai's income for awhile to see if they can manage their finances without it.

Overall, the couple appreciated Steinmetz's advice. "Her comments encouraged us to stay the course and continue to save for our future," Lai says.

 "Couple's first step: Get emergency fund going," by Christine Dugas, March 5, 2007.

Where to Stash Your Cash

Because you might need to get to your emergency fund in a hurry, keep it somewhere that's both easy to access and safe. Don't put cash in your freezer, but don't tie it up in funds like a long-term CD or in stocks whose worth may have declined just when you need the money. Fortunately, you have several good options.

Savings accounts

The most obvious place to put money that you want quick but not regular access to is a savings account. All savings accounts have three things in common (assuming they're with a reputable bank or credit union):

- they're liquid (we'll define that in a moment)
- they pay you some interest, and
- they're among the safest possible places to keep your money.

Liquidity. This means you don't have to wait a certain length of time or pay a penalty for taking your money out. If an emergency happens, you can walk right into the bank and take out the cash you need. However, the number of monthly transactions you can make, such as transfers and withdrawals, may be limited (typically to six). If you make more withdrawals, you'll pay a fee (around $5 to $15). This feature, though, may serve you well, as a handy deterrent to taking money out for non-emergencies. Also, most savings accounts require you to keep a minimum balance, though this can be as low as $1 to $100. If you dip below your minimum balance, you'll pay another fee (around $5).

> ### Maybe if we hid it in a peanut butter jar!
>
> *Oh, someone already thought of that. A whole industry exists to create "diversion safes," or containers of various sizes that conceal money and valuables within ordinary-looking objects. Fake bottles of iced tea, light switches (with a key!), dirty underwear, and heads of lettuce are just a few of your options. Of course, buying such a safe may replace the danger of burglary with the possibility of unwittingly throwing out your valuables.*

Interest. Don't get too excited about your interest rate, which may be low. That's why we don't recommend putting all of your money into savings. In fact, Sandra comments, "Until recently, investing in a bank savings account was only slightly more profitable than stashing your money in a coffee can." But, she adds, "Online banks have brought something revolutionary to the banking industry: competition. In an effort to attract new deposits, they're offering interest rates of 5% or more, compared with less than 1% for traditional passbook savings accounts." (We'll discuss online accounts below.)

And even a low interest rate can yield significant income over time, through a piece of financial magic called "compounding," in which your interest earnings fatten the amount in your account and earn their own interest.

For example, let's say you earn $45,000 a year after taxes, and decide to save 5% of that, or roughly $187 a month. If you put that money into an account earning 4% interest, you'd have approximately $46,237 at the end of 15 years. Not bad! It would have added up to only $33,660 if you'd left it in a coffee can.

> **RESOURCE**
> **See for yourself how your savings will add up with a little interest thrown in.** Use calculators on sites such as www.nolo.com/calculator.cfm (click "How much could I save over time?") or www.dinkytown.net (click "savings calculator").

Safety. The safety factor of savings accounts is important, since you can't predict when a financial emergency will strike. One reason these accounts are safe is that, by definition, the bank agrees to give you a set amount back based on what you've deposited, plus a stated rate of interest. The bank doesn't get to run around investing your cash in high-risk vehicles and passing on the risk to you. Another reason is that your savings will (or should) be insured for up to $100,000 per bank, through either the Federal Deposit Insurance Corporation ("FDIC") or the National Credit Union Administration ("NCUA") for credit union accounts. This means that even if the bank or credit union goes belly up (which has hardly happened at all since the 1930s), you'll still get your money.

Mighty Money From Little Acorns Grows

The power of compounding, over time, is one of the marvels of the universe. Consider Ben Franklin, who bequeathed 1,000 pounds each—about $4,400 in today's money—to the cities of Boston and Philadelphia. His terms: It was to be held in trust for 200 years. The trust earned $2 million for Philadelphia and $5 million for Boston.

You may not have such a long-term outlook, but every $1 you deposit for your 15-year-old today will be $11.50 when she turns 65, assuming the account earns just 5% interest per year. Earn 10% a year, and every $1 deposited today will soar to $117 over 50 years.

 "Mighty money from little monetary acorns grows," by John Waggoner, June 8, 2007.

Varieties of savings accounts. Of course, like every other financial product, savings accounts come in various flavors. A basic account is often called a "passbook" account, referring to the little book in which the bank may record your balance, transactions, and interest earnings. However, actual passbooks are going out of style, and many banks instead call their basic account a "statement account," meaning the bank sends you a monthly or quarterly statement (by mail or email) of your account activity.

But don't get too caught up in the names. Even within an individual bank, you may be offered a variety of savings account options. For example, a bank's "premium" account may pay higher interest and other accounts but also require you to maintain a high minimum balance.

Here's a name that's sure to pique your interest: "High-yield savings account." In some cases this is just a fancy name that banks give to their highest-paying accounts. The banks usually attach their strictest conditions to these accounts, such as a particularly large initial deposit, a high balance over time, and a limit on the number of transactions you can make. Some banks offer their high-yield accounts only to customers who keep other accounts at the bank.

The highest of the high-yield savings accounts can't normally be found at your local bank. They're available through online banks such as HSBC, ING DIRECT, or E-Loan. Despite some people's fears, these are perfectly reputable places to keep your money. The catch is that you normally give up the ability to walk into a local bank and interact with a human being—a particular problem if the bank's website goes down or you're not comfortable with how its website is structured. Transferring money in and out of your online account is normally done by linking it to your checking account, though some online banks also give you an ATM card.

In case you hadn't already guessed, you'll need to do a bit of shopping to find a savings account with the best rates and most suitable terms. A good resource is www.bankrate.com. When comparing interest rates, make sure you're being offered "compound," not "simple" interest. Compound interest means that, as your savings build up due to interest earned, you also start earning interest on those added amounts. Simple interest means that the bank will pay you interest only on your deposits, that is, on the "principal" in your account.

CAUTION
When you've reached your emergency fund goal, find a better place to continue saving. According to financial planners with whom Sandra spoke, it's not unusual to meet clients who have up to $100,000 in low-interest accounts. Sandra says, "That money is like dust bunnies under the bed: People know they should do something about it, but they don't." But you can earn hundreds of dollars more by investing in something offering higher interest, such as a certificate of deposit (discussed below).

What's a Credit Union?

A credit union is a nonprofit organization that is owned by its members. Credit unions function like banks in most ways, but return their profits to the members in the form of higher interest rates and lower loan rates. You don't necessarily have to be in a special club to qualify for membership—being an alumnus of a particular school, a member of a certain profession, or even a friend of an existing credit union member may be enough. Ask your friends and organizations, pop into the door of local credit union offices, or try "CU Matchup" at www.howtojoinacu.org.

Checking accounts

A checking account is another safe, FDIC- or NCUA-insured place to keep your money. The difference from a savings account is that it gives you check-writing privileges and doesn't pay much interest, if any at all. That makes it the least desirable place to keep your emergency fund. In fact, the easy access can make the money just a little too tempting ("I need an emergency haircut, quick!"). However, you'll need checking accounts for your everyday expenses, so let's briefly review how they work.

If you think savings accounts came in a lot of flavors, get ready. When choosing a checking account, you'll need to consider not only the interest rate, minimum balance requirements, and transaction limits, but any monthly service fees, the number of checks you can write

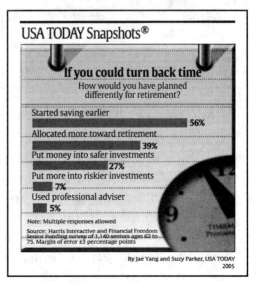

USA TODAY Snapshots®

If you could turn back time
How would you have planned differently for retirement?

Started saving earlier — 56%
Allocated more toward retirement — 39%
Put money into safer investments — 27%
Put more into riskier investments — 7%
Used professional adviser — 5%

Note: Multiple responses allowed
Source: Harris Interactive and Financial Freedom Senior Funding survey of 1,140 seniors ages 62 to 75. Margin of error ±3 percentage points

By Jae Yang and Suzy Parker, USA TODAY 2005

each month (some accounts charge for more than eight), overdraft fees, whether to get overdraft protection (you pay a fee to have the bank honor your bounced check, thus saving embarrassment with the vendor), the availability of ATMs, and whether you'll be given back your checks (or images of them) after people cash them.

"Free checking" does exist—meaning accounts with no monthly service charges or per-check fees—but usually with conditions, for example that you arrange direct deposit of your paycheck. In order to find a checking account with favorable rates and terms, you'll need to wade through a number in which the banks act as though they're doing you a huge favor for harboring your account (never mind that they're out investing your money), and charge you for every little thing.

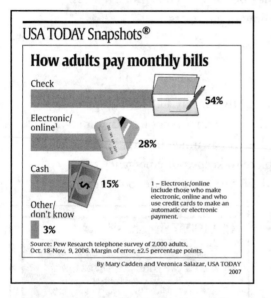

USA TODAY Snapshots®

How adults pay monthly bills

Check **54%**

Electronic/online[1] **28%**

Cash **15%**

Other/don't know **3%**

1 – Electronic/online include those who make electronic, online and who use credit cards to make an automatic or electronic payment.

Source: Pew Research telephone survey of 2,000 adults, Oct. 18–Nov. 9, 2006. Margin of error, ±2.5 percentage points.

By Mary Cadden and Veronica Salazar, USA TODAY 2007

Talk with a customer service rep at your current bank to find out whether you're in the most advantageous account. If something has changed—for example, you're now getting your paychecks deposited directly—you may be eligible for an account at higher interest or with lower fees.

Then go to www.bankrate.com to compare rates and terms at your local or online banks.

If you're willing to part with personal interactions, online banks also offer checking accounts, again at relatively high interest. As Kathy describes, "online checking-type accounts don't typically offer a checkbook or issue paper statements. You generally can't go to a teller. You pay bills online and make deposits electronically or by mail. In most cases, you'll be able to withdraw your money for free within a designated ATM network."

Bouncing Checks More Expensive Than Ever

Kathy discovered that banks are making it increasingly easy for you to overdraw your bank account. And the money they're reaping from your mistakes has likely hit a record high.

So says a report from the Center for Responsible Lending, a consumer advocacy group. Its research shows that customers are paying $17.5 billion annually in fees for overdrawing their bank accounts, up 70% from the $10.3 billion they paid in 2004. The fees—assessed when banks pay for, rather than deny, an overdraft—exceed the $15.8 billion that consumers are overdrawing.

Banks have long allowed you, for a small fee, to transfer money from a credit line or savings account in case you mistakenly overdraw an account. But you have to sign up for this protection.

In the late 1990s, banks began automatically covering overdrawn transactions—even if you didn't sign up for such protection. But there was a catch: They charged you a fee for doing so. These fees now average $34 per transaction, much steeper than the cost of the regular overdraft programs.

Banks are increasingly clearing checks from highest to lowest dollar amounts, causing consumers to overdraw more often—and to be hit with a higher total of fees, the consumer's group found.

If you have $100 in your account, for example, and you write three checks, for $15, $20 and $90, banks would clear the largest one first. You'd then be hit with two fees, rather than just the one you'd face if the bank had cleared checks from lowest to highest amount.

Not good at keeping track of your money? Sign up for an overdraft line of credit or a transfer from savings. The fees for these services are often much cheaper than what the bank will hit you with if you don't have money to cover a check.

 "Overdrafts rise, and banks are making more on fees," by Kathy Chu, July 12, 2007; "Tips offer ways to keep fees to a minimum," by Kathy Chu, October 5, 2005.

CAUTION
Always look over your bank statements. Inappropriate charges, mistaken amounts, and unrecorded deposits are far more common than you'd think. Make sure they're guarding your money well!

Money market accounts

A money market account can also be a good place to keep your emergency fund. Money market accounts (MMAs) are similar to savings accounts—in fact, they're offered by banks, are federally insured, and may include limited check-writing privileges. You earn regular interest, at a rate that's normally higher than regular savings accounts pay but lower than you'd earn on most other investments.

The disadvantages of MMAs include that they usually have higher minimum balance requirements than savings accounts, in the neighborhood of $500 to $5,000. You'll be charged a fee (around $7 to $15) if you go under that amount. And like a standard savings account, they usually limit the number of withdrawals you can make each month, often to six.

When choosing a money market account, look for one offering a combination of high interest and low fees, service charges, and minimum balance requirements. For help finding the best all-around deals, see www.bankrate.com.

Certificates of deposit (CDs)

A certificate of deposit or CD is another form of savings account, usually with a minimum deposit of $1,000 or more. Like savings accounts, CDs are federally insured for up to $100,000 per bank per depositor. The CD's key feature is that you must leave the money untouched for a set amount of time, ordinarily from three months to six years. The longer you leave your money there, and the more you put in, the higher the interest rate you'll lock in. CDs usually offer higher interest rates than traditional savings accounts, but online savings accounts are giving CDs a run for their money.

You can, in an emergency, close your CD account before its maturity date, but you'll have to pay a penalty. The amount of the penalty depends on the bank's policies and the length of the CD. Commonly, for a CD with a term of a few months to a year and a half, you'll forfeit three months' interest for an early withdrawal. If you pull money out of a two-year CD, the penalty might be six months' interest.

There's rarely a reason to choose a short-term CD over an MMA or online savings account, given that MMAs are easier to deal with—you can take your money out without penalty, and they don't require you to make any decisions at the maturity date. Long-term CDs, however, are profitable places to keep money that you know you'll need within a certain amount of time, but not before. They can be especially helpful if you want to save a certain amount for a particular goal, like a European tour or a new car.

If you do put some cash into CDs, try to stagger the maturity dates. This will give you more flexibility if you need to withdraw money earlier than you'd planned. For example, if you buy two one-year CDs, buy them six months apart, so that they mature six months apart as well. That way you'll never be more than six months away from being able to withdraw money without a penalty.

The bank will notify you a month or so before the CD is set to mature, but then the ball is in your court: Many CDs automatically renew, at the current interest rate, unless you request something different in writing. You'll probably get a grace period of a week or so after the maturity date to get to the bank and cash in the CD if that's your preference.

To shop for CDs, check with your favorite bank; it may offer you a higher rate if you have other accounts there. Or go to www.bankrate.com.

Treasury bills

Another safe short-term investment, T-bills are guaranteed by the federal government. They have maturity dates of four, 13, or 26 weeks. They'll usually give you a yield that's slightly less than you'd get from a money market fund. Over the last 50 years, they've gained about 5.4% annually; during the same period, annual inflation averaged 4.1%.

You buy T-bills at a price that's less than their face value. For example, you might buy a $1,000 T-bill for $950. When the T-bill matures, you'll be entitled to $1,000. The $50 you receive in interest is subject to federal income tax, but exempt from state and local income tax.

You can find out current interest rates and buy T-bills directly at the federal website, www.treasurydirect.gov.

If All Else Fails: Drawing From Your IRA or 401(k)

If you secretly think of your retirement savings as your emergency fund, here's a little reality check: You're going to need retirement funds for retirement. So as a general rule, you should consider those funds to be off-limits—forbidden fruit. That's because there are some serious consequences if you withdraw money from your IRA or 401(k) before you retire:

- You'll have to pay tax on the money now, instead of deferring it until you retire.
- You'll probably have to pay a 10% penalty to the IRS.
- You could jeopardize your retirement security.

However, if your current existence is threatened while you're busy protecting your future life, making an exception may be perfectly rational. And we've already said that funding your 401(k)—especially if you receive an employer match—should be priority number one, to reap the greatest financial rewards. So the question really becomes what to do if you've started saving for retirement but haven't finished setting money aside for emergencies.

There are situations in which you can take money out of your IRA without dire results. For example, you won't owe a penalty if you're age 59½ or older, you become disabled, or you withdraw the money to pay college expenses, medical expenses that exceed 7.5% of your income, child support, or alimony. You will, however, owe taxes on the money withdrawn.

Also, if you're buying your first home, you can withdraw up to $10,000 from your IRA penalty-free for a down payment. However, penalty-free doesn't mean tax-free—you must add the withdrawal to your ordinary income, and pay tax on it. Also, you must use the money within 120 days of receiving it, or else return it to your IRA. The $10,000 is a lifetime limit.

Ask your tax accountant for details on taking IRA distributions, or contact the IRS at 800-829-1040 or www.irs.gov.

Your 401(k) plan is another possible source of emergency cash. Check with your employer or plan administrator to see whether the plan allows for loans. We're not talking about taking an early 401(k) distribution, where you'd withdraw the money permanently—that would make you subject to a 10% penalty, unless you happened to fall within certain exceptions such as being over age 59½ or disabled. Instead, you'd literally be making a loan to yourself out of your 401(k) funds. You'd even collect interest from yourself, which would remain tax-free until you retired and withdrew it from the plan. Of course, you'll lose the interest you would have earned from other sources. To find out your total losses, see Bankrate.com's calculator at www.bankrate.com/brm/calc/401kl.asp.

USA TODAY Snapshots®

Americans who expect a defined-contribution plan, such as a 401(k), to be their primary source of retirement income

71% Generation X
63% Baby boomers
45% Seniors

Source: MainStay Investments of New York Life Investment Management survey of 515 respondents ages 26 to 82. Margin of error ±5 percentage points.

By Jae Yang and Dave Merrill, USA TODAY 2005

If your 401(k) allows loans, you can borrow as much as one-half of your vested balance in the plan, up to a maximum of $50,000. (Vested balance means the amount that's truly yours, without any possible subtractions for having left your job before meeting your employer's "vesting period" for matching funds.) But if you have less than $20,000 in the account, you can borrow the entire amount of your vested balance up to $10,000. Other conditions—like maximum term for repayment (usually five years), minimum loan amount, interest rate, and applicable loan fees—are set by your employer.

A loan from your 401(k) is risky for another reason: If you left your job before fully repaying it, the loan might become due immediately upon your departure. You might also owe income tax and penalties on the outstanding balance. It depends on the rules of your company plan, so be sure to find out what they are before you make a loan to yourself.

Is Your Disaster Kit Ready?

Financial planning isn't the only way to guard against the unexpected. If you have to leave your house in a hurry, perhaps because of a fire, flood, or hurricane, you may not have time to collect crucial possessions and documents. USA TODAY's Elizabeth Caldwell and Doyle Rice suggest the following steps to take in advance.

Rent a safe-deposit box

You can keep copies of important papers at home, but you need a safe place elsewhere for the original documents, such as:

- Birth certificates
- Passports
- Marriage licenses, custody papers, and other judicial documents
- Titles and deeds to houses and cars
- An inventory of your household possessions, with photographs, for insurance purposes.

Supplies to go

Keep supplies in an easy-to-carry container in case of an evacuation. Include:

- Three-day supply of water (one gallon per person per day)
- One change of clothing and footwear per person, rain gear, toiletries, blankets
- A first-aid kit, including prescription medicines
- Battery-powered flashlight and radio
- House and vehicle keys
- Nonperishable food items, manual can opener.

Is Your Disaster Kit Ready? (cont'd.)

Prepare your finances

Prepare a financial-evacuation box. Whether a lockbox or a shoe box, use it to store plastic bags containing documents and other things you'll need before leaving home, such as:

- Cash, change, or a small amount of traveler's checks. You may need cash because ATMs could shut down during an emergency.
- Identify where you are seeking refuge and keep directions and emergency contact numbers for doctors, friends, and family. Power outages may make them inaccessible.
- Copies of prescriptions
- Bank account information and other financial records
- Copies of insurance policies
- Copies of deeds, licenses, wills, and other important family documents.

 "If a hurricane comes knocking, will you be ready?" by Elizabeth Caldwell, Doyle Rice, June 20, 2007.

From Piggy Banks on Up: Your Kids and Money

The words "I want" tend to pop up early in a child's vocabulary, and they get plenty of use from then on. We've got to sympathize. Children's material desires are probably no greater than the rest of ours, and at first, they have little way to fulfill them beyond asking mom and dad. The answers they get—anything from, "No, we can't afford that," to, "But of course, Daddy will get his little precious anything," will probably shape the way they handle and relate to money in the future. And just when you've figured out how to respond to these requests, your children will get old enough to carry or earn their own spending money—and perhaps return home with things that horrify you.

Every parent struggles with where to draw the lines between wish-fulfillment and restraint, or top-down control and financial freedom. Although different parents deal with these issues in different ways, the core things you can do now to help create a financially stable, responsible adult include:

- modeling responsible financial behavior
- deciding when and whether to give your children an allowance
- teaching your children basic principles of spending and saving
- advising your teens on finding work and handling their first paychecks
- keeping the reins on college expenses, and
- deciding how much to help your kids after they've left the nest.

They're Watching You: Messages About Money

Children pick up on their parents' behavior in many ways, and money-handling is no exception. All those feelings about money we discussed in Chapter 1—aversion to the very topic, fear of risk, and more—can be easily passed to the next generation. This happens both when you're interacting with the kids (perhaps saying yes or no to a treat) and when you've almost forgotten they're nearby (grumbling about how much the credit card company charged you for being a day late on your payment).

That doesn't mean that your kids will turn out just like you. They might fall into the generation-skipping phenomenon, in which kids say, "I never wanna be like that," and go down the opposite road. With so much happening below the surface, what's a parent to do?

You're already doing the right thing, by examining and moderating your own behavior and involving your kids in your financial goal setting. The results of setting a positive example can be hard to give yourself credit for—a child who acts responsibly and unselfishly is what you expected in the first place, right?

The biggest difficulties in transmitting positive financial behavior to children often arise at the extremes, in families that are either financially struggling or quite affluent. A parent who's losing sleep over money may, for example, wish to shield the children from the same fate. But, as Harvard psychologist Dan Kindlon told USA TODAY, "If you want a child to have integrity and character, you have to toughen them up a little bit." He describes parents who bend over backward so everything is perfect for their children. "They hate when they're upset. All this attention makes children feel they are the center of the universe." Not to mention the fact that completely insulating your children is unrealistic, especially when you could use their help in meeting your financial goals.

At the other end of the spectrum, Kindlon surveyed families with incomes of $50,000 and up and found that 58% of the parents felt that their kids were at least somewhat spoiled. USA TODAY reporter Nanci Hellmich summarized Kindlon's findings: "Many indulge their kids too much, give them too much stuff, cater to their every whim and demand too little of them in return. And, in doing so, they undermine some of their children's character development—shortchanging them in vital areas like generosity, compassion, honesty, self-control and empathy."

Nanci Hellmich continues, "But stuff alone doesn't spoil kids, experts say. Some kids get lots of things, but they turn out well, partly because their parents also expect a lot from them—good grades, good behavior, respect for their possessions, says Ken Springer, associate professor of child development at Southern Methodist University in Dallas. In short, quality of parenting is more important than number of possessions."

One effective way to let kids see for themselves the value of what you're already providing them is to volunteer—preferably as a family—for people who have less. Deborah Spaide of New Canaan, Connecticut, who founded Kids Care Club (www.kidscare.org), explains how this worked for her family: "I'm living in a very affluent community and felt my children needed some balance to the wealth they were running into every day. I wanted my kids to get some perspective on life." As Nanci Hellmich describes, "The first thing they did as a family was go into a disabled woman's home and paint the walls and clean the apartment. Her kids started telling their friends what they were doing, and the friends wanted to come along to the next activity. Spaide found that kids were 'starving for these kinds of opportunities.'" And, Spaide adds, the kids learned that "Caring for others makes you feel better about yourself."

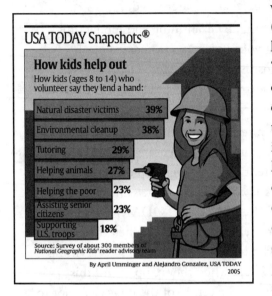

USA TODAY Snapshots®

How kids help out
How kids (ages 8 to 14) who volunteer say they lend a hand:

Natural disaster victims	39%
Environmental cleanup	38%
Tutoring	29%
Helping animals	27%
Helping the poor	23%
Assisting senior citizens	23%
Supporting U.S. troops	18%

Source: Survey of about 300 members of National Geographic Kids' reader advisory team

By April Umminger and Alejandro Gonzalez, USA TODAY 2005

From Dimes to Dollars: Allowance

Although many people think of allowances as a natural part of childhood, parents are actually almost evenly divided on whether they're a good idea. We've talked to parents who feel pride at watching their child saving up for a Game Boy—and to others who don't give an allowance precisely because they don't want their child to buy a Game Boy.

According to the pro-allowance camp, allowances give children practice at handling money and can help enforce household rules such as doing chores. USA TODAY founder and columnist Al Neuharth contends, "Allowances for kids aren't just about money to spend. They should teach money management, one of the biggest problems for most grown-ups." Kids get a chance to learn from their own small-scale mistakes, and experience running out of cash if they spend it too quickly. And besides, they say, if you don't give children an allowance, they'll come to you for cash constantly—leaving you subject to endless negotiating, manipulating, or wheedling.

In the opposing camp are those who believe that allowances are artificial, unnecessary if the child and parent make shared financial decisions, and can lead to frivolous spending. They say that, given that parents buy their children's food and major goods, the allowance too easily turns into a fund devoted to the purchase of soda, candy, and forbidden stuff. If children are really to get a good sense of how to handle money, they suggest, it's best for the parents to involve them in all financial decisions, from candy to clothing, and help them see that both parents and children must place similar limits on their spending. ("If Mom isn't buying $150 sneakers for herself, we're not going to buy them for you either.") What about allowances as a payment for doing chores? No way, they say—children should learn that helping out is just part of being a family.

> ### Here's what the neighbors are doing about allowances
>
> *A national survey by researcher Yankelovich (reported by USA TODAY) showed:*
>
> - *Fewer than 60% of children ages 6 to 17 get any allowance.*
> - *The range for 6- to 11-year-olds is $5 to $9 a week. For 12- to 17-year-olds, the average is $10 to $19 a week*

Only you know which system fits your family (or each child) best. If you do decide to give your children an allowance, you have some more decisions to make.

Allowances: When and how much?

You can start giving an allowance as soon as Junior is interested in and understands the concept of money. But you don't need a child development expert to tell you that different children are ready to handle money at different ages. We know of parents granting allowances to children as young as three, but most wait longer.

Then comes the question of how much. Many parents go with a dollar a week for each year of age. Another possibility is to take an average of how much your child's friends are getting—that is, unless your idea of what your child should be allowed to spend money on is different from your friends'.

But you really can't decide how much to give until you settle on what the allowance is meant to be spent on. If you're giving your children $4 per week, it's pretty clear that it's just for incidentals. But some parents give older children the amount they'd normally spend on their clothes, toys, books, recreation, and more.

There is, of course, a large middle ground. For example, you might decide that the allowance will be meant to cover only outings with friends, basic clothes (not coats, shoes, or outfits for special events) and incidentals. The best idea is often to start small and expand what's included in the allowance as the child gets older.

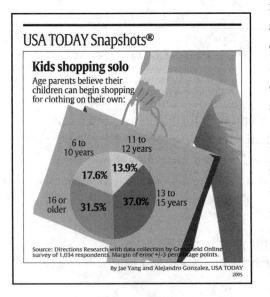

USA TODAY Snapshots®

Kids shopping solo

Age parents believe their children can begin shopping for clothing on their own:

- 6 to 10 years
- 11 to 12 years: 13.9%
- 17.6%
- 16 or older: 31.5%
- 37.0%
- 13 to 15 years

Source: Directions Research with data collection by Greenfield Online survey of 1,034 respondents. Margin of error +/-3 percentage points.

By Jae Yang and Alejandro Gonzalez, USA TODAY 2005

If you've got a preteen or teenager, why not ask what he or she thinks the allowance should cover? A kid who sits down and lists ordinary expenses—lunch, bus pass, movies, snacks, makeup, video games, gifts for friends, CDs or music downloads—may gain a new appreciation for how the small expenses of daily life add up. And the list will help both of you understand what you'll pay for and what comes from the allowance, eliminating the need for negotiations every time your child goes out with friends.

Should you attach strings? Chores and charity

Is your child's allowance his or hers to save or squander, or are there rules attached?

Chores. Most parents agree that kids should be expected to help out around the house, whether or not you write up a list of chores and tie receiving the allowance to their satisfactory completion. "Doing household jobs teaches children responsibility, lets them know that no one is the family servant, instills in them a love of order, and teaches them essential life skills," Tara Aronson, author of *Mrs. Clean Jeans' Housekeeping With Kids*, told USA TODAY reporter Nancy Hellmich. What's more, "Children who are given so much without having to work for it acquire a sense of entitlement and may not develop a work ethic, which they will need later in life," says Susan Newman, a social psychologist at Rutgers University in New Brunswick, New Jersey, and author of *Parenting an Only Child*.

If you decide to tie allowance to doing chores, you'll still have to make sure the kids follow through. Forgetting is common, even among the best of kids—who are probably busy with homework, extracurricular activities, and more. As Nanci Hellmich describes, "Aronson believes in making cleaning fun so kids want to cooperate. When her kids were young and her house needed a whirlwind cleaning, she called her kids in for a Cinderella Saturday. She gave them mops, some toilet-bowl cleaner and dust rags and put them to work for an hour or so. 'It was organized chaos,' Aronson says. Once everything was sparkly clean, they put the rags away, and the whole family dressed up to enjoy a night out."

Saving. Some parents require kids to save a certain fraction of their allowance. Does this instill a good habit, or do children perceive it as something you're doing that doesn't involve them much? Your call.

Charity. Similarly, you might earmark some of your child's allowance for a good cause of the child's choice, if you decide that enforced giving will foster genuine generosity.

One Parent's Approach

Al Neuharth, who founded USA TODAY and is now a regular columnist, says, "At our house, each child age six to 12 gets a weekly allowance in dollars equal to his or her age. Each has to save and bank at least 25%.

"When each turns a teen, rules change. Our Alexis, almost 15, has a monthly allowance that includes the money her mom and I used to spend on clothes and other necessities for her. Now she does that buying.

"Her teenage banking includes a 'debit card,' to make purchases without carrying much cash. Debit cards teach owners to spend only money they have. Credit cards encourage them to spend money they don't have. Huge difference.

"Ultimately it's more important for teenagers to be able to balance their bank account than it is for them to get straight A's in algebra or geometry."

 "Why kids should get allowances, 'cards,'" by Al Neuharth, March 24, 2006.

When Grandparents Dote: Smart Ways to Make Financial Gifts to Your Children

To help with children's future expenses (college costs and more), some parents, as well as grandparents, set money aside from early on. But what about giving money directly to the kids? Generous grandparents or other relatives may come to you wanting to make gifts but uncertain of the best way to do it.

If you have the means, Sandra advises, "Financial gifts to kids make lots of sense. They can teach kids the importance of saving and investing. And invested wisely, the gifts will continue to grow in value long after other gifts have been relegated to the back of the toy closet."

Handing over money isn't complicated when you're talking about small cash gifts on birthdays or at holidays. But when larger amounts are involved, there are lots of different ways to structure gifts to children—and possible tax consequences for the giver. It's worth getting it right.

How to give

The main ways to give children financial gifts, in addition to just handing over cash, are:

- buying savings bonds
- creating a custodial account
- setting up a trust
- donating to a tax-advantaged 529 college savings plan, and
- contributing to a Roth IRA for a child.

Buy savings bonds. It's the classic way to give money to a kid: Present a savings bond and explain that at some far-off date it will be worth a lot of money. It's like money in the bank—a locked bank.

There are two types of savings bonds. Series EE bonds come with fixed interest rates (3.4% as of late 2007). The Treasury Department also offers Series I savings bonds, which have two parts: a fixed rate that stays the same for the life of the bond, and an inflation rate that's adjusted twice a year, based on the Consumer Price Index. The combined rate for I bonds purchased through October 31 of 2007 was 3.74%.

While the interest rates may not be stellar, if you're not talking about a lot of money, it won't make a huge difference. Many givers think of savings bonds as teaching tools, to plant the idea of investment and returns—and they take pleasure from the fact that unlike many other gifts, bonds won't be broken or forgotten soon after they're received. You can check interest rates and buy savings bonds online at www. treasurydirect.gov.

Contribute to a 529 college-savings plan. If you've set up 529 plan accounts for your college-bound children, you've already got an easy way for grandparents to contribute to your children's future.

That's because anyone, not just the person who sets up the account, can contribute to a 529 plan. And the contribution limits are quite generous—many states allow accounts to contain several hundred thousand dollars. (But don't put in too much—amounts not spent on qualified college costs will be subject to tax.) Each account must be for only one child, but the money can be put toward the college expenses of others in your family if the designated beneficiary doesn't use them. (For more on 529 plans and other college savings plans, see Chapter 9.)

Set up a custodial account in your child's name. Every state allows adults to set up "custodial" accounts for minors. An adult (called the custodian) is in charge of the account until the child reaches the age set by state law—21 in most states, 18 in a few. These accounts are authorized by a law called the "Uniform Transfers to Minors Act," commonly shortened to UTMA. (A couple of states still have only the older version, the Uniform Gifts to Minors Act, which is more restrictive but works fine for lifetime gifts to children.)

USA TODAY Snapshots®

Naughty or nice
Parents who say their child's behavior affects what they receive for the holidays:

Somewhat affects
42%

Does not affect
37%

Definitely affects
21%

Source: eToys   By April Umminger and Julie Snider, USA TODAY
2005

Sandra explains that by setting up an UTMA or UGMA account, you can give money or shares to a minor and maintain control of the account until the child reaches adulthood. Most banks and brokerage firms can set up an account. When you set up an UGMA or UTMA account, you name an adult custodian—you or someone you designate—who decides how the money is invested until the child becomes an adult.

Although you control the money, UGMA and UTMA accounts are irrevocable. You can't change your mind and move the money back into your own account, even if your child announces he intends to become a drummer for a heavy-metal band. Once your child reaches the age of majority, the money automatically transfers to his or her name.

Parents, though, don't usually set up custodial accounts. After all, if you're saving for college, why not put the money into a 529 college savings plan or Coverdell account (the "education IRA"), and avail yourself of the tax advantages those plans offer? And most parents don't like the idea of the money being turned over to their offspring, no strings attached, at age 21 (or worse, 18).

Grandparents are the ones most likely to want to make gifts to your children now, with you in charge as custodian. That will work; you'll have control over the assets until the child is 21, in most states, giving you time to spend it on college before your child can get hold of it.

There are possible downsides to a custodial account:

- It might reduce the amount of financial aid your child qualifies for when it's time for college. That's because money in such an account is counted as the child's asset, not yours.

- If the person who gave the money—a grandparent, for example—dies while the child is still a minor, the amount in the account is considered part of the giver's estate, even though the money had been given away. If estate tax is a concern, the giver won't want this.

- Under federal tax law, a child's investment income is taxed at the parents' top marginal rate. This "kiddie tax" kicks in once a child's unearned income—for example, from interest and capital gains—exceeds a certain level. For 2007, that level is $1,700. Before 2006, the tax covered children up to age 13, giving parents a chance to transfer assets to their teenage children. The children could sell the assets at their lower tax rate—usually 10%—and use the money for college. But Congress raised the kiddie-tax threshold to include children 17 and younger. And starting in 2008, the tax expanded to cover children up to 19—or 24, if they're full-time students and dependent on their parents.

Set up a trust. If your child is lucky enough to be the recipient of a large gift—we're talking tens of thousands of dollars—setting up a trust is another possibility. With a trust, an adult is in charge of the money, and the giver can place all kinds of conditions on how it is used. (A trust is an arrangement where one person, called a trustee, is in charge of assets that are to be used for someone else, called the beneficiary.) You'll want to see a lawyer if a gift (or series of gifts, made over years) justifies setting up a trust.

Contribute to a child's Roth IRA. A retirement account for your teenager? It may sound nuts, yet be a great idea. Children who are already earning some income on their own are eligible to create a Roth IRA. Roths are funded with after-tax money—not a big concern when they're in the lowest tax bracket—but the eventual withdrawals are tax-free. So, for example, if your child earned $2,000 this year, and generous grandparents want to make a $1,000 gift, it could go in a Roth and start generating tax-free returns immediately. (For more information, see "Teens and retirement savings," below.)

Gift tax concerns

If someone makes total lifetime gifts over a certain amount—currently, $1 million—that person's estate can end up owing federal gift tax. (Interestingly enough, the recipients of the money don't owe a thing.) Fortunately, most ordinary gifts don't count toward this total, and as a result few people ever owe gift tax. Gifts of up to $12,000 per year, per recipient, are tax-free ($12,000 is the 2007 figure; it's indexed to go up with inflation). That means, for example, that every year grandma and grandpa could give each of their grandchildren up to $24,000 without it counting against the lifetime gift tax threshold.

If your (lucky) child gets a gift of more than $12,000 from someone during a single year, the giver is required to file a gift tax return (IRS Form 709) with the IRS. This doesn't mean that any gift tax would actually be due, because computing the gift tax debt is put off until the giver makes taxable gifts totaling $1 million or until the giver's death. (For more information, see IRS Publication 950, *Introduction to Estate and Gift Taxes*, available at www.irs.gov.)

There's one more wrinkle to the gift tax, as described by Sandra: "To qualify for the gift-tax exclusion, you must give the money with no strings attached. But what right-thinking adult wants to hand a $12,000 check to a ten-year-old?" One traditional way to get around this problem is by putting the money into a custodial account, described above. Or grandparents who want to help out with a child's educational or medical expenses can simply pay for those expenses directly—all such gifts are gift-tax-free.

Money 101:
Teach Your Children Well

Allowance or not, children need some guidance on using money wisely. And the sooner the better, given that the advertisers of the world start pelting them with tempting messages as soon as they're old enough to drool at the TV. Letting your children spend the money you allot them and then rely on you for more is of limited teaching use. So it's worth sitting them down for a few financial lessons on:

- basic budgeting
- getting the most for what they spend, and
- the power of saving.

Actually, sit-down lectures probably aren't the best forum for such lessons. If, for example, you're in a department store and can guide your child to the sale rack and show how buying two items at a 50% discount beats buying one at full price, they'll start to get the picture.

> **TIP**
> **Are the kids tuning you out?** The Web offers plenty of financial information geared towards kids, at:
> - www.younginvestor.com—games, articles, and calculators for kids of different ages, on budgeting, earning, and investing
> - www.teenanalyst.com—started by teens, to help others learn about investing and starting a business, and
> - www.kidsmoney.org—for both parents and kids, with lots of articles about allowances and more.

Basic budget concepts for kids

Which comes first, the math lesson or the budgeting lesson? It certainly helps if your kids understand addition and subtraction before they start trying to chart out how to spend their money. But their interest in seeing what their money can buy might spur their interest in learning math, so don't wait a minute longer than you have to.

Some experts suggest helping your children keep a weekly journal of where their money is spent. At week's end, you or the child can do the math and observe any trends—similar to what you did with your Family Spending Worksheet. Then you can help your child see what possibilities different combinations of spending and saving might have yielded. ("If you gave up popsicles for three weeks, you could buy a matinee movie ticket.")

If you want to see your children's interest in budgeting take off, help them find ways to earn their own money. Many children have an entrepreneurial streak and will, when they're old enough, jump at the chance to water plants for vacationing neighbors, sell crafts at a local fair, start their own egg business, or babysit.

Spending wisely

It doesn't take long for kids to get the concept that buying things cheap lets them buy more stuff. Still, they'll need your help with other bits of consumer know-how. For example, you might explain to them that quality can be as important as price, if they want what they buy to last for more than a day. (They'll probably learn this on their own after buying something cheap, shiny, and shoddy.) Clue them in to how advertising is meant to lure them with possibly false promises. And, as soon as your children have learned basic division, it's time to introduce the concept of price per amount—for example, that buying six pens for $6 is actually cheaper than buying three for $4. (Unless you'll never use all six pens.)

Is all this talk of consumerism making you antsy? Then remember that you can also use this time to develop your children's social conscience, discussing deeper issues like the resources (start with the packaging) and possibly underpaid labor that went into producing the item, and the environmental impact if they later throw it out.

Fashion Marketers Take Aim at Your Eight-Year-Old

As USA TODAY reporter Jayne O'Donnell found, Jill Brown almost cried the day her nine-year-old daughter sold several American Girl dolls at a yard sale so she could buy a Juicy Couture sweat suit.

It was a painful reminder that the emotional and psychological distance between childhood and the teen years is far shorter than ever.

"It was such an indication of her moving to a different place," says Brown, a marketing consultant in Northbrook, Illinois. "It was also a little bit of an indication that she was starting to solve things for herself."

Chalk it up to "age compression," which many marketers call "kids getting older younger" or KGOY. Retail consultant Ken Nisch says it shouldn't be a surprise or an outrage that kids are tired of toys and kid clothes by eight, considering that they are exposed to outside influences so much earlier. They are in preschool at three and on computers at six.

That's why marketers now target nine-year-olds with apparel and accessories once considered only for teens, says Nisch, chairman of the retail consulting and design firm JGA.

Generation Y, those between about eight and 26, are considered the most important generation for retailers and marketers because of their spending power and the influence they have over what their parents buy. But just as the eight- to 12-year-old "tweens" are pitched with a dizzying array of music, movie, and cell phone choices, the nearly ten million tween girls also are getting more attention from fashion, skin care, and makeup businesses. In 2006, NPD Group says seven- to 14-year-old girls spent $11.5 billion on apparel, up from $10.5 billion in 2004.

 "Marketers keep pace with 'tweens'; Fashion-minded girls prove rich, but fast-moving target," by Jayne O'Donnell, April 11, 2007.

The power of saving

The more you work with your children on budgeting and purchasing, the more they'll see that spending money as soon as they get it isn't always in their own interests. And you can help them discover this, for example by suggesting or requiring that they set aside 10% to 20% of every allowance payment for some larger future goal.

USA TODAY Snapshots®

Getting dolled up for the prom
Nearly all girls who responded to a prom survey have purchased (or plan to buy) a new dress for the prom. Average spending amounts:

Prom dress $223
Makeup, hair, nails, etc. $115
Total $338

Source: *Seventeen* Magazine. Poll of 1,382 readers of *TeenProm* and *SeventeenProm* conducted by Beta Research

By Shannon Reilly and Sam Ward, USA TODAY 2005

Saving up for a goal can actually be fun for kids, especially if you make it tangible by putting the money into a jar or writing their progress in big red numbers on a bulletin board. And when your child has saved up enough to put into a bank account, be sure to point out the line item for interest, and explain how the money will continue to grow. Unfortunately, with minimum balances on the rise, your best bet will probably be to start by adding your child's savings to one of your own bank accounts and moving it later. Call it the "First Bank of Mom and Dad," and separately write down your child's deposits and interest earned to show how the money is growing.

Burger Flipping: Summer Jobs for Teens

This just in from USA TODAY reporter Barbara Hagenbaugh: As of 2007, "Most U.S. teenagers were not working or looking for work at the beginning of the summer for the first time on record, suggesting teens are forgoing traditional summertime jobs at ice cream stands, camps and pools. Only 48.8% of teens ages 16 to 19 were working or looking for work in June, the Labor Department said .... That was down from 51.6% in June 2006 and below the 60.2% in the labor force in June 2000."

What's going on? Hagenbaugh found evidence that teens are spending more time studying, and that their parents have been more successful than ever at saving for their college expenses, taking the financial pressure off the kids. The pressure to get into a good school, however, remains—so some teens pursue résumé-enhancing travel, volunteer opportunities, or educational programs.

All this doesn't necessarily mean that you should keep your kids out of summer jobs if you can afford it. As psychologist Dan Kindlon of Harvard University advised USA TODAY, "Many parents want life to be easier for their children than it was for them. They don't want their children to have to work at hard, tedious summer jobs like they did. But, in fact, those kinds of jobs may teach the child how to tolerate boredom and make them realize how difficult some work can be."

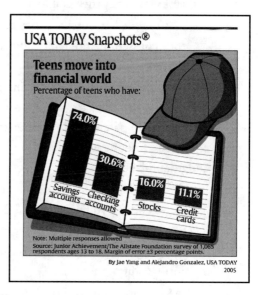

USA TODAY Snapshots®

Teens move into financial world
Percentage of teens who have:

74.0% Savings accounts
30.6% Checking accounts
16.0% Stocks
11.1% Credit cards

Note: Multiple responses allowed
Source: Junior Achievement/The Allstate Foundation survey of 1,065 respondents ages 13 to 18. Margin of error ±3 percentage points.

By Jae Yang and Alejandro Gonzalez, USA TODAY
2005

The good news is, in areas where fewer children are looking for work, your children might actually have better luck finding a halfway interesting job. But looking for a first job is never easy. Be ready to help your children scour the job listings (most likely on Craigslist or other websites), draft résumés and cover letters, and visit prospective employers. And after they start work, you'll want to help them understand new issues like tax withholding and the importance of saving for retirement.

The Perils of Being Your Teen's "Best Friend"

According to USA TODAY reporter Nanci Hellmich, surveys show that many parents would like to be best friends with their teenagers and young adult children, and they'd give their kids everything they want if they could.

Researchers with Synovate, a market research firm, surveyed 1,000 parents with kids ages 12 to 30 who are living at home and 500 children within that age range from other families. The findings:

- 43% of parents say they want to be their child's best friend.
- 40% would buy their children everything they wanted if they could.
- 73% say the last purchase they made for their kids was something they guessed their teen or young adult would want rather than something he or she asked for.

The results have both positive and negative connotations, says Ian Pierpoint, a senior vice president for the company. Some parents felt their own parents didn't understand them, and they see a best friend as someone who is fun to be around, listens, and is non-judgmental, he says.

But unlike a traditional parent, a best-friend parent "doesn't give you rules and tell you what to do," Pierpoint says.

"One mother wouldn't make her child do homework because it would make him unhappy. This is the extreme side of best-friend parenting," Pierpoint says.

The Synovate findings show that kids today aren't necessarily going to follow in their parents' footsteps when it comes to parenting, Pierpoint says. Pierpoint reports talking to one 22-year-old man who said: "There's no way I'm going to be like my mom. My mom does everything for me. She's made me lazy. There is no way the kids are going to rule my house. I'm going to be a bad-ass parent."

 "Parents want to be teens' pals; But loose style can backfire," by Nanci Hellmich, October 12, 2004.

Teens and taxes

Your teen's excitement at receiving a first paycheck may be followed by dismay at the big bite taxes took from it. You can offer consolation: Your novice member of the workforce will probably get the whole amount refunded at the end of the year. As Sandra says, "A child can earn up to $5,150 a year (2007 figure) without paying taxes, assuming she doesn't have investment income. But even if she earns far less than that amount, there's a good chance she'll have some taxes withheld from her paycheck. That's not necessarily bad, for two reasons. First, she can probably get most of the money back. Second, it will help prepare for a lifelong relationship with the IRS."

Here are a few more of Sandra's tips for your teen:

- A young worker will be required to fill out a W-4 form for every job he holds. The form includes a worksheet to figure out how many withholding allowances to claim. Most teens and college students will want to claim one allowance on the form, says Brenda Schafer, tax specialist for H&R Block.

- Most employers calculate their withholding based on annual earnings, even if an employee works for just a few months. Many young workers can get most, if not all, taxes refunded by filing a tax return next year, Schafer says. "For most kids, when they've had just one or two jobs, it's a very easy tax return," she says.

- Tips are taxable. If a student spends the summer waiting tables, he needs to keep track of his tips and report them as income, Schafer says. That way, he doesn't have to rely on his employer's estimate of tips, which might be higher than the actual amount he received, Schafer says. If he must split tips with other workers, a log will ensure he isn't taxed on someone else's income.

Teens and retirement savings

You're probably having trouble imagining your own retirement, let alone your teen's. Nevertheless, Roth individual retirement accounts (IRAs) are not, according to Sandra, just for fortysomething workers who want to save for retirement. For a young person many years from retirement, even a small Roth investment "can do amazing things down the road," says Kevin McKinley, a financial planner and author of *Make Your Kid A Millionaire*. Trouble is, there also are lots of amazing things on sale at the mall.

Why not a regular IRA for your teen? Ray Ferrara, a financial planner in Clearwater, Florida, told USA TODAY, "Go with a Roth." John explains, "A Roth won't give you a deduction for your contribution, but withdrawals are tax-free at retirement. A traditional IRA lets you, or in this case your child, deduct the contribution, but she'll later owe taxes on her withdrawals. Assuming your child isn't a part-time investment banker, she probably didn't earn enough to pay taxes on her income anyway—so the traditional IRA deduction doesn't matter. Even if she does pay taxes on her earnings this year, her tax rate at retirement will probably be much higher, Ferrara says." Also, money in a traditional IRA is locked up until age 59½—the child can't withdraw it for college.

Sandra offers this advice on how to make a Roth more appealing than Abercrombie & Fitch:

- **Explain the tax-free benefits.** Most working adults fund Roths with after-tax contributions. The tax break comes later, when they can withdraw the money for retirement, tax-free. The maximum contribution to a Roth in 2007 is $4,000. A child can earn $5,150 this year, contribute $4,000 to a Roth, wait until she's 59½ to withdraw the money, and it will never be taxed.

- **Offer to match contributions.** The Internal Revenue Service requires a child to have earned income to contribute to a Roth, but it doesn't require that the contributions come from his paycheck. For example, if a teen earns $2,000 this year, he can contribute $1,000 to a Roth, and parents can contribute $1,000. Parents feeling flush can contribute the entire $2,000. You also can front-load a Roth, giving it more time to grow. Mom and Dad could, for instance, deposit a matching contribution now, with the understanding your child will contribute a few dollars from every paycheck. One warning, though: If your child quits or gets fired, you might need to withdraw some of the money to avoid IRS penalties on excess contributions.

- **Point out the flexibility.** Ideally, parents want kids to save the money for retirement, but Roths aren't impenetrable. A child can always withdraw contributions without paying taxes or penalties. He can also withdraw up to $10,000 for a first-time home purchase without triggering taxes or penalties.

For more advice on opening a Roth IRA, see Chapter 9.

The College Years: Beyond Tuition

A college-bound child needs some financial independence, both for personal growth and everyday convenience. But this will probably be achieved using your money. So let's look at some ways to avoid expensive mistakes. (How to pay for the basic expenses, like tuition, is covered in Chapter 9.)

Start by sitting down with your collegian and estimating how much will be needed for books, food, a car or other transportation, cell phone, college-logo sweatshirts and other clothes, and any other incidentals that you won't be paying for directly. (The college website may help you with this information—and definitely check it for details like how much the college charges for parking, which can be expensive.) Create a document similar to your Family Spending

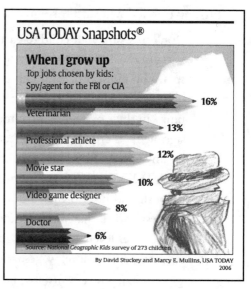

USA TODAY Snapshots®

When I grow up
Top jobs chosen by kids:
Spy/agent for the FBI or CIA
16%
Veterinarian
13%
Professional athlete
12%
Movie star
10%
Video game designer
8%
Doctor
6%

Source: *National Geographic Kids* survey of 273 children

By David Stuckey and Marcy E. Mullins, USA TODAY
2006

Worksheet, make a copy, and have your child agree to stay within the lines or get in touch if changes become necessary. Then figure out the monthly average, help the child open a bank account near campus (preferably with checking and debit card privileges), and make sure you regularly send your child checks to deposit and cover these amounts—with only a little extra, unless your offspring is particularly responsible.

> **CAUTION**
> **Watch out for credit card debt.** Around half of all college students use plastic to pay for school expenses, which only adds to their record-high debt loads upon graduation. One possibility is to add your child to your own card, so that you can keep tabs on expenses. But college students get barraged with offers from credit card companies (at high rates), so you may not be able to stop your child from getting a card. And everyone has to start sometime. Just make sure your child understands the importance of a good credit score and the reasons to avoid credit cards' high interest payments—and that you won't bail out a child who applies for a card and starts spending outside the worksheet you created.

Here are some other ways to keep your student's cash flow from turning into a downward torrent:

- **Don't pressure your child to earn too much.** Campus jobs and other part-time work can be both a learning experience and a source of spending money for your child. Studies also show that kids who help pay for their college education value it more. But there's no point in their overdoing it. Time for reading and completing assignments is crucial. And be realistic: Most students can't earn a lot anyway. As Bob Shireman of the Project on Student Debt told USA TODAY, "We hear boomers all the time say, 'Well, gosh. They should just do what I did—work their way through school.' It doesn't work that way anymore." The reasons include higher tuition, lower levels of federally guaranteed student loans per student, stagnating entry-level wages, and skyrocketing housing costs.

- **Look for cheap, one-way student plane fares.** Find them at www.studentuniverse.com.

- **Choose a flexible meal plan.** Most kids don't want to eat on campus all the time, so why waste money on a meal plan that assumes they will? A number of options are usually available, including paying for a certain number of meals in advance, or using a debit-like card to pay for on-campus meals.

- **Talk to roommates before you load up on furnishings.** A student who will be sharing a room or apartment should confer with roommates before school starts, comparing notes on who is packing what. It can help avoid arriving with multiple sets of curtains, floor lamps, and area rugs.

- **Keep your child on your cell phone plan.** That way, you'll see the bill, and can ask for repayment, voice your appreciation, shock, or dismay (whichever seems called for), or simply make sure it gets paid.

- **Check your homeowners' insurance policy.** It should cover property that's damaged or stolen while your child is living in a dorm room—but don't assume. Call the agent and find out, and while you're at it ask about coverage limits on electronics and laptops (some policies exclude them completely). Explain this coverage, and the need to call you so you can put in a claim if something is lost, to your child. If your child will be living off-campus, your homeowners' insurance won't provide coverage, so buying renter's insurance is a good idea. At approximately $15 per month, it's a bargain.

- **Check your medical insurance policy.** If the college is within the policy's coverage area and you can continue to cover your college student child under your plan (both for emergencies and regular care), great. This may be more comprehensive than coverage offered by the school (read the fine print, especially for hospitalizations and major expenses). Also make sure to sign the school's waiver on coverage, so you're not double paying.

- **Deal with auto insurance.** If your child owns a car, read over the insurance policy together so that the child understands, for example, restrictions on who can drive it. And if your child will no longer be using your car, but was named on your insurance policies, tell your company—it may lower your premiums.

Cutting the Cord:
When to Stop Supporting Young Adults

Once college is over, and you've helped your children through it, is it time to say, "No more?" After all, you're probably eager to refocus on saving for retirement. However, you got into this parent/child relationship for life, and there are reasons to maintain some flexibility, even while you encourage your children to become independent.

One reason is that kids aren't rushing into the traditional trappings of adulthood. As USA TODAY reporter Sharon Jayson describes, "Acting your age" used to make sense. Going to college, leaving home, getting married, having children and retiring took place at predictable stages. That was then. Now, it's not so easy. Not when market surveys of "American youth" routinely include ages 16-35. Age used to be an important way to organize life, but now, the picture is changing.

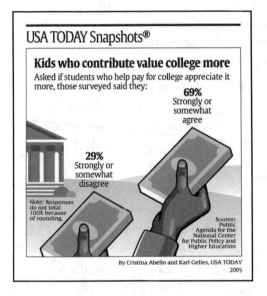

USA TODAY Snapshots®

Kids who contribute value college more

Asked if students who help pay for college appreciate it more, those surveyed said they:

69% Strongly or somewhat agree

29% Strongly or somewhat disagree

Note: Responses do not total 100% because of rounding.

Source: Public Agenda for the National Center for Public Policy and Higher Education

By Cristina Abello and Karl Gelles, USA TODAY 2005

Among the ways it's changing are that, in Jayson's words, "More young college graduates are delaying entry into a tight job market. Some opt for grad school or public service; many put off marriage and family." And many switch careers more than once, even after you thought they were settled. All of this means they may look to you for help.

Don't worry, it's not that the kids are slow or unmotivated. Jayson found that, "At the heart of these changes: increased life expectancy, which in the USA is at a record high of 77.9 years, according to the most recent preliminary data from the National Center for Health Statistics. 'All of a sudden, we have these bonus decades,' says Richard Leider, a senior fellow at the University of Minnesota's Center for Spirituality and Healing in Minneapolis. With this increase in longevity, it's no accident that ages for life events such as marriage or having a child are inching upward, says psychologist and sociologist Lillian Rubin of San Francisco. Centuries ago, when 40 was considered old age, people married as teens to make sure they lived long enough to raise children. Living twice that long alters our perceptions, she says."

Fortunately, if your college grad kids are ready to enter the workforce, employment opportunities for this age group are becoming "even hotter than the overall economy. The National Association of Colleges and Employers reported that recruiters planned to hire 17.4% more grads from the 2007 class than the '06 class," says USA TODAY's Laura Vanderkam.

If your grown children are still testing their wings, here are some ways you can help:

- **Keep them talking to you.** It's worth asking your children how they're doing financially. Otherwise, they may assume they're supposed to know it all—and get into trouble, for example by falling behind on student loan payments. (That would be your cue to help your child research alternative payment plans offered by the federal student loan program.) Remember that your children probably didn't learn much about practical finance in college, where, as Laura Levine, executive director of the JumpStart Coalition, told USA TODAY's Mindy Fetterman, "you get the bigger stuff, like the global economy. They don't teach you how to balance your checkbook." Keep sharing what you've learned about money.

- **Remind them that college grads are supposed to start out poor.** As Laura Vanderkam commented, "Too many 22-year-olds expect to start their adult lives at their parents' level of material satisfaction, without the 30 years of labor it took them to get there. Our world of easy credit and mysteriously glamorous TV apartments says you can have it all now." Buy your child a book like *Frugal Living for Dummies,* by Deborah Taylor-Hough.

- **Keep them on your health insurance policy.** As Sharon Jayson reported, "Increasing numbers of young adults are covered by their parents' health insurance policies. The National Conference of State Legislatures says at least 17 states have enacted laws in the past few years extending the time children can remain on parents' insurance; about half have considered such measures." This can save money and prevent medical problems from crippling your grown child's independence.

- **Lend money to pursue opportunities you agree with.** We'll be talking in Chapter 8 about the mutual benefits of borrowing from your family to make a down payment on a house. But at the point when you've reached some level of financial stability, it may be your children's turn to do the borrowing. If, for example, a child is trying to buy a car or house and is capable of handling the repayments, you'll do the whole family a favor by lending some or all of the money—you'll earn interest income, but will still be able to offer your child a lower interest rate than would be commercially available. Be sure to draw up the appropriate legal documents and explain the plan to your other children, including how you'll be ready to do the same for them.

- **Don't give away their bedroom.** They may be back. See "Boomerang Kids Returning to the Nest," below.

Boomerang Kids Returning to the Nest

Going back to live with Mom and Dad has lost the stigma it once had—in fact, some kids are reclaiming their bedrooms with fiancés or spouses in tow. As USA TODAY reporter Haya El Nasser tells it, many are seeking refuge under their parents' roofs from rapidly rising housing prices, mounting college debts, and more.

They're "boomerang" or "back-to-the-bedroom" kids. They leave. They come back. Sometimes more than once, often after college, between jobs, before marriage, after a divorce, or when housing costs are so exorbitant that moving in to their old bedrooms is more appealing than sharing a small, rundown apartment with three roommates.

"Your 20s are your wealth-building years," says Matthew Costigan, 24, an associate at PricewaterhouseCoopers in Pittsburgh. "If you save money, it grows. It's important to start doing things right early on." Spending $600 a month on an apartment he shared with two other guys didn't seem right, he says. Costigan prefers to commute and save to buy a condominium in the city and build up his retirement fund. And Mom and Dad are fine with the idea.

Some parents buy their children a condo or a house when they get out of college. Others let them move back rent-free to allow them to save enough money to buy a house for themselves. Jaclyn Tammaro and Brian Hanley are 23, college graduates, working good jobs, and recently engaged. They have both moved back in with their parents to save money to buy their own place. "We knew we wanted to save up some money so that seemed like the best option," Tammaro says. "If I wanted to rent something in the city, it could've been anywhere from $900 to $1,300 a month."

Books and magazines are filled with advice for parents of boomerang kids. Most suggest that adult children pay rent or contribute in some way.

Boomerang Kids Returning to the Nest (cont'd.)

But many parents never ask for money. They usually let children pay for personal expenses such as cars, insurance, and entertainment. But it helps when the children don't revert to teenage habits and expect Mom to do the laundry and clean up after them. Matt Costigan says he may not pay rent but, "they make me mow the lawn every week during the summer. That's a fair trade."

 "Why grown kids come home; High rents, college loans drive 'boomerang kids' back to nest," by Haya El Nasser, January 11, 2005.

That's Just My Co-Pay? Manage Your Health Care Expenses

With or without health insurance, medical costs can claim a punishingly large portion of your family's income. Just one injury or unexpected illness may thrust you into the land of high insurance deductibles, uncovered doctor's bills, and out-of-pocket payments. If you're reluctant to look into your insurance situation now, think how much worse it would be if you were already sick or worried about a family member's illness. So keep reading, to learn how to:

- get health coverage if your employer doesn't provide it
- claim what you deserve from your health insurer, and
- take advantage of tax benefits through flexible spending or savings accounts.

SKIP AHEAD
Super-high medical expenses may get you a tax deduction.
See Chapter 7 for details.

Going Uninsured?
That's Fine Until You're Sick

We probably don't have to remind you that the United States has no national system of medical coverage, except for the old and the very poor (and that's far from comprehensive). And although there's been plenty of discussion within state governments about how to improve the situation, not much progress has been made. Hawaii requires employers to provide their workers with health benefits, Massachusetts is struggling to implement a law requiring everyone to buy health insurance just as they would car insurance, and some other states subsidize employer health insurance payments, but that's the best of it so far.

In most states, people who are freelancing, self-employed, unemployed, or working for employers that don't offer health benefits must either find and pay for their own coverage or go without. The result is that more than 46 million Americans were uninsured at last count—or nearly 16% of the population—and the numbers have been steadily rising.

Your rights and risks when uninsured

Let's start with the good news about being uninsured: Hospitals must treat anyone who comes in the door with a medical emergency, whether or not the person has insurance. Unfortunately, that's the end of the good news. The hospitals don't treat you for free, so you're hardly off the hook. USA TODAY's Julie Appleby found that, "Just a few days in a hospital could set you back tens of thousands of dollars. Plus, because you're uninsured, you might have to pay full charges, rather than the negotiated discounts that insurers receive from hospitals and other providers." And who wants to wait until a medical condition has reached emergency levels to see a doctor anyway?

At least you're not living in 1400

Here are some reported medieval health remedies—and you wouldn't have had insurance to pay for them, either.

- *Tie a piece of black ribbon around your neck (for a sore throat).*
- *Drink wine with the lung of a fox soaking in it (to help asthma).*
- *Place a roasted onion on an aching ear.*
- *Rub an infected eye with the tail of a black cat.*

Going without health insurance is both a medical and a financial gamble. As Gary Claxton, who studies health care costs for the Kaiser Family Foundation, a nonprofit think tank, told USA TODAY, you should go without insurance "only if you can afford a serious illness, which could run $100,000 to $200,000."

Does Fido Need Insurance, Too?

When you see that little doggie in the window, you're probably not thinking about money. You should.

The expense of owning a dog can be startling if you add up everything you may have to buy—from squeaky toys to a $2,000 Sweet 16 party for 60 of your closest Chihuahua friends (as Ada Nieves of New York City did last spring for her Chihuahua, Vanilla). Okay, maybe you don't go that far. Even so, a dog can cost thousands of dollars a year once you count all the services it may need: medical care, training, grooming, kenneling, and on and on. Few people actually budget for their pet expenses, or have a firm grasp of what their dog costs them every year.

Today, many pet owners will pay for nearly the same level of medical care for their pet as they do for themselves. MRIs and CAT scans and diabetes treatment and radiation for cancer are all available. Last year, a woman in Washington state paid $38,000 for medical treatment for her pet, which had an autoimmune disease.

Pet insurance, which covers some medical costs, can run from about $30 to $45 a month, depending on what area you live in.

USA TODAY usatoday.com "Dog's life can cost an arm and a hind leg," by Mindy Fetterman, Priyanka Dayal, February 23, 2007.

What about Medicaid or state government assistance? Unless your assets and income are very low, you won't qualify. Instead, you'll probably need to look into buying individual health insurance coverage.

Before you start shopping, check out whether your state's laws give you any protections in dealing with health insurance companies. (You'll find state-by-state summaries of your legal rights at www.healthinsuranceinfo. net and http://insure.com/health/lawtool.cfm.) While your expectations shouldn't be high—insurance companies in most states can flat out turn you down if it looks like you'll cost them more than your premiums are worth—you might find small but pleasant surprises. For example, in Massachusetts, New Jersey, New York, and Vermont, insurance companies can't use poor health as a reason to refuse you a policy (though they tend to charge everyone high premiums as a result). And many states mandate that newborns be included under a parent's policy for a limited time, usually 30 to 60 days, no matter the state of their health.

USA TODAY Snapshots®

Pets at the doctor

Average veterinary-related expenses in the past 12 months for cat and dog owners:

Dog owners
$263

Cat owners
$113

Source: The Humane Society of the United States

By David Stuckey and Karl Gelles, USA TODAY 2006

Shopping for health insurance

Your success in finding a good policy, as well as the amount you'll pay in monthly premiums, will likely depend on your age, family size, medical history, what the policy covers, and where you live. Your medical history can be a big one—people have been turned down for coverage or charged higher rates due to everything from past treatment for cancer or chronic conditions to taking a cholesterol medication. In most cases there's not much you can do about your medical history, though quitting smoking and losing weight can definitely help. The lowest premium you might pay is around $40 a month, but average premiums are around $350 a month. They're not tax deductible.

When you're ready to start shopping, your most likely options include:

- **A licensed, local health-insurance broker.** Such brokers not only help you get the best price, they can also steer you toward companies with good reputations for keeping premiums stable and reimbursing policyholders without excess hassle. You don't pay them directly; instead, they receive a commission from the health insurer you choose. To find a licensed broker, contact the National Association of Health Underwriters (www.nahu.org).

- **Online price quote services.** Try eHealthInsurance.com, insure.com, or DigitalInsurance.com for immediate quotes from several brokers or companies.

- **Your state insurance department's website.** It may list companies selling individual coverage in your state, including some that aren't represented by brokers. Some states also have special programs for people turned down based on health.

- **A state program that at least covers your children.** See www.insurekidsnow.gov, run by the U.S. Department of Health & Human Services, for links to descriptions of state programs available to families that earn too much to qualify for Medicaid but can't afford private insurance.

- **Group coverage based on your membership in a professional group, club, or local chamber of commerce.** Groups representing freelance writers and journalists, for example, have come to realize that one of the biggest issues on their members' minds is finding insurance. They've negotiated group policies accordingly. The benefits of group coverage are that you might pay lower rates than if you approached insurers on your own, and you might be covered for preexisting conditions. But of course, you'll need to read the fine print to be sure.

USA TODAY Snapshots®

Medical events threaten financial health

Of the more than 1.45 million families in the USA who filed for bankruptcy[1], 54.5% blamed medical problems. Most frequently cited reasons:

Illness or injury — 28%
Birth/addition of new family member — 8%
Death in family — 8%
Alcohol or drug addiction — 3%
Uncontrolled gambling — 1%

1 – Data collected in 2001. Many people gave more than one reason. Families includes filers, non-filers and children.
Source: *Health Affairs*, February 2005

By Ashley Burrell and Marcy E. Mullins, USA TODAY 2005

Be honest and complete when filling out your applications for insurance, even if you think it will make you less insurable. A recent and unpleasant trend is for insurance companies to revoke policies because the patient allegedly lied during the application process. And what they call lies might seem like minor oversights to the rest of us, such as a forgotten emergency room visit for pain that turned out to be nothing, or an incorrect date given for a woman's last menstrual period. As luck would have it, insurance companies seem especially likely to do this after the person has racked up high hospital bills.

If you have serious conditions in your medical history, check whether your state has what's called a "high-risk insurance pool," which covers people whom commercial insurers have rejected—though at a high price.

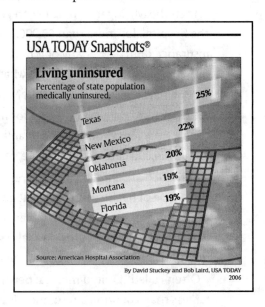

USA TODAY Snapshots®

Living uninsured
Percentage of state population medically uninsured.

Texas 25%
New Mexico 22%
Oklahoma 20%
Montana 19%
Florida 19%

Source: American Hospital Association

By David Stuckey and Bob Laird, USA TODAY 2006

If you're offered more than one policy, read "Choosing among plans," below, for tips on selecting the one offering the best value. And be sure to choose a plan that offers guaranteed renewal, so that you don't find your coverage cancelled once you've gotten sick. If, on the other hand, your search doesn't turn up any affordable coverage options, your only financially sound choice may be to find a job that comes with health benefits.

Is a Little Medical Coverage Better Than None?

Tony Camilleri rushed his pregnant wife, Bridget, to an emergency room in January, fearing she was suffering a dangerous complication with her pregnancy. Luckily, tests showed she was not.

Then the Michigan couple began getting bills from doctors and the hospital, for more than $8,000. To his surprise, Camilleri's insurance didn't cover any of it because his wife had surpassed a $2,500-a-person annual limit on what the policy would pay.

Eric Chaves, a security officer in Massachusetts, owes more than 1½ months of take-home wages for medical care this year. Two trips to the emergency room—one in an ambulance—exceeded his plan's annual $4,000 cap for doctor care, tests, and ER visits.

Both men are enrolled in an increasingly popular—and controversial—type of health insurance that gives limited coverage to more than 1 million Americans. Their cases reflect a building debate about whether such policies provide a false sense of security, and raise the question: Is a little coverage that much better than none at all?

Often called "limited medical benefit plans," the policies can cost far less than traditional insurance. But they cap what insurers will pay toward medical care, with the skimpiest plans covering as little as $1,000 a year. Some have daily caps, such as paying a few hundred dollars a day toward hospital coverage. Traditional insurance, by contrast, generally covers most medical expenses in a given year, after deductibles and co-payments.

Proponents say the limited plans should not be considered the solution to the problem of the uninsured, but rather one option to help people get basic medical care. Some patient advocates disagree, saying many of the plans leave policyholders more vulnerable to devastating medical bills than they might think.

Is a Little Medical Coverage Better Than None? (cont'd.)

Camilleri and Chaves say they soured on limited-benefit plans. "It wasn't worth it," says Camilleri, who got his insurance through the staffing agency that placed him in his job as a test engineer. The insurance cost Camilleri $400 a month and covered himself, his wife, Bridget, 33, and stepdaughter, Stephanie, 11.

 "Is a little medical coverage that much better than none?" by Julie Appleby, June 6, 2007.

Already Insured? Don't Pay More Than You Have To

If you're lucky enough to have health insurance already, most likely through your or your spouse's employer, you can relax a bit—but not too much. With a little research, both when choosing among your employer's offered plans and when making claims, you can potentially save thousands of dollars, and avoid frustration and headaches.

Choosing among plans

Most employers offer health insurance benefits to their employees. Many offer more than one plan, though the trend, Sandra says, is that "Workers who once had the choice of several health maintenance organizations may now have just one HMO." Larger employers tend to give you more offerings, partly because they themselves have more choices—some insurance companies refuse to deal with employers whose workforces are small.

USA TODAY Snapshots®

Common injuries children suffer

Top traumatic orthopedic injuries for which children are hospitalized:

Spinal 5.2%
Lower arm 14.7%
Upper arm 17%
Lower leg 21.5%
Thighbone 21.7%

Source: The American Academy of Orthopaedic Surgeons

By Shannon Reilly and Frank Pompa, USA TODAY 2004

Of course, not all health plans are created equal. And the costs of your coverage may vary between different plans, a particular concern since an increasing number of employers require employees to foot part of the basic bill. They themselves are facing premium increases that move at a faster rate than inflation. Both for cost and for medical reasons, it's in your interest to research the offerings and choose wisely.

Even if you've already chosen a plan for the year, you'll probably get a chance to rethink your choice during an open enrollment period toward year's end. If you're starting a new job, or are in an open enrollment period, it's worth reading all those glossy brochures and asking questions of any visiting representatives. Also talk to friends who've had experiences with the same plans, and see the list of America's best hospitals at www. usnews.com/usnews/health/best-hospitals/tophosp.htm.

Coverage If You and Your Partner Aren't Married

Many families rely on one wage earner's employer to provide health coverage for the entire family (though often at added cost). But this doesn't always work for unmarried couples, where one person isn't legally the other's "dependent." However, some states do require employers that provide family coverage to extend this coverage to formally registered domestic partners. Even without such a state law, some employers voluntarily offer benefits to domestic partners. About a third of such employers limit the benefit to same-sex partners, the rest don't distinguish.

If your employer offers domestic partner health benefits, expect to be asked to sign an affidavit (sworn statement) and provide other proof that you two have really settled down together. As for the children, to get them coverage under their father's health plan, Dad may have to sign an acknowledgment of paternity.

RESOURCE

Check independent ratings of your prospective health plans. The National Committee for Quality Assurance (NCQA) has done some of the work for you, evaluating health plans in every state on the basis of access to service, qualified providers, and more. Go to http://web.ncqa.org and click "Report Cards."

Here are some key issues to focus on when choosing health insurance:

- Whether you prefer traditional health insurance coverage or a health maintenance organization ("HMO"). Traditional coverage usually gives you a wide selection of doctors and hospitals (though you may have to pay more for going outside a certain network). You gain freedom and potentially quality of care, but may have to deal with more paperwork and high or unpredictable costs. HMOs, by contrast, limit your doctor and hospital choices to within a closed system, but once you're within it, it's usually easy to navigate. However, consumers allege that some HMOs pressure their doctors to save money by giving you only the minimal amount of needed care. HMO doctors can also be harder to sue for malpractice. And despite the predictable costs, you've got nowhere to run if the rates for particular services seem high.

- The company or HMO's reputation among consumers for quality medical care and good customer service.

- Your monthly contribution to what your employer pays (fortunately, this comes from pretax dollars). The average per year in 2007 was $3,281 for families and $694 for a single person's coverage.

- If your employer offers coverage to your spouse or partner and children (which not all employers do), your cost for their coverage. On average, you're likely to pay 27% of the premium your employer must pay for a family plan versus 16% for single coverage. Many employers contribute nothing at all toward family members' premiums. Still, this may be a better deal than buying individual coverage for family members, particularly if one has a preexisting medical condition.

- Your deductible amounts (the amount you pay before your insurance kicks in). The average in 2007 ranged between $401 per year for individual workers in HMOs and $1,729 for people in high-deductible plans. Higher-deductible options usually come with lower premiums; but before going with one of these policies, make sure you're ready to put money aside for out-of-pocket, possibly unexpected medical costs.

- Co-pay or coinsurance amounts (a co-pay is a set fee, such as $20, that you pay when visiting the doctor or filling a prescription; coinsurance means that instead of a co-pay, you pay a percentage of your overall costs).

- Your freedom to choose a primary doctor. For non-HMOs, focus on how many local doctors accept this type of insurance. For HMOs, focus on how often you can change doctors—an important concern, since the primary care doctor is often responsible for your referrals to specialists.

- Your freedom to choose specialists. For example, in a non-HMO, must you still choose within a particular network? If so, look at the plan's list of specialists to whom you'd have access, sorted by category (such as dermatology or cardiology). If only one or two names are given in each category, that's not much choice. In an HMO, also check on how extensive their list of specialists is, and on whether they'll let you see a specialist outside the HMO if you have an unusual condition that has exhausted the HMO doctors' expertise.

- Coverage for preexisting conditions. For example, if you already have high blood pressure or diabetes, you'll want to make sure you'll get continuing care, and without a waiting period.

- Prenatal care, psychological therapy, or care for other special needs or conditions within your family.

- Any annual or lifetime limits on coverage (yes, some policies actually cut you off after a certain dollar limit).

Going with the cheapest option isn't always wise. Less expensive plans are no bargain if they severely restrict the doctors or hospitals you may choose among or limit coverage for things like immunizations and prenatal testing.

Keeping out-of-pocket costs down

As Harvard professor Elizabeth Warren told USA TODAY, "No one reads the insurance coverage until the insurance company denies the coverage." But by then it's often too late to do anything more than negotiate a payment plan. So once you've chosen your coverage, read the paperwork again, and be alert for exclusions or limits on certain types of care, such as physical therapy or mental health services.

Get advance approvals. Be careful not to sign up for any procedures or hospital stays until you're sure they'll be covered. The administrative staff at your doctor's office or hospital can normally help you figure this out, but don't sit back and expect them to know or handle everything. "In non-emergency situations," USA TODAY's Julie Appleby advises, "See if you have choices. Ask your doctor about the cost of drugs and treatments and whether there are less-costly options. Try to choose an in-network hospital." According to Professor Warren, "There are times when having a procedure done at one hospital rather than another can mean a $5,000 difference in what the patient will be charged."

Check the bills. Question any bills that seem out of whack. Big dollars are potentially at stake here, so a little monitoring and follow-up will be well worth your time. Although your doctor's office may be doing its best, the world of medical insurance is confusing, even to those dealing with it every day. Mistakes and overcharges happen! Ask anyone who's ever called about a doctor's bill—an extraordinary number turn out to have been just plain miscalculated, or already covered by the patient's insurance.

We know someone who called about a supposedly unpaid co-pay and was told, "Oh, sorry, that was before we fired the receptionist who was stealing the cash co-pays; we'll cancel that bill." (How many people just pay these bills without question?!) Write down who you speak with and on what date, in case you get a repeat of the same bill later. And if the person on the phone isn't completely helpful, write a letter.

Dispute refusals of coverage. If your insurance company has unreasonably refused to cover a particular service, you may be able to appeal its decision to a review board (most likely internal, but possibly independent). But you must submit your appeal within the company's deadline, which is usually six months. In some states, the laws protect your right to a certain level of review; visit www.Kff.org/consumerguide to find out what rules your insurer must follow.

> **CAUTION**
>
> **Another baby on the way?** Read your policy before heading to the doctor's office or hospital. Under some plans, you must contact their administrative office for advance approval of your prenatal and maternity care, sometimes by submitting a form. And some plans even require you to call your health insurer shortly after admission to a hospital for labor and delivery (between contractions, we assume).

Getting COBRA coverage after a job loss

At last, a federal law that offers you some help: the Consolidated Omnibus Budget Reconciliation Act (COBRA). This law allows you and any covered dependents to keep your health coverage after you've either left a job (even if you were fired, as long as it wasn't for "gross misconduct") or you've cut back to a part-time schedule and thus lost your health benefits.

The main conditions are that you worked someplace with 20 or more employees (though some states' laws extend COBRA to workplaces with fewer employees) and that you're willing to pay the ongoing monthly premiums. It's all coordinated through your employer—who, unfortunately, can charge you up to 102% of your normal premiums. But that's still probably less than you'd pay for an individual policy, and worthwhile for two other reasons. First, continued coverage allows you to avoid major medical expenses that might arise while you look for a new job or new individual coverage. Second, it frees you from the worry that your next health plan won't cover your preexisting conditions for some period of time, sometimes up to a year. (Even if you're well now, don't forget that you or a family member might need medical care while you're job hunting.)

COBRA coverage lasts for up to 18 months, or 29 months if you become disabled during that period. Some states' laws extend that period even longer. If your employer's plan covered children, and you get pregnant while under COBRA, you'll also have a right to coverage for your new child, though you may have to pay additional premiums.

RESOURCE
For more information on your COBRA rights: See the U.S. Department of Labor's list of "Frequently Asked Questions about COBRA Continuation Coverage," at www.dol.gov/ebsa/faqs/faq_consumer_cobra.html.

Save Money With Flexible Spending or Health Savings Plans

A $20 doctor's co-pay here, a $15 prescription co-pay there: Even with health insurance, it adds up. In fact, a reasonably healthy person can easily spend several hundred dollars a year out-of-pocket, especially when seeking alternative treatments like acupuncture or chiropractic adjustments. That's why it's worth looking into options to reduce the hit through tax advantages, namely:

- a flexible spending account (FSA), or
- a health savings account (HSA).

Even the Insured Have Trouble Paying Bills

USA TODAY's Julie Appleby reports that, when Janet Fredrick got breast cancer in 1998, she never thought she would face bankruptcy because of medical bills: She had insurance.

But her illness dragged out, then her income plunged when she went on disability. By 2005, her co-payments for treatment, including surgery, medications, doctor visits, and hospital care, totaled about $8,000.

Such co-payments and deductibles, along with difficult-to-understand policies and complex hospital billing issues, are among the main reasons even people such as Fredrick who have health insurance can face devastating financial costs, says a report from The Access Project, an advocacy group that researches medical debt.

In October 2006, a poll by USA TODAY, the Kaiser Family Foundation, and ABC News found that one in four Americans had trouble paying for medical care during the year. Among those reporting trouble paying, 69% had insurance.

Along with deductibles and co-payments, The Access Project found other factors associated with medical debt were annual or lifetime "caps" on benefits; extra charges for "out of network" care, even when admitted to in-network hospitals; and complex billing systems by insurers and hospitals that left patients confused about what they owed.

USA TODAY usatoday.com "Even the insured have trouble paying bills," by Julie Appleby, March 22, 2007.

Flexible health spending accounts

If your employer offers a flexible spending account (FSA) benefit for health expenses, run, don't walk, to sign up. It's usually offered during the end-of-year open enrollment period, or when you first start a new job. (Self-employed people can't get FSAs.) The idea is that you choose an amount of money to set aside from your paycheck over the course of the calendar year, before any tax is withheld from it. You then draw on that money to pay your medical expenses, usually with a simple system of saving your receipts and putting in a claim. You can even draw on the money before you've deposited it, if you need to. But if you don't use all the money, you lose it—it goes to your employer.

USA TODAY Snapshots®

Treating ailments with diet, exercise

Percentage of people within age groups who treat ailments with diet and exercise:

18-24: 22%
25-44: 25%
45-54: 30%
55-64: 37%
65-74: 32%
75 and older: 24%

Age group

Source: 2005 MARS OTC/DTC Survey; based on more than 21,200 responses from adults 18 and older

By Shannon Reilly and Sam Ward, USA TODAY 2005

For example, let's say you tell your employer to set aside $1,000 of your paycheck in your FSA for the year. If, over the course of the year, you spend $100 on doctor co-pays for you and your family, $800 on a new dental crown, $40 on a chiropractic visit, and $60 on prescription and other medicinal drugs, you'll reach that $1,000, and will just need to submit your receipts to claim it. How much you'd save as a result would depend on what federal tax bracket you're in. But even in the 15% tax bracket, setting aside $1,000 a year will net you $150 in tax savings. If you're in the 25% bracket, you'll pocket $250. The maximum you can set aside depends on your employer, and a few employers will supplement your set-asides.

The type of expenses you can pay from your FSA are broader than you might expect. They're based on the IRS's rules for tax-deductible medical expenses, and include your, your spouse's, and your children's medical and dental expenses, such as prescription drugs (including birth control pills), co-pays, acupuncture, chiropractic adjustments, eyeglasses, fertility treatments, lab fees, home renovations for a disability or to remove lead paint, and more. And unlike with regular tax deductions, you can claim reimbursement for over-the-counter drugs like pain relievers and antacids (but not vitamins).

Of course, the use-it-or-lose-it aspect of FSAs makes it very important that you track your spending and claim your reimbursements, often by the end of December (though many plans give you until March). If you simply forget to submit your receipts, you're out of luck. If you haven't gone to the doctor much, you may have to make a mad December shopping trip to stock up on aspirin, diaper cream, and bandages.

How Much to Deposit to Your FSA

Sandra says that to avoid forfeiting your money, planners recommend using conservative estimates, especially if you've never had an FSA before. Here's how to get the most from your health care FSA:

- Add up your out-of-pocket costs for routine medical and dental treatment during the year. Include costs for teeth cleaning, vision exams, glasses, contact lenses, and contact lens solution.
- Estimate the cost of ongoing prescription medications not covered or only partially covered by your insurance, such as birth control pills.
- If you know you'll need elective surgery or other procedures, ask your dentist or doctor for a cost estimate. Use your plan information to figure out how much will be covered by insurance.
- Consider using an FSA to reduce your premiums. Choose a less expensive plan with a higher deductible, and use money from your FSA to pay the deductibles.

Too often, workers get caught up in the holiday bustle and forget about their FSAs, says Barbara Steinmetz of Steinmetz Financial Planning in Burlingame. Don't expect your plan to remind you to spend the money. "It's on your back to make sure you use it," she says. "This is really your money you're losing."

 "How to pay medical bills and save taxes; Flexible spending accounts do have a hitch: Use it or lose it," by Sandra Block, December 1, 2000.

RESOURCE
For more information on expense eligibility. Talk to your benefits administrator and download IRS Publication 502, *Medical and Dental Expenses*, from www.irs.gov. Also see IRS Publication 969, *Health Savings Accounts and Other Tax-Favored Health Plans*, for general information.

Health savings accounts

Instead of FSAs, some employers offer a tax-saving option called a health savings account (HSA). You can also open one on your own, in conjunction with buying individual insurance coverage (see the options at www.healthdecisions.org/hsa or www.hsainsider.com).

HSAs allow you, and your employer if it's feeling generous, to deposit money into an interest-bearing account managed by a bank or other financial trustee. The deposit entitles you to a tax deduction, and the interest is tax-free, too. As with an FSA, you later draw on this account to cover your out-of-pocket medical costs.

The downside of an HSA is that, to be eligible, your health plan must require you to pay unusually high deductibles—for 2007, it was at least $1,100 per year for individual coverage, or $2,200 per year for family coverage. Unfortunately, this has created an opportunity for employers to switch to high-deductible health plans (with lower premiums for them) and then offer HSAs. The high-deductible requirement also explains why, if you're buying insurance on your own, you'll normally set up the HSA as part of a package deal in which you choose a high-deductible policy.

The maximum you can contribute to your HSA is, in most cases, either the amount of your annual health insurance deductible, or $2,850 if you have individual coverage, $5,650 if you have family coverage (2007 figures).

As for getting your money back, you typically have a choice of either paying for coverage using an HSA debit card or checks, or using your own money and requesting reimbursement after the fact. And the best part is that you need not worry about end-of-year deadlines. Any amounts you don't use just stay in the account and accumulate toward your retirement. Once you reach age 65, you can withdraw money from the account for any purpose without penalty.

The types of expenses that qualify are the same as qualify for other tax deductions, as listed in IRS Publication 502, *Medical and Dental Expenses*. (Unlike with FSAs, however, you can't count nonprescription drugs.) And be warned: If you use the money for something other than a health care expense, the bank or trustee will advise the IRS, and you'll owe not only income tax on the amount, but in some cases a penalty fee. You're also expected to keep receipts and other records of your reimbursed expenses, just in case the IRS comes looking. ●

April Refund Showers:
Claim the Tax Breaks You Deserve

Filing your federal taxes is easier than ever, thanks to software and direct online filing. But as Sandra points out, "Even the best software program is only as good as the information you provide." The same could be said about accountants and tax preparers. So don't wait until April to start gathering your receipts and records. Many people get a smaller refund than they deserve because they either fail to keep good records or simply have no clue that doing so could gain them tax deductions or credits.

You don't need to study everything there is to know about federal income taxes. Here, we'll cover some "don't miss 'em" tax deductions and credits that can help your family—and we'll warn you about a few tax traps to avoid.

By the way, are you clear on the difference between a tax deduction and a tax credit? Here's a quick review: A tax deduction is an amount you subtract from your gross income (all the money you earned during the year) to figure out how much of your income is subject to tax. For example, if your gross income is $80,000 and you have a $2,000 tax deduction, your taxable income is $78,000. A tax credit, by contrast, is a dollar-for-dollar reduction in your tax liability. For example, in recent years the government offered a tax credit for buying energy-efficient home-heating equipment, allowing you to knock up to $500 off your tax bill if you spent that much on things like new insulation or a tankless water heater. If your taxable income is $80,000, and you qualify for a $2,000 tax credit, your taxable income is still $80,000, but you get to take the full $2,000 off the tax you ultimately owe. The bottom line: Tax credits are worth more than tax deductions.

USA TODAY Snapshots®

Who prepares your tax return?

I do my own
59%

41%
I hire a professional

Source: TD Ameritrade survey of 1,000 investors with assets of $100,000 or more. Margin of error ±5 percentage points.

By Jae Yang and Dave Merrill, USA TODAY 2007

Choosing the Best Tax Preparer

Sandra notes that, "You probably wouldn't take your W-2s and 1099s to a business that advertised, 'Tax Returns and Lube Jobs Done While U Wait.' But if the preparer works for a well-known chain, what could go wrong?"

As Sandra discovered, plenty. In early 2007, the Justice Department filed civil lawsuits alleging that employees at more than 125 Jackson Hewitt outlets filed thousands of tax returns claiming fraudulent refunds, costing the government more than $70 million.

At the Jackson Hewitt franchises named in the complaints, tax preparers were inadequately educated and poorly trained, the government said. Their compensation was directly tied to the number of returns they prepared, "without regard to the honesty or quality (or lack thereof) of the return preparation," the complaint alleged.

You are responsible for the information on your tax return, even if the guy who did your taxes is carted off to jail, so:

- **Check the preparer's credentials.** An enrolled agent is a tax professional who has at least five years' work experience at the IRS or has passed an IRS-administered two-day exam. A certified public accountant has a college degree and has passed a certification exam. Both are authorized to represent you in an IRS audit.

- **Find out if the preparer has taken continuing education courses.** Ask about the types of returns he's prepared and how long he's been in business, says Roger Harris, chairman of the government relations committee for the National Association of Enrolled Agents.

- **Ask for an estimate of the cost.** Many preparers base their fees on the complexity of your return, so the preparer might not be able to give you an exact price, Harris says. But a reputable preparer should be able to provide a range of costs, he says. If the preparer bases her fee on a percentage of your refund, head for the door. Those preparers have a vested interest in illegally inflating your refund.

Choosing the Best Tax Preparer (cont'd.)

- Make sure the preparer will be around after April 17. Some tax preparers close their doors once the tax season is over. That could be a problem if the IRS raises questions about your return.

Finally, a reputable preparer won't be afraid to tell you that you're not eligible for a particular tax deduction or credit that would reduce your tax bill. When you ask a tax preparer a question, Harris says, "You want an honest answer. Sometimes, that answer is no."

 "Don't just go to any old tax preparer: Do some checking around first," by Sandra Block, April 10, 2007.

How Much Will Tax Deductions Help You?

No one has to pay income tax on every penny earned. The IRS allows everyone a "standard deduction"—an amount you can subtract from your income to get the amount that will be taxed. (There are other adjustments to that income figure, but this is the big one.) As an alternative to claiming the standard deduction, you can list certain actual expenses on your tax return, including mortgage interest, state and local taxes (including your real estate taxes), charitable contributions, allowable medical expenses, and other miscellaneous deductions. This is called itemizing your deductions, and it requires keeping track of various expenses over the year.

If you have a lot of deductible expenses, itemizing is probably the way to go. However, there are two groups of people who don't have much to gain from itemizing their federal tax deductions. The first includes those for whom it's more financially advantageous to simply take the standard deduction. The second includes people who fall prey to an alternate tax structure called the Alternative Minimum Tax, or AMT.

Who should take the standard deduction

The standard deduction for tax year 2007 is $10,700 for married couples filing jointly or for widow/widowers, $5,350 if you're single or married filing separately, and $7,850 as a head of household. If your total possible itemized deductions don't reach the standard amount, there's no point in itemizing—you should simply take the standard deduction. Many people don't begin itemizing until they've bought a home and can claim a deduction for mortgage interest. Sandra says, "If you rent and live in a state with no income taxes, you may be better off taking the standard deduction." Your tax software will help you run the numbers.

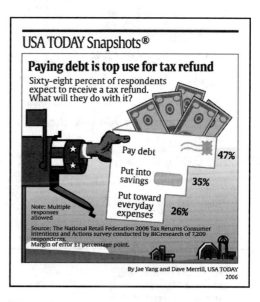

USA TODAY Snapshots®

Paying debt is top use for tax refund

Sixty-eight percent of respondents expect to receive a tax refund. What will they do with it?

Pay debt — 47%
Put into savings — 35%
Put toward everyday expenses — 26%

Note: Multiple responses allowed

Source: The National Retail Federation 2006 Tax Returns Consumer Intentions and Actions survey conducted by BIGresearch of 7,209 respondents. Margin of error ±1 percentage point.

By Jae Yang and Dave Merrill, USA TODAY 2006

Even if you take the standard deduction, you can take advantage of the various tax credits described below. And occasionally, the tax laws offer "above-the-line" deductions, which you can claim even if you don't itemize.

Who'll miss out on deductions because of the AMT

Even the geekiest of financial experts seem to hate the AMT. This messy piece of the tax code—sort of a parallel tax universe—was designed to stop high-income taxpayers from canceling out their tax obligations with lots of deductions. But it's no longer just the wealthy who are paying this extra tax. Although the AMT tax rates themselves are a little higher than under the standard regime, one of the biggest reasons you pay extra is that the only deductions allowed to you under the AMT are for mortgage interest and charitable deductions. That's right, no more deductions for supporting children or dependent parents, or for paying ultrahigh medical expenses.

Here's what a USA TODAY editorial had to say about the AMT: "If you are one of the 3.5 million people who pay the Alternative Minimum Tax (AMT), chances are you have committed at least two of the following three offenses:

- You have a family.
- You live in an area with high taxes, high real estate costs, or both.
- You own a small business.

"Because the AMT is not indexed for inflation, it captures more people each year. Currently it can hit couples earning as little as $62,550."

Sandra advises that, "Tax software programs will automatically calculate whether you owe the AMT, and an experienced preparer will be on the lookout for it. But if you continue to do your taxes the old-fashioned way, the AMT is easy to miss. The only way to figure out whether you owe it is to prepare your taxes twice—once using the standard method and a second time using AMT Form 6251. If the AMT produces a larger tax bill, that's what you owe. Even if you ignore the AMT, the IRS won't." The agency will eventually notify you that you miscomputed your taxes, and you'll have to not only make up the difference, but pay interest on your underpayment.

Strategies to avoid the AMT do exist, based on the principle of raising your income relative to your deductions. Unfortunately, simply neglecting to claim deductions doesn't seem to work. The IRS has sued people over this strategy (and won).

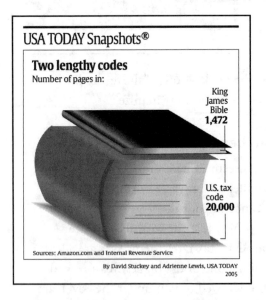

USA TODAY Snapshots®

Two lengthy codes
Number of pages in:

King James Bible
1,472

U.S. tax code
20,000

Sources: Amazon.com and Internal Revenue Service

By David Stuckey and Adrienne Lewis, USA TODAY
2005

Besides, failing to claim deductions means you end up paying a higher tax at regular rates than you would have otherwise. Talk to a tax adviser for a personal analysis—shifting your income or expenses into different tax years can help.

> ⦿ TIP
> **Congress is considering proposals to fix the AMT.** Let's hope these go through, because otherwise the number of taxpayers who owe the AMT will explode, from about 4 million in 2007 to more than 23 million in 2008. Check usatoday.com for updates.

Your Children as Tax Breaks

Although you might not guess it based on his appearance, Uncle Sam does like children. At tax time, you might be able to take advantage of the dependent exemption, child tax credit, and child care expense deductions. For each of the deductions and credits described below, a "child" can be not only your biological child, but an adopted, step, or foster child—or the descendant of one of them. In fact, one of your siblings can count as a child, or your sibling's children (your nieces and nephews).

The dependent exemption

Remember that box near the top of your 1040 income tax return, asking about your exemptions? It lets you claim one exemption per person—that is, deduct a specific amount of your taxable income—for yourself, your spouse, and if they meet certain qualification rules, your dependent children. The exemption amount is $3,400 for the 2007 tax year, and it's adjusted for inflation each year.

These exemptions may not be available at their full value if your taxable income (also known as "adjusted gross income," or AGI) is too high—that is, over $234,600 for married couples filing jointly, $117,300 for married people filing separate returns, and different amounts for singles, heads of household, and widows or widowers (2007 figures). Couples earning more must reduce the dollar value of their exemptions by 2% for every $2,500 they're over the limit (or $1,250 if married filing separately). However, you can't lose more than two thirds of each exemption's value; in other words, an exemption can't be reduced to less than $1,100. And the IRS plans to gradually get rid of this income-based reduction of the exemption; it will be gone completely in 2010.

You can claim an exemption for any child who:

- is younger than age 19 at the end of the tax year, or under 24 and a full-time student, or permanently disabled (any age)
- lived with you for more than half the year (with exceptions, for example for temporary absences or children of divorced or separated parents)
- didn't provide more than half of his or her own support for the year, and
- is a U.S. citizen, national, or resident alien (that's a tax law term for green card holders and certain legal visitors), or a resident of Canada or Mexico for some part of the year.

RESOURCE

Looking for more detailed information? There's a lot more to learn, especially if, for example, you're sharing custody of a child. See IRS Publication 501, *Exemptions, Standard Deduction, and Filing Information*, available at www.irs.gov.

The child tax credit

The child tax credit allows you to subtract a certain amount from your overall tax for each of your children. The maximum is $1,000 per child per year (through 2010). No need to save receipts for this one—the credit has nothing to do with what you spend on your children. However, the amount you can claim will be reduced, or even wiped out altogether, if your income is over a certain limit. More specifically, we're talking about your "modified adjusted gross income (MAGI)," which for most people who have no foreign income will be the same as their "adjusted gross income (AGI)"—in other words their taxable income. For 2007 filings, the MAGI limit was $110,000 for married couples filing jointly, $75,000 for people either filing singly, as head of household, or as qualifying widow or widower, and $55,000 for married people filing separately.

Your children are eligible if they're under 17 and both live with and are supported by you. If a child turns 17 during the tax year, however, you can no longer take the tax credit for that child.

So if you're responsible for $2,000 in taxes and you have two kids, you can (if your income isn't too high) reduce your tax bill to zero. But what if your tax liability is less than the amount of the credit—for example, you owe a mere $1,000 but have two kids? You may have to say goodbye to part of the credit; the IRS won't send you the extra $1,000 unless you qualify for something called the additional child tax credit. To claim this, you'll need to fill out and submit an extra form (IRS Form 8812). The IRS will send you either the unused portion of your child tax credit or 15% of your taxable earned income over an annually adjusted amount, whichever is smaller. How much will that actually gain you? You'll need to run the numbers to find out, but families with lots of kids usually benefit the most.

There's also an adoption tax credit, to help defray your adoption expenses, such as adoption fees, attorney fees, and travel costs. It's worth up to $10,960—see the resources below for details. Adopting a stepchild (your spouse's child from a previous relationship) doesn't count. But that's usually a much less expensive process anyway.

RESOURCE

Ready for details regarding child-related tax credits? See IRS Publication 972, *Child Tax Credit*, available at www.irs.gov. It includes worksheets to help you figure out the exact amount of the credit or additional tax credit you're allowed. For more information on the adoption tax credit, see the instructions for Form 8839, *Qualified Adoption Expenses*.

Child care expense credit

If you're paying for a nanny, preschool, or day care while you work, you'll be glad to know that there's a tax credit available to you. It's good for up to 20% to 35% (depending on your income) of your first $3,000 in child care costs over the year, as an offset from your federal tax liability. But you can't have the IRS send you a check for any unused part of your offset—that is, any amount over and above the tax you owed in the first place.

You can claim more expenses than just salary or wages toward the credit. For example, if you've employed an in-home caregiver, costs such as room, board, and even the employment taxes you paid may be counted.

First, let's make sure your children fit the criteria for the child care expense credit. Each child must:

- live with you for more than half the year, and
- be under age 13 when the care is given or permanently and totally disabled.

Next, let's see whether your child care provider qualifies. The provider must:

- be a licensed day care provider, preschool, nanny (one for whom you're paying employment tax), or day camp

No wonder it's tough to find a nanny!

USA TODAY reporter Del Jones found that corporate CEOs—with their combination of anxiety and wealth—are driving annual salaries of the best-paid nannies toward $100,000. "Those at the high end also get benefits such as health insurance, meals at fine restaurants, country club passes, cars with free gasoline, education stipends, cellphones, working trips aboard corporate jets to places like Hawaii and personal trips compliments of the CEO's frequent-flier miles. All that, plus room and board in a mansion . . . ." Hmm—how about free peanut butter and jelly sandwiches?

- not be someone you claim as a dependent—in other words, if your mother lives with you and provides child care, you can't pay her, claim her as a dependent, and claim the child care credit, and

- be doing child care, not other household services (at least, not for the money that you're requesting the credit to offset).

Finally, let's make sure your own situation qualifies you for the credit. You must:

- pay more than half the cost of keeping up a home in which you and your child live

- work outside the home full- or part-time, or be a full-time student; and if you're married, the same must be true for your spouse, and

- have paid for the child care in order to allow you to work, look for work, or go to school (in other words, you can't be a stay-at-home parent simply looking for a break in your daily routine).

RESOURCE
For more information on the child care expense credit:
See IRS Publication 503, *Child and Dependent Care Expenses.*

Dependent care accounts

While we're talking about lowering your taxes, another possibility if you're paying for child care is a dependent care account (also sometimes called a dependent care flexible spending account or a cafeteria plan). Similar to medical cafeteria plans, these accounts are handled through your employer, and let you set aside pretax dollars from your paycheck. After you've paid for the child care (including expenses such as fees or salary, a nanny's room and board, and day camp), you submit your receipts and reclaim your money.

If you sign up for one of these plans, you can't then also claim a tax credit for the same childcare expenses. Still, a dependent care account is, for most families, the more tax-advantageous choice.

The maximum amount that you can put into your account is $5,000 if you're married filing jointly or $2,500 if you're married filing separately. Your employer may, however, set a lower amount. Do your research before choosing the amount—if you don't spend it by the end of the year, you will, in most cases, lose it.

Do You Have a Nanny Tax Problem?

According to Sandra, "If you paid a nanny $1,500 or more in 2007, you're supposed to file Schedule H with your tax return and withhold a portion of your employee's pay for Social Security, Medicare, and unemployment tax."

But, Sandra adds, despite some high-profile cases of nanny-tax evasion, the tax is widely ignored. In 2003, the most recent year available, only about 241,000 taxpayers filed Schedule H, according to the IRS. The International Nanny Association estimates that about 1 million households employ nannies in the USA. Families bypass the nanny tax for many reasons. Some are already struggling to pay for child care and can't afford it.

Others employ undocumented workers. And some don't understand the rules, or think the tax is too complicated or burdensome, says Robert King, co-owner of Legally Nanny, an Irvine, California-based company that helps people pay nanny taxes.

But this much is clear, King says: If the IRS audits your return and finds you have an off-the-books nanny, you'll owe back taxes and interest—along with penalties for tax evasion and fraud.

 "Did you pay all your taxes?" by Sandra Block, March 6, 2007.

RESOURCE

For more information on dependent care accounts: Talk to your employer's human resources department for more information and for details on what expenses qualify. Also see the instructions to IRS Form 2441, *Child and Dependent Care Expenses*, available at www.irs.gov.

Higher education credits and deductions

Got a kid in college? There are both tax credits and tax deductions that could help you. "Yet, millions of families leave money on the table every year by overlooking valuable education tax breaks," says Sandra. She suggests, "Start by familiarizing yourself with the credits and deductions available to you." These are summarized on the "Tax Breaks for Education Expenses" table below.

They all sound so good—but you'll have to choose among them. As a general rule, Sandra advises that the education-related tax credits are more valuable than the deductions. She adds that, "Apparently, this distinction is lost on a lot of people. A Government Accounting Office study found that 21% of taxpayers who claimed a tuition deduction would have saved more by claiming the lifetime learning credit."

TIP

Keep an eye open for Form 1098-T. Your child's college must send this form to each enrolled student by the end of January, reporting either the payments it received from you or the amounts it billed you for qualified education expenses. In addition, your Form 1098-T should tell you about adjustments made for prior years, the amount of scholarships or grants, reimbursements, or refunds, and whether the student was enrolled at least half-time or was pursuing graduate studies. The information on this form will help you claim the tax credits and deductions described below.

Tax Breaks for Education Expenses (for 2007)			
Benefit	Maximum value	Income* level at which deduction or credit starts phasing out	
		Single, head of household, or qualifying widow(er)	Married filing jointly
Hope credit	$1,650	$45,000-$55,000	$90,000-$110,000
Lifetime learning credit	$2,000	$45,000-$55,000	$90,000-$110,000
Tuition deduction	$4,000	$65,000-$80,000	$130,000-$160,000
Student loan interest deduction	$2,500	$50,000-$65,000	$105,000-$135,000

* "Income" refers to "modified adjusted gross income" or "MAGI," meaning your taxable income with certain exclusions and deductions added back in.

The Hope credit. The Hope credit is meant to offset your spending on education during your child's first two years of college. (It's not available after that.) You may claim one Hope credit per dependent per year—good news for parents of twins!

The credit is worth $1,650. But before you can claim it, you must show that you—or your child—paid at least $2,200 in tuition, fees, equipment, books, and other qualifying expenses. You're not allowed to include amounts paid for insurance, medical expenses (including student health fees), room and board, transportation, or similar personal, living, or family expenses.

It's hard to imagine any family spending less than $2,200 on tuition and fees alone. But of course you can't claim any expenses that were reimbursed, for example by scholarships. And you're expected to go through a somewhat tortuous calculation using IRS Form 8863, which results in your claiming 100% of the first $1,100 of what you spent and 50% of the next $1,100, to reach that magical $1,650 credit amount. You'll submit your completed Form 8863 with your Form 1040.

For you to take the Hope credit, your child must meet certain criteria. He or she must be seeking a degree and be enrolled at least half-time for at least one academic term at an eligible educational institution. Also, any felony drug conviction will destroy the child's qualification for the credit.

If your income is beyond certain limits (listed on the chart above), the Hope credit becomes less valuable to you. Form 8863 will also lead you through calculating this. See Sandra's further advice on "Choosing Education Tax Credits," below.

The lifetime learning credit. This lets you claim 20% of the first $10,000 you pay for a child in college, or $2,000. You can't take the credit more than once in a year, for example by doubling it if you have two kids in college—the $2,000 is a per-family limit. But if you have a freshman or sophomore in college, you could claim the Hope credit for one child and a lifetime learning credit for the other.

And by the way, if you're thinking of going back to school, you yourself can take the credit. It works for any postsecondary education or for courses taken to acquire or improve job skills.

Just like with the Hope credit, you'll need to complete Form 8863 showing amounts you've actually spent and submit it with your Form 1040. The types of expenses that qualify are the same.

As for eligibility, it's fairly simple: The child (or you) must be enrolled in one or more classes at an eligible educational institution. Any colleges eligible to participate in a federal student aid program will do. The felony drug conviction bar doesn't apply to this credit.

The tuition and fees deduction. If your income is too high for either of the education tax credits, you may still be able to deduct the cost of tuition and fees. You may reduce your taxable income by any amounts you spent on qualifying educational expenses (tuition, fees, equipment, books, and supplies) at a qualifying college or other educational institution, up to a maximum of $4,000. But there's a phaseout. If your income is over $65,000 as a single filer or $130,000 if you're married filing jointly, the value of the deduction is cut in half, to $2,000. And once you hit $80,000 in income as a single filer or $160,000 if filing a joint return, no more deduction (2007 tax year figures).

The school-qualification rules are the same as for the tax credits described above. No extra forms are needed; you claim the deduction on your Form 1040. And it's an "above-the-line" deduction, so you can claim it even if you don't itemize.

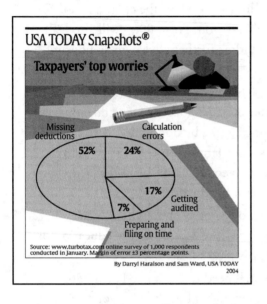

USA TODAY Snapshots®

Taxpayers' top worries

Missing deductions — 52%
Calculation errors — 24%
Getting audited — 17%
Preparing and filing on time — 7%

Source: www.turbotax.com online survey of 1,000 respondents conducted in January. Margin of error ±3 percentage points.

By Darryl Haralson and Sam Ward, USA TODAY 2004

The student loan interest deduction. If you're still paying off your own student loans, you probably know about this one. It lets you deduct a maximum of $2,500 per tax return for interest paid on a qualified student loan (for yourself or your child, or maybe both). You may include the loan origination fee as "interest," so long as it wasn't actually a fee for lender services. The deduction phases out at higher income levels, until disappearing completely if your income is over $65,000 as a single filer or $135,000 if you're married filing jointly. You can claim this deduction even if you don't itemize.

The student must have been enrolled at least half-time in a program leading to a degree, certificate, or other recognized credential at an eligible educational institution. The lender should send you Form 1098-E at the end of January, stating how much interest you paid.

Choosing Education Tax Credits

To help you play your credits wisely, consider both when you can use them and how many children you have in college or other post-secondary school. As Sandra explains (using 2007 tax figures):

The Hope credit is available only for the first two years of your child's undergraduate education. The lifetime learning credit can be taken in any year to offset the cost of college education or classes to improve job skills. You can't take both credits at the same time for the same child, so during the first two years, you need to determine which one delivers the bigger tax break. The maximum lifetime learning credit each year is 20% of the first $10,000 you spend on college expenses, up to $2,000. To get the maximum, you have to shell out at least $10,000. If your college costs are considerably lower than that, the Hope may be the better deal.

You can claim a Hope credit for each eligible student. If you have twins who were college freshmen last year, you may be eligible for up to $3,300 in credits. For the lifetime learning credit, though, the maximum applies to all eligible students in the family. No matter how many kids you have in college, the most you can claim in a year is $2,000.

 "Learning about education deductions can pay off at tax time," Sandra Block, February 21, 2006.

Your Parents as Tax Breaks

Many people find themselves squeezed into the so-called "sandwich generation," supporting both children and parents. According to Sandra, "If you're supporting an elderly parent, you may qualify to claim that parent as a dependent on your tax return. For tax year 2007, claiming an additional personal exemption would reduce your taxable income by $3,400. But to claim this tax break, you must pass the following tests:"

- **Income.** To qualify as a dependent, your parent's income can't exceed the amount of the personal exemption. For 2007, the cutoff is $3,400. In most instances, Social Security benefits aren't counted. But if your parent receives more than $3,400 from other sources, such as pension benefits, interest and dividends from investments, or withdrawals from retirement savings plans, you can't claim her as a dependent. Francis Degen, an enrolled agent in Setauket, New York, says the income requirement prevents most taxpayers from claiming a parent as a dependent, because even a small pension will make the parent ineligible.

- **Support.** In addition to the income test, you must provide more than half a parent's costs for food, housing, medical care, transportation, and other necessities, says Cynthia Jeanguenat, an enrolled agent in Virginia Beach. Even if all your mother's income is from Social Security, you can't claim her as a dependent unless you pay more than half her living expenses. Your mom doesn't have to live with you to qualify as a dependent, as long as she meets the income test and you provide more than half her financial support, says Donna LeValley, a tax lawyer and spokeswoman for *J.K. Lasser's Your Income Tax 2007*. If your mother lives with you, you can include a percentage of your mortgage, utilities, and other expenses in calculating how much you contribute to her support, LeValley says. You can find a worksheet in IRS Publication 501, *Exemptions, Standard Deduction, and Filing Information*, available at www.irs.gov.

Are you helping a parent pay medical costs? Sandra advises that, even if you can't claim your mom as a dependent, you may still get a tax break for helping pay her medical costs. The IRS lets taxpayers deduct money spent on a parent's health care, even if the parent doesn't qualify as a dependent. To claim this deduction, you still must provide more than half your parent's support, Degen says, but your parent doesn't have to meet the income test.

The deduction is limited to medical expenses that exceed 7.5% of your adjusted gross income. You can include your own unreimbursed medical expenses in calculating the total.

Most taxpayers don't have enough medical expenses to clear the 7.5% threshold. But if you're paying thousands of dollars a month for a parent's nursing home care, you might not have trouble overcoming that hurdle.

Children who pay for a parent's care in an assisted-living facility could also qualify for a deduction. Most administrators of these facilities will break out how much of the monthly payment goes toward medical services, as opposed to food and other amenities. The portion that goes toward medical care is deductible, LeValley says, once your total medical expenses exceed 7.5% of your adjusted gross income.

Deduction for Medical and Dental Expenses

We truly hope you don't qualify for the medical/dental expense deduction. It would mean that family health expenses are eating up more than 7.5% of your adjusted gross income. But if you think you might qualify, start saving your receipts now, and be sure to claim this deduction at tax time (assuming you'll be itemizing, rather than taking the standard deduction). You probably deserve a tax deduction as much as anyone possibly could, though it won't go far to offset your total expenses.

Here's how it works: Figure out your adjusted gross income (on the first page of your Form 1040), and then take 7.5% of that amount. Next, add up your out-of-pocket health care costs. (But if you've already claimed them on a flexible spending account or health savings account, discussed in Chapter 6, you can't add them in here.) The amount by which your health care costs exceed the 7.5% is the amount you can deduct, using Schedule A (Itemized Deductions) to Form 1040.

The list of eligible deductions can be found in IRS Publication 502, *Medical and Dental Expenses*, available at www.irs.gov. Read it carefully: It may include more than you expect. And although you don't need to send your receipts or proof of payments to the IRS, you should keep them on file in case of an audit.

Your Home as a Tax Break

If you had to scrape together money to buy your house, you may have been comforted by the thoughts of the homeowner's tax breaks to come. You will, in fact, get to claim federal tax deductions for various home-related expenses. These deductions can add up to some serious savings.

Mortgage interest deduction

One of your biggest deductions will be the interest you pay on your home mortgage, available for mortgages of up to $1 million for individuals and married couples filing jointly and $500,000 for marrieds filing separately. This is particularly advantageous during the early years of a fixed-rate mortgage, when most of your payment goes toward interest. If you have an interest-only loan, your entire mortgage payment will be deductible for several years.

If you bought your house within the last tax year, and you paid points, you get to deduct those, too. (Points are additional and usually optional fees paid when you first took out your mortgage, in exchange for a re-duced interest rate—which is why they're regarded by the IRS as prepaid interest.) Points are tax deductible in the year you paid them, except when refinancing, in which case you must prorate them over the life of the loan.

RESOURCE

For more information: See IRS Publication 936, *Home Mortgage Interest Deduction*, available at www.irs.gov.

Other tax-deductible house expenses

You can also deduct certain other expenses, such as:

- **State and local property taxes.** The amount varies between localities, but most people pay around 1% to 4% of the home's value each year in state and local property tax. These taxes are deductible from your federal tax. And if you recently bought your house, don't forget that you may have paid a chunk of the year's taxes at the closing.

- **Private mortgage insurance (PMI).** If your mortgage was for more than 80% of your home's purchase price, the lender probably required you to buy PMI. (You pay the premiums, but the lender gets the protection, from financial loss if you don't make your payments.) PMI is tax-deductible for mortgages taken out in 2007. However, the amount of the deduction decreases as the taxpayer's income increases. And, while it's a one-year-only law, Congress is taking steps to make it permanent. Check in with your tax adviser.

- **Interest on a home improvement loan.** If you take out a loan to make improvements that increase your home's value, prolong its life, or adapt its use (such as for older or disabled people), you can deduct the interest on that loan, with no limit. These improvements might, for example, include adding a deck, replacing the roof, or installing a handicapped-accessible shower. You can't deduct interest on loans used for normal maintenance and repairs, such as repainting the kitchen or fixing a window.

- **Interest on home equity debt.** You can deduct interest paid on a home equity loan even if the money isn't used to buy, build, or improve your home—but within certain dollar limits. The maximum if you're an individual or a married couple filing jointly is the interest on a $100,000 loan. That maximum drops to the interest on a $50,000 loan if you're married but filing separately. You could, for example, use such a loan for a child's college tuition or family medical bills. If, however, your total home equity and mortgage debt goes over the fair market value of your home, your deduction will have to be reduced.

- **Home office expenses.** If you use part of your home (whether you own or rent) regularly and exclusively for a home-based business, you may be able to deduct a portion of the related expenses—including mortgage or rent, utility bills, and home maintenance and repair costs. However, this deduction can be more trouble than it's worth. For starters, the exclusive-use requirement prevents many people from using the deduction, because they can't spare any space for exclusive business use—for example, they need the same desk area for their business as for their online shopping and personal emailing. Another issue is that if you sell, you'll have to pay capital gains tax on the profit you earn from the portion of your house used as a home office within the last two years. You won't be able to shield it under the $500,000 capital gain tax exclusion available to married couples filing joint returns ($250,000 for singles). For details, see *Working for Yourself: Law & Taxes for Independent Contractors, Freelancers & Consultants*, by Stephen Fishman (Nolo).

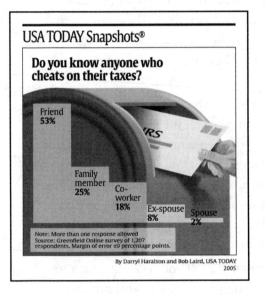

USA TODAY Snapshots®

Do you know anyone who cheats on their taxes?

Friend
53%

Family member
25%

Co-worker
18%

Ex-spouse
8%

Spouse
2%

Note: More than one response allowed
Source: Greenfield Online survey of 1,207 respondents. Margin of error ±9 percentage points.

By Darryl Haralson and Bob Laird, USA TODAY
2005

- **Moving costs.** If you move because of a new job that's more than 50 miles from your current residence, you may be able to deduct your moving expenses.

- **Prepayment penalties.** Although we advise against getting a mortgage with a prepayment penalty, if you did, and then you make a prepayment, the penalty you pay will be tax deductible.

RESOURCE
For more information: See IRS Publication 530, *Tax Information for First-Time Homeowners*, available at www.irs.gov.

The Charitable Deduction

You don't have to be Bill Gates to make a difference in the world with charitable gifts. In fact, it's not rich folks who top the charts for charitable giving. An average of 70% of U.S. households give money to some causes, and the typical donor is middle- or lower-income.

The tax deduction is rarely the number one reason that people give. But if you do give money to your favorite cause, why not claim a modest tax break? (That lets you give even more money away next year.) It's easy. The most important rules are:

- You can deduct your gifts to any "qualified organization," which in most cases means one whose purpose is religious, charitable, educational, scientific, literary, or for the prevention of cruelty to children or animals. The organization should have applied to the IRS for tax-exempt status, probably under tax code section 501(c)(3). Most organizations that you think of as nonprofits will qualify, such as your local church or place of worship, Salvation Army, American Cancer Society, the Humane Society of the United States, and the like. But people do occasionally discover that their donations to small groups collecting money for a good cause (like sending local kids to camp) aren't

USA TODAY Snapshots®

Donors prefer giving money, not time

Is it easier to give money to charitable causes or to volunteer time?

2004
Time 42%
Money 37%

2005
Time 32%
Money 50%

Source: Thrivent Financial for Lutherans survey conducted by Synovate TeleNation Research of 1,000 adults 18 or older. Margin of error ±3 percentage points.

By Jae Yang and Marcy E. Mullins, USA TODAY 2006

tax-deductible, because the group hasn't filed for nonprofit status. And political advocacy or lobbying groups can't qualify for tax exemption, so your gifts to them won't be tax deductible, either.

- You'll need proof of every monetary gift, no matter how small—not to file with your tax returns, but in case the IRS ever comes around to check. That might be a cancelled check, copy of a credit card statement, or a letter or receipt from the charity itself. In the past, you didn't need proof of gifts under $250, but that changed in tax year 2006. So if you've been putting cash into the collection plate or giving it to the actors passing the hat at an outdoor theatre, now's a good time to switch to checks.

Don't try this hard to file on time

The Darwin awards reports that, one April day just before taxes were due, a Memphis man tried to beat a train by driving around the crossing gates—only to be hit by a car coming from the opposite side, whose driver had the same crazy idea. The driver of one vehicle was killed, making this the first recorded instance of a Darwin Award winner crashing into an Honorable Mention. (See http://darwinawards.com.)

- If you get something in return for your gift (other than a token item), your tax deduction must be reduced by the fair market value of what you received. The charity should tell you that amount. For example, if you bid $60 at a silent auction for a gift basket that would normally sell for $50, you've made a $10 tax-deductible contribution.

- If you give used items to places like Goodwill, you can take a deduction for their fair market value—that is, the amount they'd sell for used. But under recent rules, you can't claim any deduction at all for clothing and household items (such as appliances and furniture) that are in less than "good" condition. (The IRS is tired of people getting tax deductions for old socks.) To help estimate the value of your gifts, see the Salvation Army's Valuation Guide at www.satruck.com/ValueGuide.aspx.

- If you donate a car whose value you're claiming to be over $500, you can't deduct its estimated fair market value. You'll have to wait until the charity sells it and tells you how much the actual proceeds were. (Some exceptions include where the charity fixes up the car first or uses it for its own purposes.)

Missed a Deduction? How to File an Amended Return

Sandra compares the feeling of realizing you neglected to take a tax deduction to "that dreadful feeling you get when you've locked your car, only to realize the keys are still in the ignition." But, she adds:

You can claim any credit or deduction you overlooked the first time around, by filing an amended return. And filing one is easier than you might think, says Bob Scharin, senior tax analyst for RIA-Thomson Tax & Accounting.

You need your original tax return and Form 1040X, available at www.irs.gov. Form 1040X has three columns. In the first column, copy the figures you reported on your original tax return. In the second column, show any changes on your return. In the third column, write the correct amount.

A tax preparer can file an amended return, but the preparer's fees may exceed the amount of the refund.

Some tax software programs include a program for filing an amended return, but you'll still have to print out the form and mail it. Form 1040X is one of the few forms that can't be filed electronically with the IRS.

The IRS recommends waiting at least three weeks after you e-file your original return, or eight weeks after you file a paper return, before submitting an amended return. "You want to make sure the IRS processes them in appropriate order," Scharin says.

Don't file an amended return if you discover you made a math error on your original return, or failed to attach some documents. Many of these errors are caught by the IRS when it processes returns. In that case, the IRS will automatically adjust your refund to reflect the correct amount. If documents are missing, the IRS will contact you."

 "Missed a deduction? File an amended tax return to get your money," by Sandra Block, April 24, 2007.

Common Tax Mistakes to Avoid

If you ask Sandra, "Some tasks, such as baking a cake and performing open-heart surgery, shouldn't be rushed. It's wise to take your time doing your taxes, too. Otherwise, you risk overlooking valuable tax breaks, which means you'll pay too much. Or you might fail to report all your income, which could trigger a sternly worded letter from the IRS." Here are some common tax-filing blunders to avoid:

- **Itemizing when you should take the standard deduction.** If you've itemized your deductions for years, you might assume that itemizing will always produce the lowest tax bill. But that's not necessarily so, particularly if you're getting on in years, says Tom Ochsenschlager, Vice President of Taxation for the American Institute of Certified Public Accountants. For example, homeowners who are close to paying off their mortgage probably don't have much mortgage interest to deduct. In that case, you might get a lower tax bill by taking the standard deduction, which is increased annually to account for inflation.

- **Reporting investment income in the wrong place.** In the tax wilderness, something that looks like a duck and walks like a duck may actually be an egret. Such is the case with earnings from money market funds, which many taxpayers mistakenly report as interest income. The IRS considers these earnings to be dividends, and that's how they should be reported on your tax return. The error won't affect how much you owe in taxes, Ochsenschlager says. But the IRS will receive a 1099 form from your brokerage or mutual fund company that says you received the money in dividends, and that won't match the information on your tax return, he says. There's a good chance you'll get a letter about the discrepancy, he says, "And you'll end up using a bunch of stamps straightening it out."

- **Leaving losses on the table.** If you sold some stocks or mutual funds several years ago that were real stinkers, you probably already know about the limits on capital losses. After you've used your losses to offset capital gains, you can deduct up to $3,000 in losses against ordinary income—but no more, even if your losses exceed that amount. You can, however, carry over unused losses to future years, when you can use them to offset capital gains. If you don't have any capital gains, you deduct up to $3,000 against your ordinary income every year until you've exhausted your losses. To take advantage of carryovers, you must keep track of your leftover losses. That means keeping good records. If you don't use a tax preparer, try tax software, because most programs will keep track of your losses, Ochsenschlager says.

- **Overlooking the alternative minimum tax.** You may think the AMT is a problem for people who own yachts and polo ponies. And when the AMT was originally created, that was the idea. But because the tax was never indexed for inflation, the number of people who have to pay it has increased every year. (See "Who'll miss out on deductions because of the AMT," above.)

- **Omitting Social Security numbers for your dependents.** Having children can reduce your tax bill, but the IRS wants evidence that the little people on your tax return are real. You must include Social Security numbers for all your dependents on your return.

Can't Pay Your Tax Bill?

Sandra suggests the following two options if your bank account is empty.

- **Charge it.** You can charge your taxes by going to Pay1040.com or OfficialPayments.com to process your payment. Both accept major credit cards. You'll pay a "convenience fee" of 2.49% of your payment, plus interest if you don't pay off your balance.

- **Set up an installment plan.** If you owe $25,000 (in 2007) or less, you can ask the IRS for an installment agreement. This allows you to make monthly payments for up to three years. You'll pay an interest rate, currently 7%, plus a $43 setup fee. Use Form 9465 to request an installment plan. Alternately, you can use the IRS's Online Payment Agreement Application, or call them at 800-829-1040.

Assuming you can pay off your bill in three years, the second option is the better one, because you'll avoid the high interest rate you'll pay on a credit card.

Whatever you do, if you owe, make sure you file a return by the deadline. Otherwise, the IRS will hit you with penalties of up to 5% a month of the amount due, plus interest and penalties.

 "Time to beat the clock before tax deadline; But don't get burned by common boo-boos," by Sandra Block, April 7, 2006.

Get a Grip on Real Estate

I f you're like many families, buying a house is tops on your financial priority list. We all want not only a stable investment, but a place to raise the kids—ideally with a yard to play in, walls they can chalk without angering the landlord (your own reaction is another matter), neighbors to bond with, and good schools.

A house is also, however, likely to be the biggest expense you ever take on as a family. And if hard times hit, it will probably be the one thing you work hardest to keep, meaning it will define your financial future. So let's take a look at:

- whether you're financially ready to buy
- how to choose a mortgage you can live with
- who can help you get the best deal on a house and mortgage
- how to get family help with your down payment
- when it's safe to use your home as collateral for other loans
- your options if paying the mortgage ever becomes a problem, and
- when and whether to refinance.

Are You Ready to Buy?

In financial terms, you'll need to say "yes" to five questions before you can feel comfortable setting out to buy.

Are houses where you want to live within your financial reach?

It's never too early to start checking out your local housing market. Browsing the real estate section of the paper isn't enough—you need to know what houses have actually sold for in the neighborhoods where you're hoping to buy. (List prices don't always mean much.) Local real estate agents can help you, and you can plug local addresses into a website that tracks recent sales—try www.realtor.com and www.zillow.com.

Start going to open houses, to get a sense of what's available and to discover what the ads really mean when they say "cozy starter home" (tiny), or "fixer-upper" (decrepit). Then, for a ballpark estimate of how much house you can afford given your monthly spare cash, use online calculators such as those at www.nolo.com/calculator.cfm (look for ""How much home can I afford?" and "Should I rent or buy?").

Could you stay in the house longer than planned if need be?

Although buying a starter house with the idea of moving to a larger or better place later is a good way to break into the real estate market, you still want to find a place you could stay in for at least three to five years. Buying a house involves a lot of upfront effort, and you won't want to have to do it again in a year or two. It also involves expensive transaction costs like loan setup fees, property inspections, and more—usually in the thousands of dollars. And if you need to move during a market slump, you might have to sell for less than you bought for, plus pay commissions to real estate agents (averaging 5% of the house purchase price, or $5,000 for every $100,000).

This doesn't mean that you need to start out buying a giant luxury home.

In the face of trends toward supersized houses, many Americans are realizing the virtues of more modest-sized homes: lower heating and cooling bills, less furniture to buy, and fewer unused or lonely rooms.

Escape rising rents!

If you pay $1,000 in monthly rent now, approximately how much will you be paying in 40 years, assuming average inflation (4% per year) and no rent control?

a. $2,500

b. $3,400

c. $4,800

d. None of the above, because I'll own a home.

Answer: c or d.

Can you scrape together a down payment?

Saving up for a down payment can be tough, but will yield lifelong benefits. And although it's usually best to put down as much money as you can, it doesn't have to be the 20% down payment that was once standard. In recent years, almost half of first-time buyers put down less than 20%—and, because such buyers are statistically more likely to default, this trend directly fueled the mortgage meltdown of 2007.

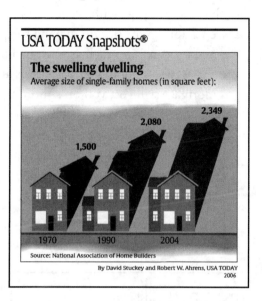

USA TODAY Snapshots®

The swelling dwelling
Average size of single-family homes (in square feet):

1,500 — 1970
2,080 — 1990
2,349 — 2004

Source: National Association of Home Builders

By David Stuckey and Robert W. Ahrens, USA TODAY 2006

The amount of your down payment affects everything about your mortgage, which means it may well affect your financial picture for the next 30 years. If you put down less than 20%, some of the consequences may include:

- The lender will insist that you buy private mortgage insurance (PMI), which protects the lender in case you default on your loan. The cost: one-half to 1% of the loan amount.
- You may have to accept a higher interest rate.
- Your monthly payments will be higher.

The down payment isn't the only upfront cost when you're buying a house. You'll also have to pony up for various "closing costs." These typically include homeowners' insurance, mortgage insurance, escrow company fees, title insurance, your share of that year's property tax, and more. The total is usually around 2% to 3% of the house price, depending on what state you live in, what kind of mortgage you get, and more. (See www.bankrate.com for a state-by-state look at average closing costs.)

If you're worried about coming up with the cash you'll need, see "All in the Family: Borrowing From Relatives or Friends," below.

Will you qualify for an affordable mortgage?

To get a mortgage with good terms, you'll need a clean credit history—see Chapter 3 for tips on making sure yours is spot-free. Then check newspapers or sites such as www.bankrate.com to see the going interest rates. What's a good rate? It changes all the time. To get an idea of what a mortgage will cost you on a monthly basis, use one of Nolo's mortgage calculators, at www.nolo.com/calculator.cfm. (There's lots more about mortgages below.)

Can you afford home maintenance, taxes, insurance, and other ongoing costs?

As you no doubt know, you'll get a tax break from owing a home—your mortgage interest is deductible—but you shouldn't expect it to cover the additional costs you take on when you say goodbye to the landlord.

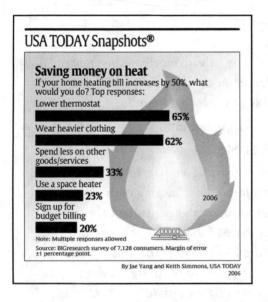

USA TODAY Snapshots®

Saving money on heat
If your home heating bill increases by 50%, what would you do? Top responses:
Lower thermostat **65%**
Wear heavier clothing **62%**
Spend less on other goods/services **33%**
Use a space heater **23%**
Sign up for budget billing **20%**
Note: Multiple responses allowed
Source: BIGresearch survey of 7,128 consumers. Margin of error ±1 percentage point.
2006
By Jae Yang and Keith Simmons, USA TODAY 2006

That's why it's worth refiguring your Family Spending Worksheet to include the monthly costs of owning a house. These will include not only the mortgage payments, but homeowners' insurance (usually between about $450 and $1,300 per year), maintenance (roughly 1% of the house's purchase price each year), property taxes (check your state's average, using the housing data on www.bestplaces. net), utilities (see the cost of living data at www.bestplaces.net), and decorating and furniture.

RESOURCE

For detailed information from a team of real estate experts: See *Nolo's Essential Guide to Buying Your First Home*, by Ilona Bray, Marcia Stewart, and Alayna Schroeder.

So Many Choices! Kinds of Mortgages

Before you start mortgage shopping, let's cover the basics. A mortgage is a loan to purchase real estate, with the property as collateral. That means that if you buy your dream home but can't make the payments, the lender (the mortgagor, in legal parlance) can recover what it's owed by foreclosing on the property—that is, taking possession of and selling it.

Naturally, lenders get into this risky business to make money. They do that primarily by charging interest over the life of the loan. They may also charge points, which are one-time fees when you take out the loan. One point is equal to 1% of the loan amount.

Mortgages come in a number of varieties—more all the time, it seems. The sections below cover the main kinds of mortgages and their risks and benefits. Narrow your search based on your willingness to accept risk and, if you go with a mortgage that has an adjustable rate, your ability to handle fluctuating mortgage payments in the future.

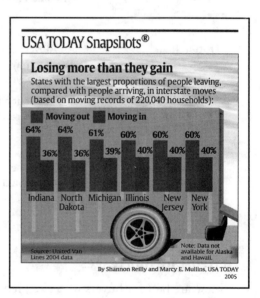

USA TODAY Snapshots®

Losing more than they gain

States with the largest proportions of people leaving, compared with people arriving, in interstate moves (based on moving records of 220,040 households):

Moving out / Moving in

Indiana	North Dakota	Michigan	Illinois	New Jersey	New York
64% / 36%	64% / 36%	61% / 39%	60% / 40%	60% / 40%	60% / 40%

Source: United Van Lines 2004 data

Note: Data not available for Alaska and Hawaii.

By Shannon Reilly and Marcy E. Mullins, USA TODAY 2005

Mortgages at a Glance	
Type of Mortgage	Description
Fixed rate	You repay at an unchanging interest rate, with identical monthly payments for the full term, usually 30 years.
Adjustable rate (ARM)	Monthly payments go up and down depending on certain market indexes, the lender's profit margin, and any built-in caps.
Balloon loan	Starts out at a fixed rate for a limited time period, after which you owe the entire loan balance.
Interest-only loan	You start out paying back only what you owe in interest, usually at an adjustable rate, for a fixed time; after that, you begin repaying principal as well, either as a lump sum or spread out.
Option loan	An ARM that gives you several choices of how much to pay each month, the lowest being a partial-interest payment.
Hybrid loan	Starts out at a fixed rate, then switches to an adjustable rate after a certain number of years.
Two-step loan	Starts at one fixed rate, then after a certain number of years, switches to another, market-determined fixed rate.

Fixed-rate mortgages

These are best for buyers who like predictability and stability. The interest rate is set when you get the loan, and it never changes. A 30-year term is normal, though if you can pay off your house faster (and want to save thousands of dollars in interest as a result), 15- and 20-year terms are also possible. Another way to achieve the same result, unless your mortgage has what's called a "prepayment penalty," is simply to pay your mortgage

Pros	Cons
Predictability, ability to lock in a low rate if you get in at the right time.	Interest rate usually starts out higher than an ARM's, and won't go down if market rates do.
Rates start out relatively low. If market rates remain low, so does yours.	Unpredictability. Caps still allow for huge rises in interest rate and monthly payments.
Predictability; starting rate usually very low.	Problems if you can't pay off that remaining chunk of the loan balance when the time comes.
Initial monthly payments very low.	Later monthly payments very high! And even the initial payments can vary, if it's an ARM. Also, during the interest-only period, you haven't reduced what you owe for the actual house by one penny.
Flexibility and very low monthly payment choices, especially useful if your income varies.	Paying the lowest amount can lead to deeper debt as you start paying interest on the unpaid interest.
Starting rate lower than regular fixed-rate mortgages. Useful if you know you'll sell the home before the loan converts.	Unpredictability after the loan turns into an ARM.
Starting rate lower than regular fixed-rate mortgages. Useful for people who know they'll sell their home before the new rate kicks in.	Unpredictability of second fixed rate.

off early by adding some money to your regular payment each month. (Prepayment penalties are not the norm, but are still fairly common.)

Adjustable-rate mortgages (ARMs)

The interest rate on an ARM can fluctuate during the loan term—and no one can predict with certainty where interest rates will go. For buyers who aren't put off by this risk, or see buying their first home as a short-term stepping stone, an ARM may be an attractive option.

Homeowners Struggle to Keep Up With Adjustable Rates

For 45 years, Robert and Lorraine Brown have lived in their ranch-style home in Florissant, Missouri. One of their four children was even born there. But for the past eight months, the couple have been locked in a sleep-wrecking race to keep up with their rising mortgage bills. They've switched to cheaper phone service, cut back on groceries, and sometimes put off ordering medicine.

When they refinanced their home two years ago to pay off some bills, Robert, now 78, was working as a deliveryman. But his employer went out of business last April. Now he and Lorraine, 72, a retired nurse, are both seeking work. The rate on their mortgage has jumped from 7% to 10.5%.

"We were having a hard time meeting bills at the time we refinanced. It seems once you get behind, you do desperate things to catch up, and you never do," says Lorraine, trying to hold back tears.

They feel alone, but they're not. America's five-year real estate boom was fueled partly by a tempting array of cut-rate mortgages that helped millions of Americans qualify for homes or refinance loans. To afford soaring home prices, many turned to adjustable-rate and other, riskier, loans with low initial payments.

Now, the real estate market is cooling, interest rates are rising and tens of thousands more Americans are starting to have trouble paying their mortgages. . . .

 Excerpted from: "Some homeowners struggle to keep up with adjustable rates," by Noelle Knox, April 3, 2006.

Most ARMs come with low initial rates, but these teaser rates may not last long. The rate is adjusted monthly or yearly, based on an economic index (the U.S. Treasury Bill index, for example), to which the lender adds a profitable margin, calculated as either a set amount or percentage. For example, your rate might be "the U.S. Treasury Bill index rate plus 1%."

How high can the rate go? High enough to make your monthly mortgage payment very different from what it was at first. There are some limits, though. One is the "life-of-the-loan cap," or the maximum on the ARM's total interest rate—usually a well-padded 5% to 6% above the starting interest rate. The second brake on the lender is the "periodic cap," limiting how much your interest rate can increase (or decrease) at any adjustment period. Look for an ARM with a periodic cap of no more than 2% to 3%.

Balloon loans

At first glance, balloon loans might look pretty attractive. Their interest rate usually starts below the market rate on a 30-year fixed-rate mortgage. You make payments for a set period of time, usually somewhere between three and ten years. However, your monthly payments are calculated as if you were going to be paying the same amount each month for 30 years, which keeps them low. (The technical way to say this is that the loan is amortized over a 30-year period.) But at the end of the fixed period, you owe the entire loan balance—so unless you've come into a very large amount of cash, you'll need to refinance (or sell). If interest rates have gone way up, you could be in trouble.

Interest-only loans

You've no doubt heard about these in the news lately; they have a deservedly bad reputation. Interest-only loans, which are usually ARMs, are set up so that you start out paying only the interest that builds up on the loan principal. This makes for very low monthly payments. The downside is that you have no equity in your home and you don't reduce your debt until a set date (years later) upon which the principal either starts getting added to your monthly payments or you pay the whole thing off.

Interest-only loans are attractive when home prices are going up fast, because buyers can either sell or refinance on better terms before the interest-only period stops. But they're a gamble. If house prices don't increase, and you can't afford the eventual payments that include loan principal, you may have to sell, perhaps at a loss.

Option loans

These loans, a type of ARM, give you the option to decide what amount you want to pay each month when you get your bill. This flexibility is supposed to give you greater control over your cash flow. Your choices are:

- an accelerated payment that will help you pay off the loan over a shorter period than the actual loan term
- a payment of principal plus interest (adjusted monthly), calculated as if you were paying off a normal, regularly amortized loan
- an interest-only payment (which, with an ARM, may change each month), or
- a partial-interest payment (called a "minimum payment") that doesn't cover that month's interest. It's usually based on a fixed rate of interest for the first one to five years, after which they'll adjust it periodically.

That last, partial-interest option makes for a low payment, all right, but it presents a major problem: The unpaid interest is added to the loan principal, and you're farther in the hole than when you started. (This is called "negative amortization.")

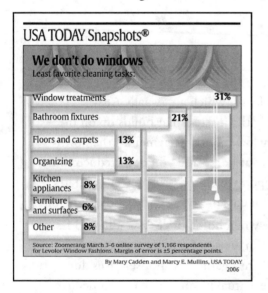

USA TODAY Snapshots®

We don't do windows
Least favorite cleaning tasks:

Window treatments	31%
Bathroom fixtures	21%
Floors and carpets	13%
Organizing	13%
Kitchen appliances	8%
Furniture and surfaces	6%
Other	8%

Source: Zoomerang March 3-6 online survey of 1,166 respondents for Levolor Window Fashions. Margin of error is ±5 percentage points.

By Mary Cadden and Marcy E. Mullins, USA TODAY 2006

The interest rate and minimum payment on an option ARM start out very low, but interest rates are adjusted frequently—every few months or even every month. An option loan might be good for someone disciplined enough to pay the accelerated or principal-plus-interest payment. But if you're that disciplined, you'd be better off with a more stable loan.

Hybrid loans

Hybrid loans, as the name implies, combine features of fixed-rate and adjustable-rate mortgages. They can be great for first-time buyers who want to break into the market but don't plan to be in their first homes forever.

For a set period of time (three, five, seven, or ten years), you pay interest at a fixed rate, usually below the rate of a comparable traditional fixed-rate mortgage. After that, the rate becomes adjustable and changes every six months or one year. If you're planning on moving within ten years, a hybrid ARM can give you stability without the relatively high interest that you'd pay for a regular 30-year fixed-rate mortgage. However, if you stay in your home after the expiration of the fixed term, your interest rate may go up significantly, and you may have to refinance.

Two-step loans

These are essentially hybrid loans with only one adjustment. For a while—typically five or seven years—the loan has a fixed rate that's usually below that of comparable fixed-rate mortgages. Then the rate adjusts to a newer fixed rate, based on the index at the time of the adjustment plus a margin. You're betting that if the rate goes up, you'll be able to afford the correspondingly higher monthly payments. You could try to refinance, but depending on the market you may not be able to do much better.

Shopping for the Right Loan

The variety of mortgage options mean you can borrow the same amount of money, but with different terms, and end up paying very different amounts back. Interest rates and points may look like tiny numbers and percentages in the beginning, but they add up to real dollars later. It's worth it to shop around. But how do you actually find the right lender and the best deal?

Advertisements for mortgages are everywhere, in newspapers, on billboards, and online. Some offer very tempting rates, too. But the interest rates you see advertised often bear no relation to what you'll actually be offered. That depends on unique factors, including:

- The type of mortgage (fixed-rate, ARM, or other).
- How risky you are as a borrower.
- The amount of your down payment. A large down payment tells the lender that you're not likely to walk away from your investment.
- How many points you pay. The more points, the lower the interest rate.

Researching mortgages online

You can check out prevailing interest rates—they change all the time—in your local paper and on sites such as www.bankrate.com, www.hsh.com, and www.freeratesearch.com. If you've got the cash to pay points in order to lower your interest rate, use calculators such as those at www.nolo.com/calculators or www.mtgprofessor.com/calculators to see how long you'd have to stay in the house to make this upfront investment worthwhile. Finally, you can research current mortgage options yourself on sites such as www.bankrate.com, www.hsh.com, and www.fanniemae.gov.

Whether to buy online is another matter. You'll need to do a fair amount of research to understand the offerings and how they compare. And some people report poor customer service from online lenders (though you can find out which are best at the website of Jack Guttentag, the "Mortgage Professor," at www.mtgprofessor.com).

Getting help from a mortgage broker

One way to save time, aggravation, and potentially money is to find an experienced mortgage broker to work with. As many as two-thirds of all buyers get their loans through a mortgage broker—a professional who will sort through the myriad financing options to help you find the best one available to you based on your income, credit score, and more. Your other primary alternative is to go directly to a bank, credit union, or other commercial lender and select one of its mortgage offerings, but then you'll have fewer to choose among.

As for compensation, mortgage brokers make most of their money by marking up the costs on the loan the wholesale lender is offering. This may get passed on to you in the form of points (again, 1% of the loan value), processing fees, or a higher interest rate. Ask the broker to tell you exactly how you'll be paying, and then negotiate any fee that seems excessively high. A good broker will save you enough money that you'll ultimately come out ahead.

The key is to find a good broker. Turn on the radio or pick up a newspaper and you'll hear stories of brokers who lied about the financing terms, failed to alert homebuyers to huge risks associated with their loans (like prepayment penalties or balloon payments) and more. These stories shouldn't make you say, "Forget the lot of them," but they should make you very choosy.

When selecting a broker (or any real estate professional), start by getting recommendations from friends and colleagues. Also search the Web for reviews (including through your local Better Business Bureau, which you can find at www.bbb.org), and double check the person's credentials with any state government regulatory agency. Many—but not all—states require mortgage brokerages to be licensed, and individual mortgage brokers can seek certification from the National Association of Mortgage Brokers (NAMB). Meet with a select few brokers in person, ask the questions we provide below, and ask for the names of three customers you can—and absolutely should—call for a reference.

> ### Questions to Ask a Prospective Mortgage Broker
>
> 1. Do you work full time as a residential mortgage broker? (Best answer: Yes.)
> 2. How long have you been in the residential mortgage business? (Best answer: Two years or more.)
> 3. Are you licensed (if applicable) and certified by the National Association of Mortgage Brokers? (Best answer: Yes.)
> 4. How many residential mortgages have you brokered in the past year? (Best answer: Ten or more.)
> 5. How many of those transactions were with first-time home buyers? (Best answer: Five or more.)

All in the Family: Borrowing From Relatives or Friends

The idea of asking family or friends for a loan may strike you as a last-ditch strategy, to be used only when you're ready to add shamefacedness to your desperation. But if you feel this way, you're forgetting two important things: First, the people close to you might actually be happy to lend you money, especially for an important purchase like a house. Second, with proper loan structuring, your lenders can benefit financially from the transaction, and with very little risk. No wonder private loans have become an increasingly popular way for people to deal with family financial issues.

Let's say you're looking at mortgages, and rates are in the neighborhood of 7%. Meanwhile, your parents, grandparents, siblings, or friends might be struggling to find a CD or other safe, short-term investment that pays more than 5%. You could satisfy everyone's needs by structuring a private loan in which you make monthly repayments at 6% interest. And looking at the bigger picture, all that interest money would stay within the family, rather than going into a bank's coffers.

Beyond the favorable interest rate, other possible benefits to your lender include:

- **Ongoing income.** Some investments just sit there and gain in value, or pay occasional dividends. With your private loan, your lender will receive regular payments from you, which can be reinvested.

- **Low risk.** Your parents or other private lender can count on your personal commitment to repay the loan, somehow, someday, even if the original repayment schedule needs to be rejiggered. You'll want to sign a formal, written agreement documenting the loan, which your lender could use in court if needed (don't worry, they're unlikely to sue you for repayment). In addition, you can offer up an item of property (such as a car or the house itself) as collateral, which in the worst case, your lender could claim and sell to repay the loan.

You, meanwhile, would enjoy the benefits of:

- **A flexible repayment structure.** Banks require a preset monthly payment schedule, but a private lender might be more flexible. For example, you might agree that you'll make quarterly (rather than monthly) payments, or delay all payments for a period of time. And if down the road you want to temporarily pause payments (perhaps while you stop working to care for a newborn), your parents or other private lender might agree to that.

- **No points or loan fees.** Institutional lenders often charge thousands of dollars in loan application and other fees. Family and friends don't.

- **Easier qualifying, with minimal red tape.** Your relatives or friends probably won't require that you have a great credit score and fill out scads of application forms. You qualify as long as your lender trusts that you'll pay back the loan.

How to approach Mom, Dad, or another private lender

Even people who are convinced that private loans are a win-win proposition may blanch at the thought of asking for one. But if you approach it like a business proposition, it's not so hard. Set up a time to talk, even if you see your parents (or brother or old roommate) regularly and the formality seems odd. You might say, "I'm trying to buy a house and am reviewing a number of ways to finance it. Can we sit down and talk soon?" If you sense resistance, back off gracefully.

From paperclip to house

Kyle McDonald set himself a challenge: to trade his way from a red paperclip to a house in Kipling, Saskatchewan. He succeeded by bartering on Craigslist, working his way up through a pen, a doorknob, and a camp stove. It took McDonald only 14 trades (one with actor Corbin Bernsen) and about one year to reach his goal of home ownership. Read his story at www.oneredpaperclip.blogspot.com.

If you get a positive response, schedule a specific time to meet. Then prepare a one-page list of things to discuss, including:

- **How much you want to borrow.** Take into account both how much you need and how much you think your relative or other private lender can spare.

- **The interest rate you're offering to pay.** For practical as well as tax reasons, it's best to choose a rate that's higher than the minimum rate set by the IRS (see "Too-Low Interest: A Potential Tax Problem for Your Lender," below), but lower than what you'd pay to an institutional lender. Websites such as www.compareinterestrates.com, www.bankrate.com, and www.hsh.com will give you a sense of current institutional rates.

- **Your proposed repayment schedule.** For example, you could go with a simple amortized schedule, in which you pay the same amount each month; a schedule in which you wait a period of months before beginning to make payments, or during which you pay interest only; or whatever other variant you and your lender agree on. Loan calculators will help you compare the possibilities.

For example, at www.virginmoneyus.com, click "Real Estate Loans," then "Payment Calculator." (After you run the initial, simple loan calculation, you'll be given a chance to compare other payment plans.)

- **How much you have available for the down payment.** The higher your down payment, the lower the lender's risk of loss.

- **Your financial ability to make monthly payments.** Even without setting rigid qualification rules, your lender will want this reassurance, so be ready with pay stubs, credit card and bank statements, and any other documents you feel comfortable using to show you've got the cash needed.

- **The legal and financial protections you'll offer the lender.** These should include a promissory note (your written promise to pay) and possibly a "security interest," that is, collateral or a mortgage (all described below).

- **The financial benefits to the lender.** Show how your proposed interest rate compares to money market and CD rates.

When you meet, don't sound as if you feel entitled to the money. ("If you love me, you'll lend to me!") Give the potential lender ample time to ask questions, and don't expect a decision on the spot.

TIP
Is your family member reluctant to charge you interest or even let you repay the loan? For example, parents who were already planning to leave you money might figure this is a good time to transfer it your way. Tell them they can always decide later to "forgive" (cancel) some or all of your loan payments, of not only interest but principal. To do so, they should write you a letter referencing the loan and stating the amount they're forgiving. That's because forgiven loan payments are considered gifts, and gifts of more than a certain amount (currently $12,000) to any individual in a calendar year raise federal gift tax considerations.

! CAUTION

Never try to disguise a gift as a loan. If the transaction you're calling a loan is really a gift—that is, you don't intend to repay the loan, and the lender doesn't expect you to—don't try to pass it off to the IRS as a loan. That is just a fraudulent way of avoiding gift tax, by making a one-time gift look like it's actually stretched out over several years of forgiven loan repayments, and the IRS is well aware of this ploy.

Too-Low Interest: A Potential Tax Problem for Your Lender

The IRS sets a minimum rate for private loans, called the "Applicable Federal Rate" (AFR), each month. In mid-2007, the rate averaged around 5%. See the IRS website at www.irs.gov for the latest AFR.

What's the big deal if a private lender charges you less than the AFR—or even no interest at all? No problem for you (who wouldn't want a low interest rate?), but there may be tax ramifications for the lender. This is mainly an issue if you're borrowing a substantial amount of money or receiving a loan on top of a gift that exceeded the lender's $12,000 annual gift tax exclusion. If the interest rate doesn't meet the AFR, the IRS will "impute" the interest to your lender—meaning it will act as though your lender really received AFR-level interest on the loan. The question then becomes, where did the interest money go? Aha, reasons the IRS, your lender gave it right back to you, as a gift. Then the IRS can demand that the private lender file a gift tax return for any amount over the annual gift tax exclusion.

A private lender who charges you less than the imputed interest rate must report interest income at the imputed rate. If the lender doesn't and is audited, and the IRS discovers the omission (unlikely), the IRS will readjust your lender's income using the imputed interest rate and charge the tax owed on the readjusted income plus a penalty.

How to protect everyone's legal interests

If a relative or friend agrees to lend you money, don't seal the deal with just a handshake. Finalize the loan with the proper legal paperwork, to clarify your agreement and avoid later disputes and memory lapses.

Another important reason to go beyond the handshake is that, if you're offering a home mortgage or other collateral to back up the loan, you need to record (file) the paperwork in your county's land records office. If you don't, the lender could be left out in the cold if some other lender or creditor foreclosed on the house or reclaimed the collateral—your relative or friend wouldn't be entitled to any of the proceeds. And finally, having written proof that you're paying home mortgage interest allows you to deduct it at tax time.

To make your agreement legally binding, you'll need these documents:

- **Promissory note.** You'll need to sign a note for the amount of the loan. Include the rate of interest, repayment schedule, and other terms, such as penalties for late payments. You can find several promissory notes on Nolo's website (www.nolo.com). If you're borrowing no more than a few thousand dollars, a promissory note may be all you need. But for larger loans, it makes legal and financial sense to also prepare a mortgage, putting the lender in line for any foreclosure proceeds. (Without it, your lender has no recourse other than to take you to court if you don't repay.)

- **Mortgage (or "deed of trust," in some states).** For home purchases, a mortgage gives your lender an interest in the property to secure repayment of your debt (per the promissory note). It needs to be recorded (filed) with your county's land records office, sometimes called the registry of deeds.

- **Security interest and U.C.C. Financing Statement.** If you're giving the lender a security interest in property you own other than the house, you could grant the security interest either within the promissory note or as a separate document. In addition, to advise the world about your lender's interest in the property (and protect your lender's place in line for any proceeds), you'll want to file what's called a U.C.C. (Uniform Commercial Code) Financing Statement with the appropriate government office. Check your state government's website; most offer a standard U.C.C. form and instructions. Also, if the collateral is a car or boat, you'll probably need to add the lender to the asset's certificate of title, to put any potential buyers on notice.

For the paperwork, we recommend you get an expert's help. Consult an attorney or check out Virgin Money USA (www.virginmoneyus.com), a company that specializes in administering "person-to-person" loans between relatives, friends, and other private parties.

Borrowing Against Your Home

If you've already owned your home for a while, you have probably built up some equity—the portion of the property's value that's yours

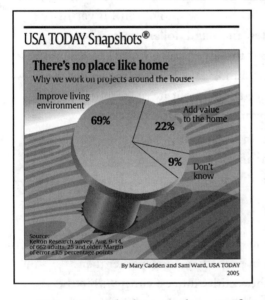

USA TODAY Snapshots®

There's no place like home

Why we work on projects around the house:

Improve living environment 69%

Add value to the home 22%

Don't know 9%

Source: Kelton Research survey, Aug. 9-14, of 662 adults, 25 and older. Margin of error ±3.5 percentage points

By Mary Cadden and Sam Ward, USA TODAY 2005

and yours alone. To figure out how much equity you've got, take the amount your house is currently worth and subtract how much you owe on it. For example, if you think your house would fetch $300,000 if you sold it now (never mind that you bought it for $189,000), and you owe $100,000 on it, you already have an impressive $200,000 in equity. All or part of that equity can be borrowed against, using a home equity loan or line of credit.

You can use the borrowed money for any purpose you want, not just remodeling, though that's a popular one. Many people borrow against their homes to fund their kids' college educations.

First, the difference between loans and lines of credit: A home equity loan is also called a second mortgage, because you borrow a certain amount in addition to your existing home mortgage. It usually has a fixed interest rate and must be repaid in monthly payments over a set time period, usually ten, 15, or 20 years.

By contrast, a home equity line of credit (HELOC) is a revolving line of credit from which you can draw (by phone, check, or credit card), up to a certain maximum and for a set time period. The dollar limit is set by taking a percentage, usually around 75%, of your equity (you'll have to get the house appraised to determine just how much equity you have). HELOCs are available only as variable-rate loans, though you might find one with a low introductory fixed rate, say, for the first six months. Your repayment amounts will depend on how much you've drawn out, what the current interest rate is, and whether you're in the early or late years of the loan. Early on, you can still draw out money and repay only the interest. In the later years, you must stop borrowing and start paying off the principal.

USA TODAY Snapshots®

Just like new

Number of households that had work done to their homes in prior 12 months (by remodeling project):

Remodel bathroom **15.5 million**

Roof **11.6 million**

Carpet **10.8 million**

Remodel kitchen **10.7 million**

Remodel bedroom **8.1 million**

Source: Census Bureau

By David Stuckey and Bob Laird, USA TODAY 2006

Home equity loans and lines of credit are attractive because their interest rates are usually only a little higher than regular mortgage interest rates and far lower than credit card interest rates. Plus, ordinarily you can deduct your interest payments at tax time. The details are complicated, but you'll most likely be able to deduct interest on any loan of $100,000 or less, and possibly more interest if you use the money for home improvements. (See a tax adviser for a full, personal analysis.)

But there's one giant disadvantage to both home equity loans and lines of credit. Taking out a loan that's secured by your house means you can LOSE YOUR HOUSE if you fail to repay it. That's right, the lender can foreclose on you just as fast as if you didn't repay your primary mortgage.

> **CAUTION**
> **Don't use a home equity loan to pay off credit cards.** Never enter into a home loan if you're just trying to shift around debt that you have little hope of repaying. If you truly can't pay your credit card debt, you could, if necessary, get it erased in bankruptcy. Not so with loans secured by your home. So if you turn credit card debt into debt tied to your house, you could end up losing your house unnecessarily.

Avoiding Foreclosure

According to Sandra, "If you're lying awake at night, fretting about whether you'll lose your house to foreclosure, you may not be the only insomniac on your block."

More than 2.1 million Americans with home loans missed at least one payment in 2006, according to the Mortgage Bankers Association. Even more troubling, the rate of new foreclosures hit a record.

But be aware: Even if your mortgage has become an intolerable burden, letting the bank foreclose could lead to a lifetime of hurt. Losing your home is just the beginning. A foreclosure will wreck your credit report for years, making it impossible—or at least extremely expensive—to buy another home, says David Jones, president of the Association of Independent Consumer Credit Counseling Agencies. If the proceeds from the sale of your home don't cover your loan, your lender might sue you to recover the unpaid balance.

Many borrowers who lose their homes to foreclosure haven't tried to negotiate with their lenders. That's unfortunate, because lenders are usually willing to work with borrowers to avoid foreclosure, says John

Lamb, co-author of *Solve Your Money Troubles*. "With the number of foreclosures on the horizon, lenders are going to be more willing to work with people, because it doesn't do anybody good to have a glut of foreclosed houses on the market."

Ideally, you should call your lender before you miss your first payment, says Bob Walters, chief economist for Quicken Loans. If your payment is due on the first of the month, call before the 15th, which he says is usually when your lender will report the late payment to credit-reporting agencies. The longer you wait, the fewer options you'll have. Once your loan is declared in default, typically after you've missed three or four payments, you're "past the point of no return," Walters says. At that point, most lenders won't accept a partial payment of what you owe. Unless you can come up with the money to cover all your missed payments, plus any late fees, your lender will start foreclosure.

If you're suffering a temporary financial setback, your lender may offer programs that will help you get back on track. They include:

- **Forbearance.** This is an agreement that lets borrowers make a reduced payment, or none, for a specific period. You might have to make larger payments once the crisis has passed. To qualify, you might need to show that you're expecting a bonus, a tax refund, or other income that will let you catch up.

- **Reinstatement.** You agree to pay the full amount of your missed payments by a specific date. Reinstatement is sometimes combined with forbearance.

- **Modification.** Your lender agrees to change the terms of the loan to make payments more affordable. Your lender may agree to add missed payments to your loan balance or extend the term of your loan, reducing the size of your payments.

Before asking for forbearance or loan modification, be prepared to show that you are making a good-faith effort to pay your mortgage, says Jim Svinth, chief economist for LendingTree.com, a website that helps consumers shop for mortgages. If you can demonstrate that you've reduced other expenses, the lender will be more inclined to negotiate, he says.

Svinth warns, though, that your ability to negotiate will also depend on which institution owns your loan. If your bank still has your loan in its portfolio, it can modify the terms or offer forbearance. But many lenders sell loans into the secondary market, where they're repackaged as mortgage-backed securities. In that case, Svinth says, the company that's servicing your loan might be unable to change the terms.

Moving on. If you're in a home you can't afford, loan forbearance isn't going to solve your problem. But even if you have to move, you can take steps to avoid foreclosure:

- **Put your home up for sale.** This may be the best choice, Walters says, if you've been in your home for several years and have built up some equity. If your local real estate market is strong, your lender may agree to forgo payments until the house is sold, says John Jones, a financial specialist at ComPsych, an employee-assistance program. The proceeds from the sale might cover your mortgage and selling costs.

- **If you have no equity or your local real estate market is depressed, ask your lender to consider a "short sale."** In a short sale, the lender agrees to accept the proceeds from the sale of your home, even if they don't cover the amount you owe.

- **Ask your lender to accept a deed in lieu of foreclosure.** If you can't sell, your lender may agree to take the deed to your home and cancel your debt.

There's one serious drawback to a short sale or a deed in lieu of foreclosure: You could find yourself stuck with a hefty tax bill. In most cases, debt forgiven by a lender is considered taxable income. Unless you have your debt eliminated in bankruptcy or can prove you're insolvent, you'll have to pay taxes on the canceled debt, says John Roth, senior analyst for tax publisher CCH. Many people don't realize that canceled debt is taxable, Roth says, until they receive a Form 1099C from their lender; a copy goes to the IRS.

So why opt for a short sale or a title transfer instead of foreclosure? For one thing, foreclosure won't get you off the hook, either. If the lender sells your foreclosed house for less than you owe, it might sue you for the balance. And if the lender writes off the remaining debt, you could still end up with a tax bill, Roth says.

Though a short sale or a title transfer will hurt your credit report, you might still be able to work with your lender to reduce the damage—which isn't possible with a foreclosure, Lamb says.

"Foreclosure is really a bad thing to have to go through," he says. "You have all this emotional baggage, as well as the financial consequences. It's certainly better to have some control over the process."

When to Refinance—and Why

Some people never think about their mortgage after getting it, except to write a monthly check and claim the tax deductions. Others watch the mortgage interest rates like hawks and refinance every time the rates take a dip. The safest course is somewhere in the middle. Done wisely, refinancing can be one of those, "Whoa, I just earned tens of thousands of dollars for a few hours of work!" tasks. But done blindly—without paying attention to the fact that every new mortgage costs you upfront fees and possibly points, and stretches your loan back to a full 30 (or however many) years of interest payments—refinancing can actually lose you money.

TIP
Can you just modify your existing loan? Sandra notes that it's possible to "ask your lender if you qualify for loan modification. With these deals, you keep your existing loan and pay your lender a fee in exchange for a reduction in your interest rate." However, loan modification is available in only a small minority of cases (for what are called "portfolio" loans, that the bank hasn't resold on the secondary market), and you may not get as low an interest rate as you would elsewhere.

When should you consider refinancing? You might have heard an old rule of thumb that, for fixed-rate mortgages, the time is right when interest rates have dropped by two percentage points since you got the loan (for example, from 7% to 5%). But that theory dates from a time when closing costs were consistently higher than they are now and tended to undo the benefits of refinancing. So run the numbers, as described below, even if the drop is as low as 0.5%. Another good time to refinance is if you're tired of the fluctuations in your adjustable-rate mortgage and want to switch to either another ARM with better terms or to a fixed-rate mortgage.

You'll need to take two important steps before deciding whether to refinance:

- find out how much a refinance will cost you up front, and
- calculate your total savings.

As with your original mortgage, you should also shop around, both with your current mortgage company and by comparing rates online and with local lenders. A good mortgage broker can help you with this, as well.

> ⓘ **CAUTION**
> **Watch out for prepayment penalties on your current mortgage.** Technically, when you refinance, you pay off your existing mortgage—meaning you'd also have to fork over any prepayment penalty fees.

How much will your refinance cost up front?

Although refinancing can save you thousands of dollars over the life of your loan, Sandra warns that, "Transaction costs and junk fees can eat into your savings." Many of these transaction costs are the same as you paid when you first bought your home, such as title insurance and escrow fees, lender fees, points (optional), appraisal fees, credit reporting fees, and any payments needed to bring your insurance and tax obligations up to date. So why do you have to pay them all over again? Because your new lender wants to hear for itself that if you don't make your payments, the house can be sold for enough to cover your loan balance. However, more than a few lenders pad the standard fees with various processing fees, which have earned the name "junk fees." Sandra adds, "While some lenders explain their costs to borrowers, others bury them in the mortgage documents."

Sandra advises, "That doesn't mean you're defenseless. Tell lenders and mortgage brokers upfront that you want to keep transaction costs down. Excluding points, total closing costs should not exceed 2% of the amount of your loan. Some fees, such as title insurance and a credit check, are standard in any mortgage. But a lender who wants your business might agree to waive other fees, such as document preparation and processing costs." You might also be able to lower the title insurance fees by using the same company you did when you first bought the house. And some lenders skip the appraisal if you bought the house fairly recently or you have so much equity in the property that they're all but guaranteed to get their money back in a foreclosure.

After all these warnings, your ears may perk up when you hear advertisements for "no-cost" mortgages, promising zero closing costs. But another name for these might be "no-free-lunch" mortgages. They usually charge comparatively high interest or roll your closing costs into the loan amount. That said, one good time to go for a no-cost mortgage is if you plan to stay in your house for only a short while, in which case you won't have time to save much on interest, but will have saved a lot on the closing costs.

Your willingness to pay a share of the standard, reasonable costs, and perhaps points, should make you eligible for a competitive interest rate. Just pay close attention and watch out for unexpected or extra-high fees as the process goes along. The best way to do this is to compare the Good Faith Estimate (GFE) of your costs that the lender will give you when you first apply to refinance, and compare that to the actual amount you're told to pay at closing. And, as discussed below, figure out how the closing costs and the interest rate will balance each other out over time.

Loan Comparison; 30-Year Fixed Rate Loans for $200,000

	Refinance loan 1		Refinance loan 2		Lessons learned
Interest rate	7%		6.5%		
Points	0		1		Paying points and higher costs can lower the interest rate.
Closing costs	$2,000		$2,500		
Monthly payment	Spread out over new, 30-year loan term	Sticking to original loan term	Spread out over new, 30-year loan term	Sticking to original loan term	A lower interest rate will always lower your monthly payments—but check what you'll owe in total interest when all is said and done.
	$1,331 ($213 reduction)	$1,414 ($130 reduction)	$1,264 ($280 reduction)	$1,350 ($194 reduction)	
Break-even point	10 months	16 months	18 months	26 months	Yes, it takes a lot longer to break even if you pay extra each month—but it's a truer breakeven, because you haven't taken on months of additional payments.
Total interest difference; new 30-year term	You'll pay $15,928 MORE in interest!	You'll save $39,022 in interest!	You'll save $8,001 in interest!	You'll save $57,966 in interest!	Lower monthly payments aren't everything!

Will the savings be worth the costs?

Never just calculate what your new monthly payment would be after a refinance and say, "Great, it's lower than our current monthly payment, let's do it!" Even assuming you're comparing apples to apples (such as a fixed-rate 30-year mortgage to another fixed-rate 30-year mortgage) you'd be leaving out one vital fact: Starting over with a new 30-year mortgage means adding several months or years to your payment schedule. Thought your mortgage would be paid off by the time you retire? You may have just nixed that hope. And the more time you take to pay, the more interest you'll owe in total.

USA TODAY Snapshots®

American homes
Cities with the largest and smallest average household size:

4.33 — Santa Ana, Calif.
2.07 — Cincinnati
2.60 — U.S. average

Source: Census Bureau

By David Stuckey and Alejandro Gonzalez, USA TODAY 2006

If your math anxiety is starting to kick in, don't worry; online calculators can help you. To compare fixed-rate mortgages, the best calculator we've found is at http://realestate.yahoo.com. (Click "Home Loans," then "Should I refinance my home mortgage?") To calculate whether to switch from an ARM to a fixed-rate mortgage, go to www.mtgprofessor.com, click "Calculators," and scroll down and click "Mortgage Refinance Calculator: Refinancing an ARM into a FRM."

These calculators ask you to input data such as your existing loan balance and terms, how long you have left to pay off your mortgage, any upfront costs and points to refinance, and the new interest rate. You'll then find out your new monthly payment amount, your total interest savings, and your "breakeven point." This means the number of months or years it will take you to work off your initial closing costs by saving on interest each month. If you think you'll stay in your home for less time than it takes to reach your breakeven point, the refinance definitely isn't worth it.

But even reaching your breakeven point soon enough isn't necessarily a green light on refinancing (despite what many online calculators imply—especially those created by mortgage lenders). Sure, you've saved on interest month by month, and lowered your monthly payments. But that doesn't negate the problem we've already described, in which you're now looking toward a full 30 years of paying off your loan. Because of added interest, you may end up eventually paying more to the bank than you would have if you hadn't refinanced. You can get around this by paying extra principal each month, so that you're done by the same date you'd originally planned. And here's why we like the Yahoo! calculator: It tells you what your monthly payments, overall savings, and breakeven point would be if you did just that.

Imagine that you bought your house five years ago and still owe $200,000 on your 30-year fixed-rate mortgage at 8%, which you'd thought would be paid off in another 25 years. Your current monthly payment is $1,544. But interest rates have dropped to 7%, and if you pay two points, you can get a loan at 6.5%. The table above shows how these two refinance options might play out, comparing paying over the full, new 30-year term to adding to your monthly payments so you can stick with your original, 25-year loan payoff date.

The lessons are pretty clear: Keep your upfront costs down unless paying them will lower your interest rate significantly. And if you really want to save on interest, create a repayment schedule that sticks with your old end date. Why not just take out a 15-year mortgage instead? You could, but you're likely to get as good a deal on a 30-year mortgage, which lets you go back to the required payment structure in a financial emergency.

For more complex comparisons between mortgages, talk to your mortgage broker. ●

College or Retirement?
Get Your Savings Goals Straight

Setting aside an emergency fund was hard enough. Now how are you supposed to save up the sums needed for your kids' college education, your own retirement, and everything else? No matter what anyone says, collecting the pennies you find under couch cushions is not going to get you where you need to be. But that doesn't mean you can't start small, or with manageable steps—and eventually pull off what looks like the impossible. This chapter will help you:

- prioritize your goals
- learn about 401(k)s, IRAs, and other retirement savings options, and
- look at options for paying for your kids' college education.

Honey, Remind Me Why We're Saving?

Yes, there's a reason you're doing this. But what is it? For most couples, their main savings goals include their children's college educations and their own retirement. But if saving for both at once seems impossible, which should come first? The answer may surprise you: You should save for your retirement first.

As Sandra explains, parenthood is all about sacrifices. When your children are babies, you give up sleep. When they're teenagers, you surrender your sanity. But there's one thing you shouldn't sacrifice for the kids: your retirement security. All too often, parents postpone saving for retirement or reduce contributions to retirement plans so they can save for their children's college education. A survey by Allstate (2005) found that 46% of parents were saving equally for retirement and college, while 14% were saving primarily for college. Low-income parents were more likely to put off saving for retirement in favor of their children's college education.

As heartless as it may sound, your retirement should come first, financial planners say. Here's why: Your child can borrow money to pay for college. You can't borrow to pay for retirement. Many parents don't want their children to graduate in debt, and most students aren't thrilled with the idea, either.

But the alternative may be worse, says Robert Smith, a planner at Comprehensive Financial Advisers in Exton, Pennsylvania. If you fail to save for retirement, your children could end up supporting you later in life, when they've got their own family obligations, he says. The federal student loan program provides low-interest loans to college students. And there are other ways to raise money for college or reduce the cost. Your child can apply for scholarships and financial aid, attend a less expensive school, get a part-time job, or live at home for a couple of years.

Making up for a retirement savings shortfall is much harder. Brian Jones, a financial planner in Fairfax, Virginia, tells clients who are determined to trim their retirement savings for college that they should plan on working a few more years. Catching up on retirement savings is harder than you think. Many parents say they'll start saving for retirement once their children are out of college. But that means giving up your most powerful investment tool: time. The earlier you start saving, the more you'll benefit from compounding.

T. Rowe Price analyzed a hypothetical couple with a combined income of $100,000 who invested 6% of their salary each year. The analysis covered 36 years and assumed an 8% average annual return and a 3% salary increase. If the couple split their savings between college and retirement for the first 18 years, and saved only for retirement during the second 18 years, they ended up with $126,000 for college and $1.65 million for retirement. If they devoted all their savings to college for the first 18 years, then switched to retirement savings, their college fund totaled $253,000, but their retirement savings fell to $759,000. And that assumes their employers matched 50% of their 401(k) contributions. Without the company match, their nest egg shrinks to $506,000.

Saving for retirement will improve your chances for financial aid. From a financial aid standpoint, sheltering money in a 401(k) or similar retirement plan is a smart planning strategy. The federal financial aid formula doesn't include money invested in retirement accounts when calculating how much your family can afford to pay for college, says Kalman Chany, author of *Paying for College Without Going Broke*. In general, assets owned by the parents are counted much less heavily than the child's assets, Chany says. If maxing out on your 401(k) is unrealistic, at least contribute enough to qualify for any matching funds your company provides. Matching funds will fuel the growth of your savings at no cost to you. And when you're juggling competing demands of college and retirement, the last thing you want to do is turn away free money. Still determined to put your child's education first? Make sure you understand the consequences, says Amy Noel, a financial planner in Boulder, Colorado. Are you willing to retire later, or have less money in retirement? she says.

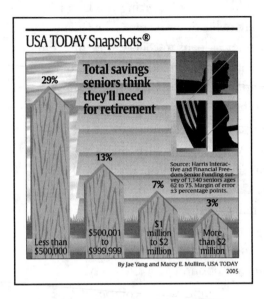

USA TODAY Snapshots®

Total savings seniors think they'll need for retirement

29% Less than $500,000

13% $500,001 to $999,999

7% $1 million to $2 million

3% More than $2 million

Source: Harris Interactive and Financial Freedom Senior Funding survey of 1,140 seniors ages 62 to 75. Margin of error ±3 percentage points.

By Jae Yang and Marcy E. Mullins, USA TODAY 2005

Looking Ahead:
Retirement Saving Strategies

No matter how old you are when you stop working, you'll want to feel reasonably secure that you can coast along, comfortably paying the bills for your living expenses, health costs, and travel and recreational activities. This will require having money tucked away in various places, from banks to retirement accounts to other investments. We'll address general investment strategies in Chapter 10. But let's start with three core financial issues regarding retirement, namely:

- how much money you'll need
- how much you'll get from Social Security or an employer pension plan, and
- your options for retirement-specific, tax-saving plans.

How much you'll need for retirement

Exactly how many dollars you'll need to live on in retirement is the question of the hour. Different financial planners will tell you very different things. Some say you'll need to either save a few million bucks or keep working until you keel over; others swear that these are just scare tactics by a financial industry bent on making you buy its products. The truth is probably somewhere in between. Complicating matters, you can't be sure how high inflation will go by the time you're retired, or how long you'll live. And the concept of a "retirement age" has changed radically over the years—while some people now aim to retire at age 45, others never want to stop working, at least on a part-time basis.

USA TODAY Snapshots®

Part-time job might make retirement better
Percentage of respondents who said retirement is better than expected because of:

34% — Not working
45% — Working part time
35% — Working full time

Source: 2006 Merrill Lynch New Retirement Study of 2,180 respondents 65 and older. Margin of error ±2 percentage

By Jae Yang and Keith Simmons, USA TODAY 2006

But you can get ballpark figures by using online calculators, of which there are many. We say "ballpark" because these calculators can give wildly different results, to the tune of tens of thousands of dollars. It's no wonder, given that they have to work in assumptions about such things as the rate of inflation, your investment returns, future tax rates, and how long you live.

That said, one of our favorite calculators is the one at www.choose tosave.org (click "Ballpark E$timate," then "Interactive Ballpark"). One thing we like about this calculator is that it not only has you input key information like the amount in your 401(k), your expected Social Security earnings, and your assumption about inflation (3% is widely considered a safe assumption), but it lets you decide how much money you'll need to live on each year, expressed as a percentage of your current income. While most experts say you'll need 65%-85% of your current income in retirement, and some calculators automatically input a number, like 70%, this one lets you make your own decision. In fact, plenty of people live happily on as little as 40% of their pre-retirement income.

How can that be? When you think about it, the working life demands that you spend a certain amount just to support it—or at least to reward yourself for getting through it. For example, commuting guzzles gas and wears out your car. You probably buy more or better clothes for office wear—and then pay to have them dry cleaned. On busy days, you may pick up coffee and a muffin rather than making breakfast at home, and do the equivalent at lunch. And you wouldn't be the first person to deal with a frustrating day by going out at lunchtime for some "retail therapy." All of this adds up—and much of it will disappear in retirement. Picture yourself making your own muffins and taking long walks instead of fighting rush-hour traffic.

To get a realistic idea of what percentage of your current income you'll need in retirement, take a look at your Family Spending Worksheet. Start by identifying which of your current expenses are directly related to getting up and going to work each day. Subtract those from your total expenses. Then subtract any debts that you'll have paid off by the time you retire, such as your home mortgage. If your kids will have left the nest by then, you can also subtract the costs of their care, unless you'll be paying college expenses while you're retired.

Of course, you'll also need to add in any expected major new expenses, such as a vacation home, a yacht, or golf club membership. If you'll be moving to a different state, factor in any changes in property or income tax rates.

And, although it's not as much fun to think about, you'll need to estimate your post-retirement medical expenses. Many retirees rely largely on Medicare, a federal program for which you'll probably be eligible based on your work record (it doesn't depend on financial need). However, Medicare leaves almost half of all medical costs unpaid, with limitations on things like hospital stays and long-term care. So retirees are all but forced to supplement Medicare with a private "medigap" insurance policy, or with Medicare Advantage, a managed care option. Prices for such policies vary widely, depending on your geographical location, age, physical condition, the comprehensiveness of the policy you choose, and more. If your employer has promised you health coverage in retirement, that's even better (though some employers are reneging on their promises).

In any case, chances are also good that you'll spend more for medicines and unreimbursed medical care than you do now. According to Kathy, "Fidelity Investments estimates a 65-year-old couple retiring today will need $215,000 to cover medical costs in retirement. (This assumes the couple has no employer-sponsored retiree health coverage and that the husband lives 17 more years and the wife 20.)"

As Bugs Bunny said

(while testing shells for duds by hammering them)

And just think, in thirty years I can retire.

— FROM *FORWARD MARCH HARE* ANIMATED SHORT

Finally, calculate what percentage of your current income you think you'll need in retirement. Now you're ready to go back to those retirement calculators and get a sense of how much you'll need to save for retirement.

RESOURCE
For more information and updates on retirement and Medicare, see:

- The Social Security & Retirement articles on Nolo's website (in the Property & Money section) at www.nolo.com.
- USA TODAY's retirement page, which will keep you abreast of any changes that might affect your planning, at www.usatoday.com/money/perfi/retirement.
- Government websites, including www.socialsecurity.gov and www.medicare.gov.

Your Social Security income

Hey, you're partway to funding your retirement already! If you've been working, you'll probably be entitled to monthly Social Security retirement benefits one day. However, these benefits may not be enough to comfortably live on—the Social Security Administration (SSA) says they replace only 40% of yearly preretirement income for the average worker—and that assumes the system won't be overhauled, which only time will tell.

How much you are personally entitled to will depend on the average dollars you put into the system over your working years. (Remember all those payroll deductions?) The longer you worked and the higher your income over the years, the more you'll get back—it has nothing to do with your financial need.

It's easy to get an estimate of how much you'll receive in Social Security benefits. In fact, you may have already received a Social Security Statement in the mail. The SSA keeps a database of your earnings record and work credits and is supposed to send you a statement, which details your contributions and expected payments, every year. But if you haven't received one lately, go to www.ssa.gov or call 800-772-1213 to request a copy.

As you review your Statement, you'll notice one important thing: The size of your Social Security benefit check will depend on whether you start claiming benefits before or after your so-called "full retirement age." And if you thought retirement age was 65, think again. In a cost-cutting measure, SSA now won't start paying full benefits until you're 67 if you were born in 1960 or later. Most people born earlier will have to wait until age 66, depending on the year they were born.

But you can retire as early as 62 if you're willing to receive lower benefits (permanently lower—the amount won't go up when you hit your full retirement age). And if you can hold out beyond your full retirement age to start receiving benefits, you'll set the permanent amount of your check even higher, until the possibilities top out when you're age 70. The calculators at the Social Security website will help you figure out what retirement age makes more financial sense for you, at http://ssa.gov/planners/calculators. (Unlike your Social Security Statement, the calculators let you click on "break-even age" to find out how long you'll need to live in order to make delaying your benefits worthwhile.)

One more SSA rule to factor into your plans: The age at which you start claiming Social Security benefits doesn't have to be the age at which you stop working. You could, for example, start claiming benefits at 62 but work until you're 68. However, the SSA will deduct a portion of your benefit payments based on your income until you reach your full retirement age. The deduction is one dollar of your benefits for every two dollars you earned over a set yearly limit ($12,960 in 2007).

Employer pensions

If your employer provides you with a retirement pension plan, count yourself lucky. For the most part, pensions are going the way of the dinosaurs, though many federal, state, and local government employees are still in line for generous pensions. For details on what you'll be entitled to, check with your employer's benefits administrator. Be attentive to details like how many years you'll need to work to qualify for different benefit levels.

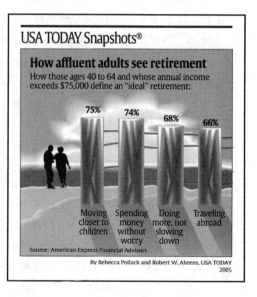

USA TODAY Snapshots®

How affluent adults see retirement

How those ages 40 to 64 and whose annual income exceeds $75,000 define an "ideal" retirement:

75% — Moving closer to children
74% — Spending money without worry
68% — Doing more, not slowing down
66% — Traveling abroad

Source: American Express Financial Advisors

By Rebecca Pollack and Robert W. Ahrens, USA TODAY
2005

Options for retirement savings

You've got three main options for tax-advantaged retirement accounts:

- 401(k) plans
- individual retirement accounts ("IRAs"), and
- Roth IRAs.

Try to think of these as "don't touch 'em" accounts—once the money is in them, taking it out before retirement will usually negate any tax advantages, and possibly subject you to financial penalties.

401(k) plan. If your employer offers a 401(k) plan (called a "403(b)" if you work for a nonprofit), it's worth signing up as soon as possible. These retirement plans offer reduction of income taxes and a convenient way to meet your retirement goals. You'll tell your employer how much to withdraw from your paycheck and deposit into your plan. The withdrawal amount is limited by an annual maximum, set by the IRS, though your employer may reduce it. For 2008, the IRS limits are $16,000, or $21,000 if you're 50 or older.

Your employer will deduct the amount of money you specify from each paycheck and put it into your retirement plan. And it will do so without deducting any taxes from it—401(k) contributions are not, for the most part, figured into your taxable income. Even better, many companies will match your contributions, up to a set amount. Over one third of all companies match 100% of your contributions. If you're self-employed, you can set up a solo 401(k), to which you'd contribute whenever you choose, up to certain limits.

Your employer should offer you a range of investment options to choose among. You can change your investment choices at any time. See Chapter 10 for tips on choosing investments—or if you don't have time for that, keep it simple by choosing a broad-based index fund, which invests in a sort of market sampler.

Should You Invest in Your Company's Own Stock?

Your 401(k) investment choices may include stock in your own company, perhaps at a discounted rate. But don't let loyalty or misplaced optimism lead you to put most of your 401(k) fund into that stock. You'd be making a common investment mistake—witness the Enron meltdown, in which many employees lost not only their jobs, but their retirement savings. Like them, you'd be placing all your hopes on the success of one company. Okay, you might argue, but you've got insider's knowledge of what a great company it is. There's just one problem: Your company's ongoing success will be affected by factors outside your knowledge and control, such as the economy and consumer fads or preferences. If the main 401(k) investment choice offered by your company is its own stock, push for additional options. As John advises, "You shouldn't have more than 10% of your 401(k) assets invested in your company stock."

Your employer doesn't deduct any taxes from your 401(k) contributions, so you'll see a lower overall tax bite on your paycheck. And you're gaining a second tax advantage: Unlike ordinary savings accounts, you won't be taxed on any earnings on your 401(k) investments, such as interest or dividends.

You will eventually owe income tax on the money in your 401(k), when you withdraw it from the account. But the idea is that by then you'll be retired, and in a lower tax bracket.

How much should you deposit into your 401(k)? For starters, don't miss out on the chance to collect your employer's matching amount, if any. After that, we recommend putting in as much as you can, while still paying your bills and saving for emergencies. Even if you get part way through the year and realize you're having too much taken from your paycheck, you can change your mind and reduce it. (You can also do the opposite if you feel you're having too little withdrawn, but are you really going to remember to do that?)

CAUTION

Don't cash out if you switch to a new job. The moment your money leaves your 401(k)—even if it's because you get a check in your name that you plan to deposit into your next employer's 401(k)—it's considered a distribution, and subject to not only income tax, but a 10% penalty if you're under age 59½. Make sure to do what's called a "rollover," using a "trustee-to-trustee transfer," either into a new 401(k), or better yet, according to Sandra, into an IRA: "Your money will grow, tax-deferred, until you take withdrawals. And you'll have more investment options than those offered by your 401(k) plan." You can still open a new 401(k) at your new job.

Traditional individual retirement account (IRA). An IRA is a retirement plan that you set up for yourself, perhaps because your employer doesn't offer a retirement plan for you at work, or perhaps because you want to put even more toward your retirement than your 401(k) allows. The keeper of your account, called a trustee or custodian, must be a trust company, bank, federally insured credit union, savings and loan association, or other IRS-approved entity. You might receive a tax deduction for the amount you contribute, although the value of your deduction will be reduced if you contribute to your employer's 401(k) or other retirement plan. You're allowed to contribute up to $5,000 a year ($6,000 if you're 50 or older; 2008 figures).

Your bank will most likely offer a broad range of possible investments for the money in your IRA, including mutual funds, index funds, stocks, and bonds. Any interest or other earnings will be tax-deferred, meaning you won't have to pay taxes on them until you start withdrawing the money. The earliest you can start withdrawing without a financial penalty is age 59½, but you must start taking minimum withdrawals at age 70½. These mandatory distributions are based on your statistical life expectancy as set out in IRS tables.

RESOURCE
For more information on both traditional and Roth IRAs, including the latest contribution limits: See IRS Publication 590, *Individual Retirement Arrangements (IRAs)*.

Roth IRA. A Roth IRA is in some ways the mirror image of the traditional IRA. Instead of getting a tax deduction when you deposit your money, you deposit after-tax dollars. It's your eventual withdrawals, including any interest or gain, that will be tax-free, so long as you have:

- held the account at least five years, and
- reached age 59½.

A Roth IRA offers unusual flexibility in that you can withdraw your contributions—that is, the principal in your account, before interest or gains—at any time, tax-free and without penalty. After all, you've already paid tax on it. (You can see why Roth IRAs are used by many people to save for their children's college education.) If, however, you withdraw any of your earnings before you're 59½, you will (except in certain special circumstances such as first-time home purchases) not only owe income tax on that amount, but also have to pay a 10% penalty.

Similar to a traditional IRA, you can open a Roth at a bank or other IRS-approved entity, are allowed to contribute up to $5,000 a year ($6,000 if you're 50 or older; 2008 figures), and you'll be offered a broad choice of investment options.

Not everyone can open a Roth IRA, however; there are income limits affecting who can contribute, and how much they can contribute. As of 2007, the income phaseout begins at $156,000 for couples filing jointly, and at $166,000 you're no longer eligible to contribute. If your income is currently well below these limits but you expect it to take a healthy rise later in your career, now might be the time to contribute to a Roth IRA, when you've got the chance. And given your lower tax bracket, you probably won't pay much tax on the income now.

TIP

If your income is too high, plan for 2010. That's the year in which everyone, regardless of income, will be allowed to convert traditional IRAs into Roth IRAs. The income limits for Roth conversions will be suspended from then until 2012. Although you'll pay income tax when you convert, it may be worth it to gain the tax savings in later years when you make withdrawals. Some experts advise putting money into a regular IRA now in anticipation of converting.

John calls the Roth IRA "your best bet to avoid taxes," explaining that, "Income tax rates are at their lowest point in decades, but government debt is at its highest ever. It's a good bet that sooner or later, Congress will have to raise taxes. By paying taxes now on your contributions, you may avoid paying at a higher tax rate at retirement."

Where to Invest the Money in Your IRA (Traditional or Roth)

Ah, the tyranny of choices: You'll have a lot of options for directing the money within your IRA. We'll talk more about investment strategies in Chapter 10, but here's some simple advice from John: "The more time you have before you retire, the more stocks and stock funds you should have in your IRA. This has nothing to do with taxes. Over a long period, stocks tend to fare better than bonds or risk-free investments, such as Treasury bills or bank CDs."

TIP

Keep your ongoing IRA fees to a minimum. John points out, "Suppose the Wombat fund earns 10% annually, but takes 2 percentage points a year in fees. The Bull Moose fund also earns 10% a year, but takes just 1 percentage point of that a year in fees. After 50 years, a $10,000 investment in the Wombat fund will grow to $469,000. Your Bull Moose fund investment will grow to $754,500—nearly $286,000 more."

Tuition, Room, and Board: Who'll Pay?

Now that you've got your retirement savings on track, it's time to think about your kids' education. At first look, the cost of sending children to college can be bone chilling: Tuition and fees at four-year private colleges average around $22,000 per year. But wait: Four-year public colleges remain a relative bargain, with tuition at around $6,000 per year. And one way or another, the majority of students attend four-year schools with annual tuition and fees below $9,000. This might be easier than you thought.

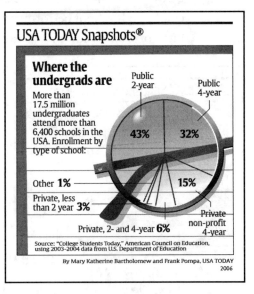

USA TODAY Snapshots®

Where the undergrads are

More than 17.5 million undergraduates attend more than 6,400 schools in the USA. Enrollment by type of school:

- Public 2-year **43%**
- Public 4-year **32%**
- Private non-profit 4-year **15%**
- Private, 2- and 4-year **6%**
- Private, less than 2 year **3%**
- Other **1%**

Source: "College Students Today," American Council on Education, using 2003-2004 data from U.S. Department of Education

By Mary Katherine Bartholomew and Frank Pompa, USA TODAY 2006

RESOURCE

But they're still in diapers! Curious how much college will cost when your little ones have grown taller than you? Go to www.finaid.org (click "Calculators," then "Cost Projector"). This free, comprehensive, and unbiased website also offers useful information about financial aid, loans, scholarships, and more.

Financial aid, loans, and savings plans

Let's imagine that your child is fated to attend a pricey private school such as George Washington University, which tops the tuition charts at nearly $38,000 per year. Then you'll need to get serious about your financing options. The three basic ways to pay for college include:

- **Financial aid or scholarships.** The main sources of these are the federal government and the colleges themselves. Both view their role as supplementing, not replacing, payments by parents. No matter how low your income and assets, or how impressive your child's high-school performance, your odds of covering all or even most of your child's college expenses through aid and scholarships are slim. Also, the hope of qualifying for financial aid through low assets is certainly not a reason to avoid saving—your retirement accounts, for example, won't be counted into your assets. For a calculator showing your family's expected contribution, see www.finaid.org. And for eligibility rules, lists of programs, and more, see the website of the U.S. Department of Education's Federal Student Aid program at http://studentaid.ed.gov.

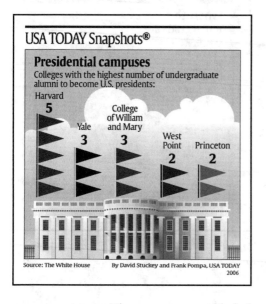

USA TODAY Snapshots®

Presidential campuses
Colleges with the highest number of undergraduate alumni to become U.S. presidents:

Harvard **5**

Yale **3**

College of William and Mary **3**

West Point **2**

Princeton **2**

Source: The White House   By David Stuckey and Frank Pompa, USA TODAY 2006

- **Loans.** These are a more likely bet for families at all income levels. The majority of students or their parents use some sort of loan—whether from a federal or a private source—to get them through college. The federal loan programs offer relatively low interest rates (in late 2007, between 6.8% and 8.5%) and flexible repayment plans. Of course, you or your child will have to pay the loans back someday. Again, www.finaid.org is a good resource for loan providers and advice.

- **Your own savings.** If you have the means to help with your child's education costs, a number of savings programs can make the job easy, and offer tax advantages. See the table, "Best Ways to Save for College," below, as well as, "New favorite college savings plan: The 529," later in this chapter.

> **TIP**
> **Credit card rebate programs can add a few bucks.** Certain credit cards or rebate programs will put cash into your child's college savings plan for every dollar you spend with affiliated merchants. Some programs require you to use a special credit card; others just keep track of your current credit cards. And the most popular ones, like UPromise and BabyMint, have no annual fee. For a complete list, go to www.finaid.org and search for "credit card rebate and loyalty programs."

New favorite college savings plan: The 529

Although families have been socking money in tax-advantaged 529 savings plans for years, Kathy observes that, "they are fast becoming the principal way for parents and grandparents to save for college."

Why? Costs have dropped. Investment options have improved. Perhaps most significantly, Congress has permanently extended the most enticing feature: All the money you pull out of 529s for college—your contributions, plus the earnings—is free of federal tax.

State-sponsored 529 savings plans let you invest in a menu of stock and bond funds, just as 401(k) plans do. Forty-eight states and the District of Columbia offer at least one 529 savings plan. The plans aren't limited to in-state residents; you can generally invest in any state plan you want. But your state's plan will often reward you with a deduction or other state tax break.

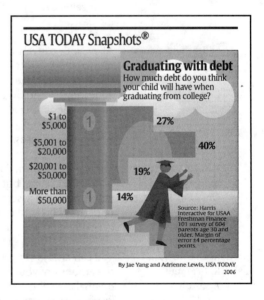

USA TODAY Snapshots®

Graduating with debt
How much debt do you think your child will have when graduating from college?

$1 to $5,000 — 27%
$5,001 to $20,000 — 40%
$20,001 to $50,000 — 19%
More than $50,000 — 14%

Source: Harris Interactive for USAA Freshman Finance 101 survey of 604 parents age 30 and older. Margin of error ±4 percentage points.

By Jae Yang and Adrienne Lewis, USA TODAY 2006

Best Ways to Save for College		
Plan type	**Description**	**Pros**
529 Plans	These state-sponsored plans allow you to invest for college tuition and other expenses.	You can save up to around $300,000 per child (the amount varies from state to state). Grandparents and other relatives can also contribute. In many states, you get a tax deduction when you contribute to your state's plan. And as long as the money is used for college, withdrawals are tax-free, so you don't pay tax on the growth.
Prepaid Tuition Plans	Let you buy tuition shares at state-funded colleges and universities, which are guaranteed to retain their value even if tuitions increase.	You won't lose your money if the stock market declines. Even if your child goes to a private or out-of-state college, the plan will pay out the average of in-state tuition rates.
Education Savings Accounts (ESAs); also called Coverdell ESAs or CESAs	Allow you to invest in mutual funds or other investments for your child's education. Withdrawals are tax-free as long as the money is used for education expenses.	You can design your own portfolio. Savings can be used for primary and secondary school tuition as well as college expenses.
Uniform Gifts to Minors and Uniform Transfers to Minors Accounts	These are established in your child's name, but you control the assets until the child is 18 or 21, depending on your state.	You determine how the money is invested, and it can be used for anything that benefits your child.
Roth Individual Retirement Account	You can always withdraw the amount of your original contributions without paying taxes or penalties. If you withdraw more than that to pay for college, you'll pay taxes on gains, but the 10% early withdrawal penalty will be waived.	You decide how to invest. Any money you don't use for college will continue to compound until you retire.

Cons	For more information
Some 529 plans carry large expenses and fees. Returns aren't guaranteed: If your investments perform poorly, you could lose money.	Check out www.collegesavings.org (by a nonprofit group; has a handy plan comparison tool); www.savingforcollege.com; and www.morningstar.com.
Most prepaid plans are limited to state residents. Not all states offer them.	See www.collegesavings.org.
Contributions are limited to $2,000 per year per beneficiary. A married couple must have adjusted gross income of less than $190,000 to contribute the full amount.	See www.savingforcollege.com/coverdell_esas, IRS Publication 970, *Tax Benefits for Higher Education*, at www.irs.gov, and www.babycenter.com (click "Articles & Tools," then "Baby," then "Family Finances.")
Your child controls the assets after reaching the age of majority. The money is considered the child's asset, which might reduce the amount of financial aid available.	
The maximum you can invest in a Roth this year is $5,000, or $6,000 if you're 50 or older. (2008 figures; annual income limits also apply.) Diverting money from a Roth will reduce the amount available for your retirement.	

Best Ways to Save for College (cont'd.)		
Plan type	Description	Pros
U.S. Savings Bonds	Interest from savings bonds used to pay for college might be tax-free.	Savings bonds are a risk-free investment.
401(k) Loan	Many employers allow workers to borrow from their 401(k) plan.	You pay interest on the loan to yourself, not a lender.
Home Equity Line of Credit or Loan	Many homeowners in hot real estate markets have a large amount of equity in their homes, providing a potential source of funds for college tuition.	Interest rates on home equity lines are low, and the interest is usually tax deductible.

For procrastinating parents, 529 plans offer particular appeal. That's because parents together can front-load in one year up to five years' worth of contributions—currently $120,000—without being subject to gift taxes. They can do this if they don't add any more money for the next five years.

Money withdrawn from 529 savings plans can be used at any accredited college nationwide. (The somewhat similar 529 "prepaid" plans also allow you to go outside your state, but are meant to lock in tomorrow's tuition at today's prices at state public schools.)

The 529 savings plans aren't without their problems. Some states' plans still impose high fees and have poor investment options. Regulators have expressed concern that, to score higher commissions, some brokers are selling clients on a more expensive out-of-state 529 savings plan rather than an in-state plan with tax breaks. And though it's become easier to compare plans from different states, it still isn't simple.

Cons	For more information
The tax break is limited to parents who meet income limits. Savings bonds must be in the parents' names, not the child's.	See www.savingsbonds.gov.
Borrowing from your 401(k) will limit the growth of your retirement savings. If you leave your job, you'll have to repay the balance to avoid taxes and early withdrawal penalties.	
Rates on home equity lines of credit are variable and will go higher if interest rates rise. If you fall behind on payments, you could lose your home.	

Yet, financial advisers are increasingly likely to recommend these plans. Lisa and Christopher Fitzgerald, of Albany, New York, say they like 529 savings plans because they can change the account beneficiary. They began saving last year in New York's 529 plan for their sons, Aidan, 4, and Christopher Jr., 16.

"If Christopher doesn't need it, then it's there for Aidan," says Lisa, 42. "And, if 14 years from now, Aidan turns out to be an amazing football player and doesn't need it because of scholarships," she will put the money into a retirement account. (Investors generally have to pay income taxes and a 10% penalty for using 529 money for non-educational purposes.)

Some employers now allow automatic deductions into 529 plans. The popularity of 401(k) plans derives partly from the fact that "you check a box, and the (pretax) money is gone," says James Boyle of College Parents of America. "There's starting to be a movement of companies doing the same for 529 plans" on an after-tax basis.

Here are Kathy's additional tips for stress-free 529 investing:

- **Look at your state's 529 plan first.** Thirty-one states and the District of Columbia offer benefits such as tax deductions to residents for investing in their plan, according to Savingforcollege.com.

- **Weigh tax breaks against investment features.** If your state provides a tax break for its own 529 savings plan but has no low-cost investment options, go elsewhere. "If you found a plan with better investment options and lower fees, you would certainly be better off" in the long run, says Gail Fialkow, a financial planner in Fairfax, Virginia.

- **Compare 529 plans.** A comprehensive source of 529 data can be found at www.savingforcollege.com. College Savings Plans Network, made up of states that sponsor these plans, provides information and links to different states' 529 plans at www.collegesavings.org.

- **Consider direct-sold 529 plans.** About 80% of 529 savings plans are sold by financial advisers. But plans that you open directly with individual states are often less expensive and have similar investment options.

Invest Intelligently (Without Obsessing About It)

At some point, the amount you're saving to meet your goals for retirement, your children's education, and the rest will overflow your piggy bank—or, more accurately, your regular bank accounts, where your dollars are probably earning a mediocre rate of interest. That's when "saving" starts to morph into "investing." You'll want to put your cash into assets that have the potential for higher earnings.

But let's not get ahead of ourselves. If you're still in the early days of getting your finances in order, you don't need to worry much about principles of investing. And the last thing you should be doing is playing the stock market if you're still whittling down your credit card debt or setting aside an emergency fund. But when you're ready to invest the money that you're putting into your retirement plan or an account earmarked for college costs, it's time to pay attention to your options and make choices about whether to put your money into stocks, mutual funds, or other investment vehicles whose names you may not now recognize. If you don't, you'll miss out on a lot of growth. That's risky to your long-term financial health, too.

So let's take a look at the world of investment choices and your simplest, best strategies at this busy phase in your life.

Where to Begin? Your Investment Choices

There are a million different places to invest your money. Flip through any personal finance magazine and you'll see articles every month about the best stocks, the best mutual funds, and the best market sectors (real estate? pharmaceuticals? solar power?) to invest in right now. But unless you're going to make a second career out of tracking the market and trying to predict its ups and downs, you're better off adopting and sticking to a simple investing strategy. And the truth is that a sensible, simple approach is every bit as likely—no, more likely—to give you good investment results as a fancy one is.

You do need to know something about the basic range of investment choices, though. Let's start with the safest options and move toward the riskiest. That fits nicely with the way you want to approach investing, anyway. For example, you'll keep your emergency fund in accessible cash, earning interest at a steady but unimpressive rate, without any risk of losing it. When you've got more money to invest and some time to leave it alone, you can investigate investment options that have the potential for greater gain—and come with greater risk.

Investment Choices	
What you've got to invest	**Options to consider**
Emergency funds (cash)	Savings account (including high-interest online options) Short-term CD Money market fund
Your contributions to retirement plans (IRA, 401(k))	Mutual funds Individual stocks
College savings funds	Tax-advantaged savings plans administered by the states that offer you a choice of mutual funds Mutual funds (taxable)
Money available to invest after you've maxed out tax-advantaged options such as your 401(k)	Mutual funds Individual stocks

Cash investments

Everyone needs some cash on hand, whether to buy food and supplies or bail you out in minor (or major) emergencies. We've already talked about the importance of keeping your everyday money in a checking account (preferably interest-bearing) and setting up a savings account, CD, or money market account (MMA) for your emergency fund (Chapter 4). All of these are considered cash investments. They do, after all, earn interest, though at a relatively low rate—possibly lower than the inflation rate, which means that you're actually losing a little spending power every year.

But once you've got your emergency and everyday needs covered, it's financially wise to move out of this safety zone (unless you're super risk-averse). With just a little more risk, you can probably raise your potential returns significantly. A major mistake that young investors make is being too conservative in their choice of retirement plan investments—or just letting their savings pile up, forgetting to shift money into retirement or college savings accounts at all. Financial planners with whom John spoke say, "Young investors should take the most risk with their investments. A young investor saving for retirement has plenty of time to make up a large loss. A 59-year-old has less time. And in general, your potential rewards increase with the amount of risk you take."

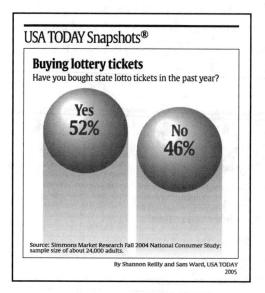

USA TODAY Snapshots®

Buying lottery tickets
Have you bought state lotto tickets in the past year?

Yes 52%

No 46%

Source: Simmons Market Research Fall 2004 National Consumer Study: sample size of about 24,000 adults.

By Shannon Reilly and Sam Ward, USA TODAY 2005

Of course, John warns, "High-risk investments don't guarantee higher returns. Otherwise, planners would urge you to invest in Powerball tickets."

Bonds

Investing some money in bonds is a safe, sound approach when you're starting to invest. A bond, as John explains, "is a long-term IOU issued by a company, a state or local government, or the U.S. government. It's not much different from a car loan or a mortgage—except you're the lender. You collect the interest until the bond matures, at which point you get your principal back." Although the returns might not be eye-popping, the fixed interest rate on a bond can look great when interest rates fall or the stock market declines. Also, bonds are relatively low risk, especially when they're from the government. Examples of government bonds include U.S. Treasury bonds (with minimum investments of $1,000, and minimum terms or "maturities" of ten years or more) or municipal bonds, such as when your local government needs to fund a new highway project.

But low risk doesn't mean no risk, especially when you buy the bonds from companies with low credit ratings. Not coincidentally, these tend to offer the highest interest rates—you're running the risk that the company could default either on your interest or capital payments, or both. Fortunately, bonds are rated by agencies like Moody's and Standard & Poor's (S&P), with AAA (S&P) or Aaa (Moody's) the best. You probably don't want to risk anything rated below BBB. (Remember "junk bonds"? There's a reason they're called that.)

Although you can go out and buy bonds directly, you're more likely to buy into a bond fund, perhaps within your 401(k). This is simply a mutual fund that invests primarily in bonds or similar debt securities. Although this is convenient, it offers less certainty than just buying a bond and sticking with it. That's because there's a separate market for bonds. John offers this example: "Suppose . . . you'd bought a ten-year T-note (a note issued by the U.S. Treasury) that yielded 15% back in 1981. By 1986, yields on newly issued T-notes had tumbled to about 7.5%. Suddenly, your 15% T-note would have looked very attractive to other investors—so much so that they would pay more for your T-note than you did. Quite a bit more." The result for mutual funds, John cautions, is that they have to "calculate the value of their bonds every day. When bond prices fall, so will your fund's share price. If you own a bond fund, your principal losses in a bear market will erode your fund's income. Inflation will, too."

Apart from your IRA or 401(k), you can purchase bonds or bond funds directly from their sources (for example, see www.savingsbonds. gov for U.S. Treasury bonds) or through brokers.

Mutual funds, Part 1: The basics

A mutual fund pools money from many investors and invests it in stocks, bonds, cash, or a combination of these asset types. There are all sorts of mutual funds: You can find mutual funds that invest only in South American companies; in biotechnology stocks; in municipal bonds; or in U.S. companies with market values of less than $1 billion—and that barely scratches the surface.

Mutual funds make money for investors in two basic ways:

- Income from fund assets—for example, dividends from stocks held in the fund (shares of the profits paid to the companies' stockholders) or interest earned by cash assets or bonds. Funds distribute this income to shareholders, usually twice a year.

- Profits (capital gains) from stocks or bonds that the fund has sold or that have gone up in value. Capital gains are also distributed every year.

Depending on what assets funds invest in, they can concentrate on producing income or on growth in the underlying value of the investments. What you're going to be looking for depends on how old you are, whether or not you're going to need money soon (for your children's college, for example), and other personal factors. Every mutual fund has a manager, who makes investments to meet the particular fund's goals—for example, long-term growth, high income, or slow growth with little volatility. You can find a mutual fund for just about any kind of company you want to invest in and at any risk level you're comfortable with.

Why are mutual funds so popular? There are several reasons:

- **They're easy.** It's simple to invest in a fund or move your money from one investment company to another. You can do it online, by mail, or over the phone. And you've always got access to your money, because fund shares are sold every business day. Most mutual fund companies give you good records of your transactions, making tax time much easier.

- **They're inexpensive.** There's a lot of competition for individual investors' money—and a lot of readily accessible information about various funds' performance and costs. You can easily find a fund that matches your investment goals and has low management fees. You get a professional managing your money, for less than you'd pay a traditional stockbroker.

- **They let you diversify your investments.** Spreading your money among different kinds of assets is a cardinal rule of investing (discussed more below). And every fund, even ones focused on a particular region or type of assets, own many different securities, often hundreds or thousands of them. This reduces your risk greatly.

Does this mean mutual funds are perfect? Well, nothing's perfect. Keep in mind that although, over the long term, the stock market has always gone up, there's no guarantee that a particular mutual fund will make money. The value of your shares will almost surely go up and down in the short term. You've got to do your homework and pick a fund that fits your goals and risk tolerance. And no investment is safe from a general decline in the economy.

You've also got to make sure that you don't invest in funds that charge high management fees—that's a mistake that can really cost you over the long term. Look for funds that charge no more than 1.5% of your assets each year (that's the average fee) and preferably much lower. You'll probably also want to go with "no-load" funds,

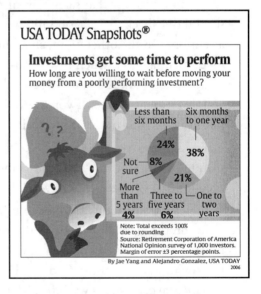

which simply means that you're not charged an upfront commission when you invest. The commission can eat up around 3% to 6% of your investment, and for most people it's not worth it. Fortunately, it's easy to compare funds' costs online.

You've probably heard of many of the big mutual fund companies, such as Vanguard, T. Rowe Price, and Fidelity, all of which offer many different funds. To invest in a mutual fund, you buy shares of the fund. Like the price of an individual stock, the price of a share in a mutual fund fluctuates daily, depending upon the performance of the underlying investments. Many funds are actively managed, meaning the fund managers are buying and selling investments all the time.

Your 401(k), IRA, or 529 (college savings) plan will no doubt offer you a wide selection of mutual funds. You can choose one or more to invest in and buy shares from the fund company directly or through a broker.

Most mutual funds want you to invest a minimum of $1,000 to open an account. Those that let you start smaller are usually sold through brokers. John points out that, "There are two drawbacks with broker-sold funds, at least from the point of view of a small investor. The first is the sales commission, or load, which will consume up to 5.75% of your initial investment. In theory at least, you'll get a broker's specialized advice in return for that sales commission. Which brings us to our second drawback: 5.75% of $500 won't buy you much of a broker's attention. On the other hand, small investors may not need a lot of investment advice, which is why no-load funds are generally a good deal. No-load funds don't charge a sales fee, or load, and they don't give you investment advice. If you know where you want to invest, you can put more of your money to work in a no-load than in a load fund."

If you don't have $1,000 to plop into a mutual fund, set yourself a plan to save up for it. Stash $100 a month in your high-yield savings account (see Chapter 4), and you'll be there before long.

There's a tremendous amount of information about specific mutual funds on the Web. For advice and ratings of various mutual funds, go to www.morningstar.com. You have to pay for some of Morningstar's information, but you can find much excellent advice there for free. Another favorite site is www.fundalarm.com, about which USA TODAY wrote, "Ask most people in the fund industry when to sell a fund, and they'll say never. FundAlarm disagrees: Kick that sucker out when its performance lags behind its peers for the past one, three, and five years. FundAlarm's list of most alarming funds is a terrific guide to the very worst funds."

Deciphering Mutual Fund Descriptions

Here are some words you're sure to encounter when choosing a mutual fund:

- **Core:** Mix growth and value strategies. Lipper classifications (Lipper being a Reuters company that provides mutual fund information): large-company core (LCC); midcap core (MCC); small-cap core (SCC); multicap core (MLC). International funds (which invest in all world markets outside the U.S.) are preceded by an I, as in ILC for international large-cap core. Global funds (which invest worldwide) are preceded by a G.

- **Equity-income (EI):** Seek income and growth by investing in bonds and dividend-stocks.

- **Growth:** Invest in companies whose earnings are expected to grow faster than average. Lipper classifications: large-company growth (LCG); midcap (MCG); small-cap (SCG); multicap (MLG).

- **Midcap (MC):** Invest in midsize companies with market values of less than $5 billion.

- **Multicap:** Can invest in stocks of any size company. Lipper categories: multicap growth (MLG); multicap value (MLV); multicap core (MLC).

- **Small-cap (SC):** Invest in companies with market value of less than $1 billion.

- **S&P 500 (SP):** Mirror the Standard & Poor's 500 stock index.

- **Value:** Buy stocks of out-of-favor companies selling for low prices relative to earnings. Classifications: large-company value (LCV); midcap value (MCV); small-cap value (SCV); multicap value (MLV).

- **Mixed-asset target (MXX):** Invest in stocks, bonds, money market securities. (XX is the target year; M40 fund's target retirement year is 2040.)

Mutual Funds for Doomsayers

The bull market in stocks, now roaring into its fifth year, leads some investors to assume the party will run forever. For others, a long-running bull market just means a bear market is lurking nearby.

If you want to bet your money on a bear market, the mutual fund industry has rolled out dozens of funds that rise only when the stock market tumbles. The number of bear-market funds, in fact, has exploded in the past three years.

Just beware: It's best not to bet your retirement account on a bear market. Consider instead using a small portion of your non-retirement portfolio to buy any of dozens of bear-market funds of a wide variety, including bond funds.

 "Bear funds unfurl when market's cloudy," by John Waggoner, July 6, 2007.

TIP
No time to read? If you can't stand the thought of putting any more energy into learning about investments, one of your best options is an index fund, described next.

Mutual funds, Part 2: Index funds

Index funds are a type of mutual fund. However, instead of being actively managed, their investment portfolios are set up to match, or track, the stocks in a market index such as the S&P 500. (That's a Standard & Poor's measurement of the stock prices of 500 large-cap, blue-chip, low-risk, mostly U.S. corporations.) The only time the fund manager buys or sells a stock is when the index itself changes.

But guess what? Index funds have a record of outperforming most actively managed mutual funds. In other words, you can summarize a perfectly sensible investment strategy for many people in one sentence: Put your money in an index fund and leave it there.

Part of the reason for index funds' success is simply that you don't have to pay for all the time the managers would otherwise spend trying to outguess the market. (Lower costs = higher returns.) Another reason is that, because the fund does less buying and selling of stocks, it owes less in capital gains tax and doesn't need to pass on those costs to you.

A third reason, explains John, is performance: "If all fund managers are investing in the same pool of stocks, it stands to reason that the average fund will do no better than the market's average performance. After all, you wouldn't expect an average person to be taller than average. By choosing an index fund, you'll get average performance, which is better than 50% of all other funds. More important, comparing the S&P 500 to the average stock fund is like

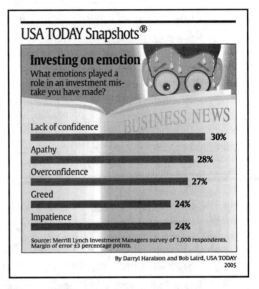

USA TODAY Snapshots®

Investing on emotion
What emotions played a role in an investment mistake you have made?

Lack of confidence — 30%
Apathy — 28%
Overconfidence — 27%
Greed — 24%
Impatience — 24%

Source: Merrill Lynch Investment Managers survey of 1,000 respondents. Margin of error ±3 percentage points.

By Darryl Haralson and Bob Laird, USA TODAY
2005

comparing apples and hippos. The S&P 500 measures the performance of the largest U.S. stocks. But the average stock fund figure includes funds that invest in large, small and midsize companies."

So, if you're interested in index funds, your first possibilities may be within your 401(k), IRA, or 529 plan. Or you can buy index fund shares directly from the fund company or through a broker.

But before you buy, realize that not all index funds are created equal. Although each fund chooses an index to guide its investments and then sticks with it (regardless of what the market does), the choice of index itself can reflect very different investment allocations. Some index funds invest partly in bonds, to lower the risk. Some have introduced a bit of active management. Others specialize—for example, by choosing only socially responsible investments within a major index. The result is that different index funds present different levels of risk and potential returns. See John's tips for choosing an index fund, below. And because these are mutual funds, you can find further information in the websites mentioned in the first part of our mutual fund discussion, above.

Choosing an Index Fund

As John describes it, science-fiction writers in the 1950s used to fret that machines would replace humans. Lately, their worries seem to be coming true. Supercomputers have clobbered chess masters. Copy machines have replaced monks. And unmanaged index funds have steamrolled fund managers.

That's why you should have at least part of your stock fund portfolio invested in index funds. But bear in mind, too, that not all index funds are alike—nor are all good investments.

Some index funds just don't make much sense. Consider QQQ, an exchange-traded fund that tracks the Nasdaq 100. That index measures the performance of the 100 largest stocks traded on the Nasdaq stock exchange.

Logically, however, it doesn't make much sense to buy stocks simply because they are traded on the Nasdaq. Where a stock is traded doesn't really have anything to do with its prospects. There's no similar fund that buys the 100 largest stocks on the New York Stock Exchange. Why? Because that would be dumb.

What kind of index fund should you choose? If you just want exposure to the stock market, buy a fund that tracks the broad-based Wilshire 5000 index or the Russell 3000. You'll get large and small stocks, all in one fund. Want big stocks only? Buy one that tracks the S&P 500.

You could create an entire portfolio of index funds, and there's nothing wrong with that. But if you still have some faith in humanity, consider keeping half your stock portfolio in an index fund. Use the rest for the actively managed funds. If your managers fail, you'll lag the index slightly. If your managers win, you might be able to buy that robot you've been eyeing.

 "Index funds' low cost makes them a solid place to start," by John Waggoner, February 27, 2004.

Mutual funds, Part 3: Target funds

The "hottest new breed of mutual fund in years," as John describes them, are target funds. What's all the excitement about? Sandra explains that target funds "invest in a mix of stocks, bonds, and money funds, based on when you plan to retire. The fund will periodically rebalance investments and shift to more conservative funds as you near retirement." John adds, "Because stocks typically fluctuate more than bonds, they can produce bigger short-term losses. If you're 30, you can afford to ride out bear-market losses. But if you're 55, a downturn in stocks can deliver a serious dent to your retirement plans. Target funds make those decisions for you—they reallocate your mix of stocks and bonds in the fund as you age." The closer you get to retirement, the more bonds in your fund.

At first glance, target funds look like the perfect choice for people too busy to keep an eye on their changing financial needs from now until retirement. No wonder that, as John says, "Investors, weary of making so many decisions and spending so much time managing their assets, have flocked to these funds." But, John warns, "before you put your portfolio on autopilot, check the fund's flight plan."

How quickly a fund moves from stocks to bonds is called its glide path. Just how the fund family arrives at the glide path is a mixture of mathematics and philosophy. Putnam's RetirementReady funds, for example, use a mathematical formula to determine their glide paths. The formula considers a person's earning power and financial assets as two parts of one portfolio.

"Early in their careers, investors have a small financial portfolio—the majority of their wealth is tied up in future earnings," notes Jeff Knight, manager of the RetirementReady funds. At that point, they have time to take a great deal of risk in their investments. At retirement, though, income from your job ends, and the assets in your portfolio take over. So the Putnam funds move out of stocks fairly quickly as retirement approaches.

T. Rowe Price takes a more aggressive approach. Its assumption is that a retiree could live an additional 30 years or longer—long enough for the stock portion of the portfolio to significantly boost overall returns.

Try the board game!

That's right, "Mutual Mania" gives you and up to five other players $25,000 in paper money, then tests your ability to increase your net worth—promising "the thrill of Wall Street" in the face of market turmoil, Middle East instability, and other influences.

Target funds have expenses, of course, and so do the funds they own. Naturally, the higher the expenses that your fund charges, the less you keep. If you buy a no-load fund, you'll pay expenses, too—just not ongoing commissions. Still, expenses can be significant.

Finally, you might not want to entrust your entire retirement plan to just one target fund, no matter how diversified it is. A truly well-rounded retirement portfolio would mean owning at least two target funds—just to be sure.

Exchange-traded funds (ETFs)

You might have heard recent buzz about exchange-traded funds (ETFs). These are close cousins to index funds (though they're not mutual funds), but were created mostly for professional investors. They've grown more popular, though, and are even showing up in investment choices small businesses offer to their 401(k) plan participants.

Most ETFs track an index that is designed to change with economic conditions or cover a niche area such as biotech or commodities. ETFs are traded like regular stocks on an exchange, going through price changes throughout the day. In buying and selling ETFs, you have to pay broker commissions just as with any ordinary stock. So what's the advantage over an index fund? Because they require little management (managers aren't constantly trading their holdings, but instead simply tracking an index), costs are low.

Individual stocks

We've all heard stories about someone who bought a stock—Coke, Microsoft, Google—at the right time and rode it to an unimaginable high. But of course people aren't always so eager to discuss the stocks they thought were sure things but weren't, even though just about anyone who invested in individual stocks during the dot-com craze of the late 1990s picked at least one big loser.

If you think this sounds like gambling, you're right. Picking individual stocks, unless you have solid information about the industry and a bit of good luck, is too risky to be anything but an add-on to your basic investing strategy of appropriate diversification and allocation. So unless you've already banked an emergency cash fund, fully funded your 401(k) at work, socked away money for the kids' college costs, and put some money into solid mutual funds, don't start dabbling in individual stocks.

Or if you're determined to invest in a company you have good reason to believe is going to rise in value, think of it for what it is: a gamble. And don't invest money you aren't prepared to lose.

How Does Stock Investing Work?

For those who've forgotten Econ 101, here's the basic concept: You buy an ownership share of a company. Your money helps the company grow and prosper, and you gain a proportional (small) share of control over the company. Because there's a public market for these ownership shares, you can wait until stock in your chosen company is selling at a higher price and then sell your shares. Also, if you hold onto your stock for a year or more, the company may decide to send you an annual dividend. Of course, the price of your shares may also go down, either because the company is doing badly or because other investors believe it's going to do badly. You could lose your entire investment.

Can They Retire Young and Rich?

Last year, Kathy interviewed Luke and Hannah Wickham, a couple with "lofty financial aspirations." One goal is to amass $10 million by the time they retire in their 50s (she's now 28, he's 30). The Wickhams were already saving 20% or more of their income per year, and had built up $157,000, with nearly $44,000 sitting in eight individual stocks, $50,000 in bank accounts in case of emergencies (but earning only about 2%), and the rest in a mix of funds in their Roth IRA and 401(k) accounts.

On the liabilities side, they owe $471,000 on four real estate investment properties, have $10,000 in student-loan debt, growing at a 4.63% rate, but no credit card debt.

Kathy asked a financial planner, "Are the Wickhams on their way to riches?" The answer:

The Wickhams have made "tremendous" strides in building their portfolio, but they should minimize investment risk to protect it, says Charlie Fitzgerald, a financial planner in Maitland, Florida.

This means: Diversifying assets. Cutting expenses. Rethinking investment expectations.

The planner recommends that the Wickhams reduce their investment risk by getting out of the eight individual stocks. Over time, they should redirect this money into no-load stock funds from providers such as Vanguard and Barclays, he says.

The Wickhams' portfolio is overweight in large-company stocks and funds. They should consider revamping it by putting 40% in large-company funds and 20% each in midsize, small-company, and foreign-stock mutual funds, Fitzgerald says.

A pure stock portfolio is fine for now, according to the planner, but they should gradually add bonds to their portfolio as they get older. He recommends a 60% stock, 40% bond mix when the Wickhams retire.

Can They Retire Young and Rich? (cont'd)

Fitzgerald says the Wickhams' goal of having $10 million when they retire in their 50s seems "overly ambitious." The planner points out that the couple would actually need $18 million upon retirement to have the spending power of $10 million today, assuming a 3% annual inflation rate.

Fitzgerald suggests the Wickhams focus instead on the amount of money they'll need each year to achieve their desired lifestyle in retirement. For instance, because they want to travel during retirement, if they plan to spend $150,000 a year in retirement—double what they're spending now—they would probably have enough money to quit working when they turn 60, Fitzgerald says.

The planner's estimate assumes the couple continue saving at least $30,000 a year and their retirement accounts and real estate investments grow annually by 10% and 4%, respectively, to a combined $10.6 million (or $4.4 million in today's dollars, after adjusting for inflation.)

The Wickhams can maximize returns on their $50,000 cash stash by transferring however much they don't need for daily expenses into a money market account.

That could bring in hundreds of extra dollars per year, according to Fitzgerald, because money market accounts pay as much as 4.7% interest right now. These accounts are also liquid, so the funds are easily accessible.

 "Can they retire young and rich? Goal is $10M by their 50s," by Kathy Chu, January 8, 2007.

Three Things to Remember When You Invest

There's no magic investing strategy that works for everyone. You have to decide what feels right, based on all sorts of factors that are unique to you and your family: what you're saving for, how much you can afford to invest, how much risk makes you uneasy, and more. But no matter how you want to direct your investments, some basic principles apply:

- diversify and balance your holdings
- keep costs low, and
- don't panic during downturns.

Maybe there's actually a fourth principle, one to remember when all your choices threaten to become overwhelming: Keep it simple. As John advises, "Simplicity is a virtue, especially in investing. You can build a simple and powerful portfolio with no more than five funds." Don't make yourself crazy!

Diversify and balance your portfolio

Everyone gets the basic concept of not putting all your eggs in one basket. In the investment context, that means putting your money into a mix of different investment types, in order to reduce your overall risk. It doesn't just mean choosing a bunch of different stocks, or even a bunch of different mutual funds. True diversification means deciding on a percentage of your money to put in higher-risk investments such as stocks, and lower-risk investments such as bonds. So even if all your holdings are in some form of mutual fund, you've got to look at where those funds are investing and make sure they collectively give you the diversification you want.

Here's how John illustrates the basic concept: "If you own several different types of stock funds, you'll probably find that diversification breaks down when you need it most—in a big decline. If the stock market has a big down day in New York, for example, international funds won't help you much, because overseas markets will probably crumble, too." Bonds, however, will often hold their value during a stock market decline.

How should you divvy up your money? To some extent, the answer depends on your tolerance for risk. It also depends on your age. If you expect to have many years ahead to catch up from downturns in high-risk investments, you can take more chances, betting on higher returns. However, the closer you get to retirement, the more conservative you need to be. You don't want all your money in volatile investments when you might need to take it out soon. John advises, "If you have ten years or more before retirement, most of your money should be in stocks, which usually return more than bonds over the long haul. One rule of thumb: Subtract your age from 125. The remainder is the amount you should have in stocks. So if you're 50, you should have 75% of your assets in stocks, with the rest in bonds."

Even after choosing your funds based on John's formula, you'll need to revisit your choices regularly, and do some "rebalancing." The reason your investments can't simmer along unattended is that, if one sector does particularly well, such as stocks, its value will expand within your portfolio, and add up to a greater percentage allocation. Sandra explains, "Suppose your strategy is to invest 60% in stocks and 40% in bonds. If the stock market fares well for several years, you could end up with 70% in stocks and 30% in bonds. That might be a riskier portfolio than you want."

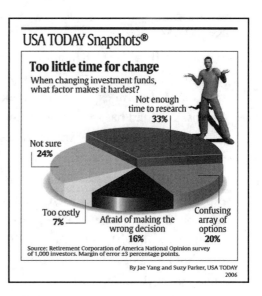

USA TODAY Snapshots®

Too little time for change
When changing investment funds, what factor makes it hardest?

Not enough time to research
33%

Not sure
24%

Too costly
7%

Afraid of making the wrong decision
16%

Confusing array of options
20%

Source: Retirement Corporation of America National Opinion survey of 1,000 investors. Margin of error ±3 percentage points.

By Jae Yang and Suzy Parker, USA TODAY 2006

Rebalancing may not be fun: As Christopher Davis, an analyst with Morningstar, told USA TODAY, it's "a painful thing for some investors to do. It means selling your winners and putting money into the laggards." Most planners suggest rebalancing once a year or if your allocation falls more than five percentage points out of whack. That way, adds Davis, "you're giving yourself some leeway to let your winners run but not taking on too much risk." Of course, John adds, "don't stick with long-term losers." If a fund has been doing worse than your other choices over the last two to three years, dump it.

TIP
With 401(k)s, you can let someone else do the rebalancing.
Sandra notes, "More than a quarter of 401(k) plans offer automatic rebalancing. This lets employees choose an investment mix for their portfolios; the plan then rebalances it each quarter to keep it in line with the target portfolio. An easier option is to invest in a target retirement fund," as described above.

Keep costs down

Between your 401(k), IRA, and regular, taxable investments, it's likely that you'll put most of your money into mutual funds, including index funds. But, as John explains, funds, like any other business, incur expenses. A fund has to pay for prospectuses, managers, and teak-paneled conference rooms. To pay those expenses, the average fund charges about 1.5% of assets each year in fees, which reduces your returns.

Over time, fees add up. Suppose your fund earned 11.5% before expenses. A $1,000 investment would become $26,000 in 30 years. But you actually earned 10%, after your fund took its 1.5 percentage points, so your $10,000 became $17,500—a $7,500 difference. Rather than holding a dozen average funds, you'd be better off owning a single highly diversified low-cost index fund as your core holding.

To find out what fees a mutual fund is charging, check a document called its "prospectus," where federal law requires its fees and expenses to be disclosed. Your employer probably won't hand you a stack of these if you're investing through your 401(k), but you can normally find fund prospectuses online.

Ride out the market's ups and downs

One of the biggest mistakes made by novice investors is to panic and sell any fund that goes down in value, or madly shift all their holdings into one that goes up. But this short-term approach will often lead only to higher transaction costs and a loss of long-term profits.

In fact, as Sandra explains, "Rearranging your 401(k) every time the market has a good (or bad) day isn't rebalancing. That's market timing, and it rarely works. Because market trends don't change overnight, there's no harm in keeping your front-runners for a while."

One of the biggest areas of volatility will be your stock funds. But, as John counsels, "The stock market's ups and downs are one reason that, over time, it produces higher returns than, say, ultrasafe Treasury bills. Risk and reward are two sides of the same coin. Your best bet, if you're a long-term investor, is to try to ignore the market's short-term ups and downs. Over long periods of time—ten years or more—you'll get your best returns from stocks."

The key is to keep your eyes on the long term. As someone who is working toward future goals, you actually have an advantage over those investors who may need to get in and out of the market quickly. You can hang on through down times, potentially reaping greater rewards than those who buy in only when they realize that the market is already on the rise.

Getting Help: Financial Planners, Advisers, and Brokers

Try as you might to keep your investment approach simple, the financial world can confound your efforts, with its cryptic terminology and perpetual new product offerings. No wonder an increasing number of Americans look for professional advice. (You might hear a rule of thumb suggesting you see an adviser after your income hits $100,000, but this really depends on your own comfort level with financial matters.) Yet the professionals themselves come with a confusing array of titles and an alphabet soup of acronyms after their names. The one thing that unites many of them is intense competition for your business. Financial advice-givers fall into three main categories:

- **Financial planners,** who look at all aspects of your financial life, from investment to tax to retirement, and come up with a plan to coordinate them. The best ones are "fiduciaries," meaning they have a legal obligation to put your interests first (especially important if they earn commissions on your stock trades).

- **Investment advisers,** who give investment advice about stocks, bonds, or mutual funds. They're all legally obligated to act solely in your best interests, as fiduciaries.

- **Brokers (or stockbrokers),** who are licensed to buy and sell securities (stocks, bonds, or mutual funds) for you. They're not fiduciaries, but must choose investments that are "suitable" or "appropriate" for you.

Some people do more than one of the above things at a time, or call themselves, for instance, financial planners when they're really acting as brokers. To sort through the possibilities, ask friends and colleagues for recommendations. Then find out these four things about anyone you consider hiring:

- What are the person's credentials?
- How will you pay for services—flat fee, commission, or percentage fee?
- What services will be included?
- Will the person be serving your interests (in a fiduciary relationship) or can this person also act as a salesperson for certain products?

Unfortunately, you won't be able to check client references, for confidentiality reasons. But you can ask for names of professional references—that is, peers who know of this person's work—preferably from a different firm or brokerage house.

Credentials

It's possible for someone to graduate from college with a degree in fashion, take a few training courses, and become a financial adviser—then carry on without any government regulation, having fallen between the cracks of a patchy system. As a result, says Sandra, "the woods are littered with folks who think they can manage your finances because they made a few smart stock picks in 1998." While there's nothing wrong with people who've made career changes, you obviously want someone with more than a few months' experience.

> *The human brain gets more impulsive, not less, as you age—which can be dangerous when investing!*

A college and graduate degree (such as a Ph.D., MBA, or JD) with a concentration in finance, investing, tax, or estate planning, is a good grounding. Also look for years in the business—preferably at least five.

Next, look for training and membership credentials. A certified financial planner (CFP) designation is, says Sandra, "widely considered the gold standard for those who give financial advice." It requires taking "a two-day exam that defeats nearly half of all candidates, adhering to a code of ethics, and devoting at least 30 hours every two years to continuing education."

Other excellent credentials include the ChFC (chartered financial consultant), PFS (personal financial specialist), and NAPFA-registered financial adviser (NAPFA is the National Association of Personal Financial Advisors). You can double-check the person's credentials by contacting the appropriate organization.

You may see a whole host of other acronyms beside an adviser's name (over 35 were possible at last count), like CPA (certified public accountant), CLU (chartered life underwriter), CFS (certified fund specialist), and personal financial specialist (PFS). Rather than spend too much time deciphering these, go for a more-is-better approach—many planners get multiple certifications over the course of their career.

Finally, ask whether the adviser is registered with a government body, such as the SEC (federal Securities and Exchange Commission), a state regulatory body, or the Financial Industry Regulatory Authority (FINRA, the largest nongovernmental U.S. regulatory organization for securities brokers and dealers). If the adviser isn't registered with anyone, walking away is your safest route, because no one is overseeing the adviser's activities. If the adviser's registered with the SEC, ask to see a copy of their "ADV Form," which describes the person's background, fee arrangements, and more. Or look for the form on the SEC's website (at www.sec.gov; click "Check out Brokers and Investment Advisers").

Paying an adviser

How fees are charged is a bigger deal than it sounds. Historically, advisers and brokers charged a commission on every transaction made on an investor's behalf. But complaints arose that this model created an incentive to move your money around for little reason other than to charge you more. That led many advisers to try out new fee models. "Fee-only" is a highly regarded one, meaning the advisers' charges are based on either the size of your portfolio under management, an hourly rate, a flat-fee basis, or a combination. "Fee-based" advisers charge a hybrid of commission and fee. Below are Kathy's tips on how to pay for advice.

Which fee structure you choose will depend on the level of advice you're looking for, says James Barnash, past president of the Financial Planning Association in Denver. If you have some investment knowledge and have identified a specific area where you need help, such as buying an individual stock, then commissions or hourly fees might be appropriate.

Some investors are just "looking for a person who can provide them with a second opinion," Barnash says.

If, on the other hand, you need ongoing advice about reaching your financial goals, you might consider a fee-based adviser who charges a flat annual fee, a percentage of the assets being managed, or even a mix of commissions and fees.

Paying a percentage of assets under management can "align the interests of the adviser and the investor better because there's no incentive to churn," or trade excessively to generate commissions, says Mary Schapiro, chief executive of FINRA. Asset-based fees typically range from 0.75% to 2% of assets. When the value of your investment portfolio rises, your adviser gets greater compensation.

Services offered

As Kathy says, "Fees arc only a starting point in evaluating an adviser. Make sure you also understand the individual's approach and areas of specialty." Don't just rely on what they call themselves—as we've mentioned, words like planner and adviser can mean different things when used by different people. Ask for a detailed rundown of what the person will do for you.

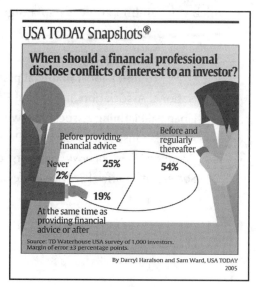

For example, the adviser's services might include goal setting, planning a budget, developing personalized tax, investment, estate, and insurance strategies, helping implement your plans (for example, by having authority to trade your assets), providing continuous oversight and advice, and more.

Whose interests come first?

Everyone will tell you that they'll give you advice that's good for you—but that may not be enough. What if, for example, an adviser sells you a perfectly respectable mutual fund that helps you save for retirement by giving you an average 6% return—but you find out later that the adviser hadn't mentioned another fund that would have given you better returns and wouldn't have given the adviser a fat commission?

This is not an unlikely scenario. Kathy found that, with brokerage houses in particular, you may be steered in the direction of the house's own products, while, "Independent advisers who don't work at large financial-services companies have less incentive to push in-house products that might not be right for you."

For these reasons, it's best to look for advisers who have a fiduciary duty to you; in other words, who will put your interests first and foremost, even when your interests conflict with the adviser's. All registered investment advisers have this duty. For other financial planners, NAPFA suggests asking them to sign a "Fiduciary Oath," which you can find at www.napfa.org.

RESOURCE

To find a local financial planner or adviser, contact:

- National Association of Personal Financial Advisors, at www.napfa.org
- Financial Planning Association, www.fpanet.org
- American Institute of Certified Public Accountants/Personal Financial Planning Division, www.aicpa.org, or
- Society of Financial Service Professionals, www.financialpro.org.

Protect Your Family

The beginning of each new year, suggests Sandra, is a good time to "take a moment to think about all the things that could go wrong in the next 12 months. Fire. Theft. Untimely death." No, she's not trying to ruin your holidays; there's a reason for this gloomy exercise. By taking steps to minimize the effects of such calamities on you and your family—unlikely though they are—you'll sleep easier the whole year round. The most important steps include:

- drafting your will
- choosing a guardian for your children
- buying life insurance
- buying disability insurance, and
- making sure you have enough homeowners' insurance.

Planning Your Estate: The Three Documents You Need (and One You Might Want)

"Estate planning"—even the term sounds fancy. And difficult. And probably expensive. The good news is that although every family should do some estate planning, it doesn't have to be complicated, hard, or costly. To take care of your family in the event of your disability or death, you need these three legal documents:

- a will
- a durable power of attorney for heath care, and
- a durable power of attorney for finances.

Those are the Big Three. You may also wish to create a living trust, which we'll also discuss. And you can confidently create all these documents yourself, without paying a lawyer. So if you're among the procrastinating majority, let's get to work.

Number 1: A will

Writing your will isn't hard to do—and think how good you'll feel when it's done. Here are the hows and whys.

I don't need a will ... do I?

"Unless you relish the thought of your relatives squabbling about your estate, you should have a will," says Sandra. "If you die without one, a court will decide who will raise your children, manage your property, and inherit your lava lamps. As unsettling as that sounds, less than half of all Americans have a will."

Many people wait until they're getting on in years to write a will.

> ### *No, you can't leave it to your pet*
>
> *Pets are considered property (sorry, we don't make these rules), and you can't leave property to property. But you can set up a trust to care for the pet (like Leona Helmsley did for her Maltese—a whopping $12 million) or give the pet—along with some money—to one of your beneficiaries.*

Before that, they may figure that their assets aren't valuable enough to worry about. Or they may have heard that state law will give everything to their relatives anyway.

But relying on state law may be worse for your family than you think, as described by Sandra: "Your state will distribute your assets, based on what's known as 'intestate succession' laws." These laws usually give the property to your closest living relatives, including your spouse, children, or parents. That's a problem if you'd like to leave, say, a memento to a dear friend, or a gift to a more distant relative or a charity. And to avoid postmortem embarrassment, maybe you'd prefer your childhood diaries or other incriminating items to be burned before anyone inherits them.

CAUTION
Part of a nontraditional couple? Sandra found that, "Most states don't recognize unmarried partners, even if you've been in a committed relationship for years. If you want your partner to inherit your estate, you need a will."

How wills work

A will is basically a set of legally binding instructions that you leave behind. It's your chance to:

- specify who you want to inherit your property
- name someone (a guardian) to raise your young children in the unlikely event that you and the other parent can't
- arrange for an adult to manage any property the children inherit, and
- name someone to be your executor (also called a personal representative), to gather your property and distribute it according to your wishes.

Appointing a personal guardian for your children

Every kid loves to read stories about orphans who make their way in the world—Anne of Green Gables, the Baudelaire siblings, Harry Potter, and more. But no child really wants to live like them. That's why with your will, you should make sure your children would be placed in nurturing and preferably familiar circumstances if the worst happened.

To do this, you use your will to name a "personal guardian" for the children. This is the person who would raise your children and be legally responsible for them. You can name an individual or a couple to take on this role. (Ask them before committing their names to paper!) Don't, of course, name two unrelated people—you want your children settled in one home. If there are two people you want to appoint for this job, name one as your first choice and the other as an alternate, to take over if necessary.

Although many parents choose a sibling or their own parents as personal guardian, others would sooner see their kids with the Dursleys (remember Harry Potter's aunt and uncle?). It's most important, of course, that you choose someone your children love and who loves them. Some other factors to consider include the person's age (you must choose an adult, at least 18 years old), reliability, location, family situation (if they already have three children, could they take on yours as well?), experience with children, and physical abilities. And if you're counting on this person to provide for your children financially, because you might not leave enough money to cover the costs of raising them, consider financial resources as well.

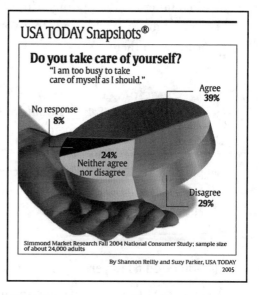

USA TODAY Snapshots®

Do you take care of yourself?
"I am too busy to take care of myself as I should."

Agree 39%

No response 8%

24% Neither agree nor disagree

Disagree 29%

Simmond Market Research Fall 2004 National Consumer Study; sample size of about 24,000 adults

By Shannon Reilly and Suzy Parker, USA TODAY 2005

This is a very tough choice for many parents. If you're having trouble, keep in mind that you can always revisit your decision in a few years, when the children are older and their relationships with your family members may have changed.

Appointing someone to manage the money

What if your best choice for personal guardian isn't much good at handling money? This is an important concern, since someone needs to manage your children's inheritance so that they're well cared for at least until adulthood. Fortunately, you can give this financial responsibility to someone other than the personal guardian.

The easiest way to name a financial guardian and ensure that this person will manage your children's inheritance in the way you choose is within your will. You can also do so using a living trust, as discussed below. You'll designate the person you've chosen as either the "custodian" of the property you leave to a child, or the "trustee" of a trust that will be created if you die while your children are still young. Either way, the adult will be in charge of investing the money your children inherit and spending it for their needs. Once the children become adults or reach an age that you specify, whatever's left will be turned over to them.

> **RESOURCE**
> *The Busy Family's Guide to Estate Planning*, by Liza Weiman Hanks (Nolo), is a great guide to the choices young families need to make. There's a whole chapter on choosing a guardian, with thoughtful, practical tips on how to get over common stumbling blocks. It also explains how to leave money to your children with a trust or custodianship.

Do you need a lawyer?

A will doesn't need to be written in fancy legal language. Nor does making one usually require hiring a lawyer, who will probably charge around $500 to $1,000 for a straightforward will, and more to deal with complexities. You can write a legally valid will yourself using a high-quality book, software program, or online service, for less than $100. Once you've created the document, follow the signing instructions carefully (you must sign your will in front of two witnesses) and you'll have a legally binding document.

You may, however, need more than a simple will. Lawyers can help you with additional documents or strategies designed to help you with specific goals such as saving on federal estate tax or making sure a child with a disability is always eligible for important government benefits. You'll want to get expert help, or at least more information, if:

- You expect to leave a very large amount of assets (say, over $2 million) and they may be subject to estate tax unless you do some tax planning.

- You want to make complex plans—for example, leaving your house in trust to your spouse for life and then having it pass to your children from a previous marriage.

- You are a small business owner and have questions as to the rights of surviving owners or your ownership share.

- You must make arrangements for long-term care of a child with a disability.

- You fear someone will go to court and contest your will on grounds of fraud or claim that you were unduly influenced or weren't of sound mind when you signed it.

- You don't want to leave your spouse much of your property (perhaps because your spouse is already well-provided for and you want most of your estate to go to children from a prior marriage). It's usually not possible to do this if your spouse objects, but a lawyer can explain your spouse's rights.

The Federal Estate Tax: Don't Worry

Many people have heard about the federal estate tax and what a big bite it takes out of property left to the next generation. But the truth is that it affects only the country's wealthiest families. According to most estimates, only about 1% of estates ever owe federal estate tax. (Some states impose their own estate taxes, but the rates are generally low.)

Through 2008, you can leave $2 million free of federal estate tax. That amount goes up to $3.5 million in 2009, and in 2010 the estate tax is scheduled to go away for a year. After that, it depends on what Congress does—but it's very unlikely that the estate tax will ever affect people of moderate wealth.

RESOURCE

Here are three highly-regarded ways to create your own will without paying a lawyer:

- *Quicken WillMaker Plus* (software developed and published by Nolo) is easy to use even if you're not computer oriented, but sophisticated enough to let you make a valid will and living trust, powers of attorney, and medical directives, that meet your wishes and are valid no matter which state you live in.

- *Nolo's Simple Will Book*, by Denis Clifford (Nolo), lets you choose a will form or assemble a customized will from a selection of clauses. All the forms are included as tear-outs and on a CD-ROM.

- The NoloNow will is an online service offered at www.nolo.com. To create your will, you just go through a simple interview online. Legal information is available at every step to make sure you understand your choices.

Number 2: Durable power of attorney for health care

It's not pleasant to think about, but a time could come when you are unable to communicate your choices about medical treatment. Accidents (car, mostly) happen.

No need to dwell on this possibility, though—just take care of it with simple documents called "durable power of attorney for health care" and "advance medical directive." (In some states, these are combined into one.) Creating these documents will let you both express your wishes about end-of-life medical care and give someone—most likely your spouse or partner—authority to carry out your wishes and make decisions for you if you're incapacitated.

Creating a power of attorney means you appoint someone to act on your behalf if you can't. That person is called your "attorney-in-fact." (It's important that the power of attorney be "durable" because that means that unlike a regular power of attorney, it will still be be effective if you become incapacitated.) Your spouse or partner will probably be your first choice. But you should also name a backup person, just in case.

These documents may never be used. But if they do ever come into play, your family will be profoundly grateful for any guidance you offered them. It can head off family fights, uncertainty, and guilt over these tough decisions.

Many healthy folks think there's no reason to prepare an advance directive or durable power of attorney for health care. But remember that it's often younger people who face the most difficult end-of-life issues, precisely because their relatively healthy bodies can be kept alive longer— giving family members more time to agonize and perhaps, argue.

> **RESOURCE**
> *Quicken WillMaker Plus* **(software developed and published by Nolo)** lets you make durable powers of attorney and medical directives, tailored to the law of your state.

Number 3: Durable power of attorney for finances

There's one more thing you should take care of when you're getting your estate planning documents in order: giving someone the authority to handle your finances if you're ever unable to do so.

You do this with a durable power of attorney for finances, an important but easily overlooked document. Designating such a person in advance can save your family the hassle and expense of obtaining a court order later, in the midst of an emergency. (And if you and your partner aren't married, obtaining this court order could be especially troublesome.) If you were, for example, in the ICU under heavy sedation, you'd want someone to be immediately able to write checks on your accounts to pay your bills or suspend your gym membership.

As Sandra explains, "Married couples often assume their spouses will handle their financial affairs if one becomes incapacitated. It's not always that simple. Without durable power of attorney, your spouse may not be able to sell property that is in your name or jointly owned. Your spouse can ask to be named your conservator, and judges usually grant those requests. But awarding durable power of attorney makes that unnecessary." However, "For the person with durable power of attorney to have access to your bank and brokerage accounts, you may need to fill out forms from those institutions." And they may require you to update the forms regularly, so pay close attention to their rules.

Sandra adds, "You can draft the power of attorney so it becomes effective as soon as you sign it, or you can specify that it won't go into effect unless a doctor certifies you're incapacitated. The latter is known as a 'springing' durable power of attorney." You can also make the power as broad or as limited as you want.

> **RESOURCE**
> *Quicken WillMaker Plus* **(software developed and published by Nolo)** lets you make a durable power of attorney for finances that meets the requirements of your state's laws.

Number 4: A living trust

A living trust does almost everything a will does, though rarely does it completely replace your need to write a will. The reason to create one is that it lets your family avoid costly and lengthy probate court proceedings after your death. The probate court process, during which assets are gathered, creditors paid, and property eventually distributed, can drag on for months, leaving property in limbo and heirs frustrated. Living trusts can usually be wrapped up much more quickly, with much less expense. And the small amount of property left to be dealt with under the will probably won't need to go through probate, as many states have "small estate" exceptions.

A living trust is pretty simple to create and maintain. You create a document called a declaration (or instrument) of trust, which looks a lot like a will. It creates your trust and names you as trustee—the person in charge of trust assets. As trustee, you have total power over the trust during your lifetime. You are free to transfer ownership of your bank accounts, real estate, and other property into and out of the trust, or even dissolve the trust altogether. If any of the trust property earns income, you simply report it on your regular tax return—you don't need to file a tax return for the trust.

Is there any reason not to create a living trust? Despite their undeniable benefits, they aren't for everyone. Here are some things to consider:

A little more work up front. Compared to wills, trusts take a bit more work to set up. That's because you must officially transfer assets into the trust, which requires preparing deeds and filling out paperwork for every bank account, house, car, or other item of property you want transferred into the trust.

No benefit now. If you're in your 40s or 50s, you've probably got a long time to live—and the living trust doesn't confer any benefits until after your death, when it makes things easier on your family. You may want to wait until later in life to take on this task.

You'll still need a will. Making a trust doesn't let you off the hook for preparing a will; the will covers any property that you don't get around to transferring into the trust during your life, and lets you name a personal guardian for your children—something you can't do in a trust.

There may be easier ways to avoid probate. If probate avoidance is on your mind, check out other ways to accomplish the same end for certain items of your property. As Sandra suggests, "You can set up payable-on-death accounts at your bank, which will automatically transfer money in your bank to your heirs upon your death. Most states will let you establish transfer-on-death accounts for stocks, mutual funds, and other investments. Joint ownership of shared assets is another option." Just make sure to review these regularly—unlike a living trust, these arrangements may not allow you to name alternate beneficiaries in case one dies.

If you decide you need a living trust, you can easily create it yourself. But hire a lawyer if your estate is large or complicated. The lawyer will probably charge you at least $1,000.

RESOURCE
Some great options to help you form a living trust include:
- *Quicken WillMaker Plus* (software developed and published by Nolo) provides a reliable, inexpensive way to make a valid living trust.
- *Make Your Own Living Trust*, by Denis Clifford (Nolo), shows you how to create a living trust and hold property in trust. All the forms are included as tear-outs and on a CD-ROM.

Where to keep your will and other important documents

Once you've drafted your will and other estate planning documents or instructions, keep the signed originals in a safe but accessible place. If you keep the originals in a safe deposit box, your family may not be able to get to them without your permission—a huge problem if you're incapacitated. Give copies of the health care documents to your doctor. And don't forget to tell your spouse, or whomever you've named as your "attorney in fact," where the documents are.

And, as Bob Clyatt, author of *Work Less, Live More: The New Way to Retire Early* (Nolo), told John, "As you're collecting your documents and putting them in one place, make sure your spouse knows the passwords to your online financial accounts. It could make a hard time a bit easier."

RESOURCE
For help getting your records in order: See *Get It Together*, by Melanie Cullen and Shae Irving (Nolo). This workbook provides a complete system for structuring and organizing a records binder.

Do You Have a Disabled Child?

If you have a child with special needs, one of your primary worries may be how the child will be cared for once you're gone. But, Sandra says, nearly a third of such parents have made no plans for their child's financial future, according to a MetLife survey.

And while 60% of parents said their special needs child will require lifetime care, the majority hadn't even prepared a will, says Nadine Vogel, founder of MetLife's special-needs division.

For a child with special needs, the consequences of poor financial planning can be catastrophic. If you die without a will, your child may inherit some or all of your estate. A disabled individual with more than $2,000 in assets is ineligible for most government benefits, such as Supplemental Social Security and Medicaid.

While you may not like the idea of relying on the government to care for your child, most families have no other choice, says Ron Pearson, a Virginia Beach financial planner and father of two adult sons who have developmental disabilities.

Housing and medical expenses for a disabled adult who lives in a group home typically exceed $50,000 a year, he says. To generate enough annual income to meet those costs, you would need a minimum of $1 million in savings, he says.

A financial alternative that will preserve your child's eligibility for government programs is a special-needs trust, sometimes known as a supplemental trust. The money can't be used to pay for necessities, such as food and shelter. But it can be used for non-essential expenses, such as vacations, DVDs, and movies.

To prepare a special-needs trust, you'll need professional help, such as a financial planner, and an attorney who is knowledgeable about your state's laws. Advocacy groups, such as The Arc, can suggest qualified professionals.

 "Securing future for a disabled child," Sandra Block, June 24, 2005.

RESOURCE

For more information on protecting a child with disabilities, see:

- *Special Needs Trusts: Protect Your Child's Financial Future*, by Stephen Elias (Nolo), which explains how special needs trusts work and how to set one up so that you won't jeopardize eligibility for important government benefits.
- The Arc of the United States, www.thearc.org, which represents people with mental retardation and their families.
- Special Needs Alliance, www.specialneedsalliance.com, a network of lawyers specializing in disabilities law.
- Financial Planning Association, www.fpanet.org, which can give you names of certified financial planners who specialize in special-needs issues.
- MetLife's special-needs division, which offers a calculator to help estimate your child's future expenses, at www.metlifeiseasier.com/metdesk.

Get Life Insurance

As Sandra says, "Nobody wants to talk about life insurance"— that is, insurance that pays, at your death, a specified amount to the beneficiaries you've named. But, she advises, if you have young children or others who depend on you, you should have it. Millions of Americans have no life insurance, and millions more don't have enough to provide financial security for their loved ones. That's a shame, because if you're reasonably healthy, you can buy a lot of life insurance without spending a lot of money. Average premiums for individual life insurance have been falling about 5% a year since 2000, according to the Insurance Information Institute. In 2007, a 40-year-old male non-smoker who buys a $500,000, 20-year term insurance policy will pay an annual premium of $615 if he qualifies for the "standard" rate, the institute estimates. If he qualifies for the "preferred" rate, which has more stringent health requirements, he'll pay $340, the institute says.

Life insurers have reduced their premiums because people are living longer, lowering the risk that the insurers will have to pay benefits to survivors, says Steven Weisbart, an economist for the institute. Insurers have also developed more sophisticated ways to measure the risks of certain lifestyles and diseases, says Michael Kalen, executive vice president for The Hartford's individual life division.

Here are some additional tips from Sandra for buying life insurance:

- **To save money, buy term insurance.** There are two types of life insurance: term and permanent. Term provides a benefit only if you die during the period covered by the policy. Permanent life insurance remains in effect as long as you pay the premiums. Part of the premium goes into an investment account. You can withdraw some of that money or borrow against your policy. Premiums for permanent life insurance are considerably higher than premiums for term insurance. If your goal is to provide financial security for your children until they're old enough to support themselves, a term policy is probably all you need. If you still need insurance at the end of the term, some insurers will let you renew your coverage, but you may have to undergo a medical exam to get the lowest rate. Permanent policies are appropriate for people

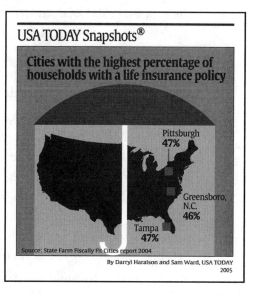

USA TODAY Snapshots®

Cities with the highest percentage of households with a life insurance policy

Pittsburgh
47%

Greensboro, N.C.
46%

Tampa
47%

Source: State Farm Fiscally Fit Cities report 2004

By Darryl Haralson and Sam Ward, USA TODAY 2005

who use insurance as part of an estate-planning strategy and want the policy to last until they die, Kalen says.

- **Don't rely on your employer's life insurance policy.** Many companies offer life insurance as a benefit, but it's usually not enough to provide financial security for your family, Kalen says. Most workplace policies cover one to two times your annual salary. Financial planners generally recommend buying enough insurance to replace seven to ten times your annual salary. In addition, most employer-provided policies aren't portable. If you change jobs, there's no guarantee your new employer will offer a life insurance benefit. If you've had health problems, the cost of buying an individual policy may be prohibitive. Buying your own life policy while you're young and healthy "is a much more stable financial strategy," Weisbart says.

- **If you have health problems, don't assume you're uninsurable.** Advances in the treatment of cancer and other diseases have led insurers to lower premiums for people once considered high-risk. In the past year, Hartford has reduced premiums for women who have been treated for early-stage breast cancer and men who have had surgery for moderate levels of prostate cancer. Prudential announced that it will lower premiums for people who have been successfully treated for heart disease.

- **Shop around.** Though insurance companies have reduced premiums for some people, they've also tightened the criteria for their lowest rates, Udell says. Even if you're healthy, you may not qualify for the best rates—often known as "preferred plus"—if one of your parents suffered from a serious illness at an early age, or if you enjoy skydiving. The standards for the best rates vary among insurers, so it pays to work with an insurance agent or broker who deals with several companies. On a $500,000 term policy, getting the lowest rate on premiums could save you $100 to $250 a year, Udell says. "Over 20 years, you're talking about a lot of money."

> **TIP**
> **Got life insurance?** In that case, John advises, "You probably don't need credit insurance" (also called "credit life insurance"—it's designed to pay off certain of your debts if you die). It's widely viewed as a ripoff, with the premiums too high to justify the likely payoff. John advises, "Just make sure you have enough life insurance to cover your debts."

In Case You Can't Work: Get Disability Insurance

Lack of disability insurance is "consistently the most gaping hole that we see in someone's financial affairs," says Mark Bass, a financial planner in Lubbock, Texas, talking to USA TODAY reporter Mindy Fetterman. Other planners agree that it's the one insurance item that tends to slip through the cracks for people in their 40s who are busy raising kids, working, and paying mortgages. Disability can be "economic death," Bass says. "You need to either live or die. In between is deadly."

Here's how a team of USA TODAY writers describe the problem—and the solution:

Many people don't realize that you're much more likely to become disabled than to die during your working years.

Disability insurance gives you income to meet daily expenses if you can't work because of injury or illness. Employers typically provide some disability coverage as part of a benefits package. But women are less likely to be eligible for this benefit because they work part time, earn less, and rely on spousal health care coverage more than men do.

The risk of not having this insurance is that if the unexpected occurs, you'll have to tap your retirement savings to support yourself and your family.

"One-third of Americans will have a disability that will cause them to stop working for at least 90 days before age 65," says Todd Katz, senior vice president at MetLife. "People don't think about that. They think, 'It's not me. I'm healthy.'"

Social Security provides disability benefits based on your salary and the number of years you've been covered under the program, but only if you can't perform any "gainful" job—not just the one you were doing when you became disabled.

To see if you have enough income to support yourself without tapping retirement funds, add up the benefits you expect to receive from group disability coverage and the government. Throw in any monthly income from investments and alimony.

If this monthly income exceeds your share of the family's expenses, then you have enough to support yourself and your family should you become disabled. If you fall short, consider shopping for more disability coverage.

"When you think about your most important asset, it's your ability to earn an income," Katz says.

How much you'll need to spend for a quality disability insurance policy depends on factors such as your age, line of work, and the level of benefits you'll receive. On average, however, you can expect to pay between 1% and 3% of your annual salary.

RESOURCE

More on disability insurance. You'll find insurance carriers that sell this product at www.healthdecisions.org, and tips on disability policy terms and restrictions at the Life and Health Insurance Foundation for Education's website, www.life-line.org.

Own a Home?
Double-Check Your Homeowners' Insurance

If you own a home, you no doubt already have homeowners' insurance. The standard policy includes:

- hazard insurance, to cover physical damage or loss involving your property and possessions (as required by mortgage lenders), and
- liability insurance, to cover injuries to people on your property or caused by members of your household (including pets).

But how closely have you read your policy? And have you updated it lately? Many homeowners are shocked, after the fact, to find that it doesn't cover them for certain types of major damage (think Hurricane Katrina) or pays an inadequate portion of their loss. Review your policy using the guidance below. Then talk to your insurance rep about changes, or shop around for better—or cheaper—insurance. No one says you have to keep the same policy forever. And there's no need to wait for your annual renewal: As Kathy advises, "In most cases, you can update your homeowners' policy and have new coverage limits take effect immediately."

USA TODAY Snapshots®

Property crime rates dip

Property crimes per 1,000 households, by region: 1994 2004

236.6
107.1 Northeast

436.1

295.2
168.8

204

West   Midwest

288.6 South
158.3

Source: Bureau of Justice Statistics

By David Stuckey and Dave Merrill, USA TODAY
2005

Are you at risk for damage your hazard insurance won't cover?

The list of damage and disasters your hazard insurance probably compensates you (and your lender) for is surprisingly long: physical damage to your property and its contents caused by fire and smoke, wind, hail, lightning, explosions, volcanoes, riots and vandalism, theft, water damage, and similar events.

Nevertheless, that list doesn't cover everything that could happen. Check the boilerplate section of your policy called "exclusions." Flooding and earthquakes are commonly excluded from coverage—even though many homeowners assume otherwise. It's also typical for policies to exclude damage caused by mudslides, police activity, power outages, sewer backups, dry rot, vermin, war, nuclear perils, losses if your house is vacant for 60 days or more, or losses caused by your own poor maintenance or your failure to preserve or protect the property after it's been damaged.

Insurance companies often don't want to sell you coverage for these high-risk, high-expense types of damage. But there are exceptions, where you can buy extra coverage from your insurance company or from another source (as is common with flood and earthquake insurance). The key is to buy added coverage for hazards that can cause huge damage (like sewer backups), or are big risks in the area where you live—like earthquakes in parts of California, hurricanes along the Gulf Coast and Eastern Seaboard, or local concerns such as sinkholes in parts of Florida.

Would your hazard coverage pay to rebuild your house?

Let's take the most unlikely (but scary) scenario: A fire or other hazard ruins your house. You might then expect your insurance company to pay for it to be rebuilt, just as it was; but what will actually happen depends on the terms of your policy.

The norm: replacement cost coverage. If your house is destroyed, the amount you receive to rebuild under a standard policy, with "replacement cost" coverage, will be a set dollar figure, which you'll see in the policy. That figure was calculated in advance, without an insurance representative actually seeing your property. Remember that long phone call or questionnaire when you first got the policy, in which you described your house's size, location, number and type of rooms, building materials, amenities, and more?

But your replacement cost figure could be way off the mark, par-ticularly if building costs have gone up, a widespread natural disaster increases demand for contractors, or your house has historical features that will be hard to recreate. In fact, Kathy found that "Close to 60% of U.S. homes are undervalued—with the average home undervalued by 22%, according to Marshall & Swift/Boeckh, which provides building-cost information. That means homeowners often don't have enough insurance to rebuild their home if disaster struck."

Ask a local contractor how much a house of a similar size, with similar features, would cost to build. If your insurance will be low, either work with your insurance rep to raise your replacement cost figure or buy an "inflation guard," which raises the stated value of your house by a set percentage annually.

The ideal: guaranteed replacement coverage. If you look hard (and pay more), you may find a policy that guarantees payment of 100% of your repair or rebuilding costs, without any limits. This rare creature is called a "guaranteed replacement cost" policy. If your house has historical features that are hard to reproduce, finding such a policy will be especially difficult.

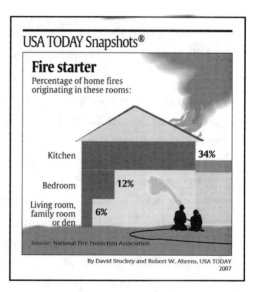

USA TODAY Snapshots®

Fire starter
Percentage of home fires originating in these rooms:

Kitchen — 34%
Bedroom — 12%
Living room, family room or den — 6%

Source: National Fire Protection Association

By David Stuckey and Robert W. Ahrens, USA TODAY
2007

To be avoided: actual cash value coverage. If your insurance policy pays the "actual cash value" of your house, start looking for new coverage. Cash value policies are sometimes pushed on people with older houses or ones with an inadequate water supply (a fire danger). You'll get the house's replacement cost minus any depreciation or wear and tear that it's suffered since being built. For example, notes Kathy, they might deduct for a roof that needed to be replaced. Experts agree you're likely to end up with an insufficient amount with which to rebuild.

> **TIP**
> **Advise your insurance company about remodels or upgrades.**
> Sandra discovered that, "Nearly 40% of Americans who have made
> significant home improvements since 2003, such as adding a room or
> deck, said they hadn't updated their homeowners' insurance, or weren't
> sure if they had. That could be disastrous if your home is destroyed,
> according to Madelyn Flannagan, a spokeswoman for Trusted Choice (a
> network of insurance agencies). If your policy is based on the value of
> your home before you remodeled, you may not recoup the money you
> spent to add a bathroom or update your kitchen." By the same token,
> some changes may qualify you for a discount, such as your having
> stopped smoking, or having installed deadbolts or a burglar alarm.

Would your living costs be covered while your house is being rebuilt?

If your house needs major repairs or rebuilding, you probably don't
want to pitch a tent on your property. Standard policies include a "loss
of use" provision, to cover the extra costs of living elsewhere. Hotel bills
and restaurant meals, for example, would be covered for up to one year,
under typical policies. Two years would be better, giving you time to find
an architect or contractor (which can be tough after a major flood or
wildfire), develop plans, and actually build.

Some policies place a dollar limit (instead of a time limit) on your
living expenses, often 20% of the total insurance on your house. If that's
the case with yours, calculate the average rental and utility costs in your
area and figure out whether the amount will be enough.

Will your coverage be enough to replace personal possessions?

You'll want to be able to replace the stuff inside your house—jewelry,
television, refrigerator, and more—if they're lost, stolen, or damaged.
See whether your policy offers "replacement value," meaning the actual
cost of buying a new item. The alternative, "actual cash value," is far less

satisfactory. You'll get the amount your stuff would sell for used, taking depreciation into account. It's not far from estimating how much your things would sell for on eBay.

Got expensive items needing separate coverage?

Talk to the insurance rep if you've acquired any big-ticket items such as jewelry, cameras, sports equipment, musical instruments, electronics, furs, firearms, coins, or silver. In a standard policy, separate limits may apply to these if they're stolen, usually between $1,000 and $2,000 in total. You'll need to pay more for endorsements insuring each such item for its appraised value—but it may be well worth it, because thefts are among your most likely losses. This extra coverage will also take care of "accidental disappearance," such as dropping your emerald ring overboard while fishing.

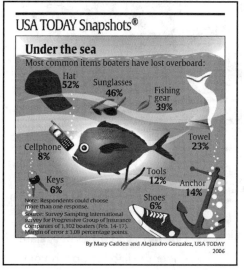

USA TODAY Snapshots®

Under the sea
Most common items boaters have lost overboard:

Hat **52%**
Sunglasses **46%**
Fishing gear **39%**
Cellphone **8%**
Towel **23%**
Keys **6%**
Tools **12%**
Anchor **14%**
Shoes **6%**

Note: Respondents could choose more than one response.
Source: Survey Sampling International survey for Progressive Group of Insurance Companies of 1,102 boaters (Feb. 14-17). Margin of error ± 3.08 percentage points.

By Mary Cadden and Alejandro Gonzalez, USA TODAY 2006

Will your liability coverage be enough if someone is injured?

Liability insurance compensates you and the people who visit your property for two things:

- **Medical payments to others.** This pays the medical bills of people from outside your household who are accidentally injured while on your property or by you or a household member, including a pet, whether on your property or elsewhere.

- **Personal liability.** If you're sued, this covers your legal fees and any amounts a court orders you to pay, such as medical expenses and lost wages, to someone who was injured or whose property was damaged by someone in your household (human or animal).

USA TODAY Snapshots®

Watch where you lay things

Top five possessions dog owners said their dogs damaged because of chewing habits:

Shoes	39%
Furniture	38%
Clothing	26%
Kids' toys	20%
Electronic equipment	15%

Source: TheHealthyChew.com   By David Stuckey and Dave Merrill, USA TODAY 2006

Standard homeowners' policies have traditionally provided around $100,000 in liability coverage. However, that's going up, and for good reason. You can easily imagine how someone's medical bills could top that amount. And if you're sued, you could end up paying even more. Rather than putting your house at risk of being sold to pay a court judgment, simply make sure your liability coverage is at a realistic level, between $500,000 and $1 million.

How Badly Do You Want That Puppy?

Dog bites and other pet-related injuries are supposed to be covered under the liability portion of your homeowners' insurance. However, if after buying the policy, you bring home a dog with a history of aggressive behavior, or whose breed the company (fairly or unfairly) considers likely to bite, your company might be able, under the terms of the policy, to refuse coverage if the dog causes an injury. And some companies will then raise your premium or cancel the entire policy.

So check with your insurance company before you bring home a rottweiler, Doberman, German shepherd, chow chow, pit bull, husky, or other breed whose reputation has been questioned.

Also be prepared to pay more or have your liability coverage cancelled based on your snake, alligator, spider, or exotic bird.

Is your deductible too low?

A deductible is the amount you must pay after a loss before your insurance company steps in. Most homeowners agree to a $500 deductible (for the hazard portion; liability insurance doesn't normally carry a deductible). However, raising your deductible can be a great financial move. It not only allows you to significantly reduce your premium costs, but also prevents you from being too quick to call your insurer for coverage. The more claims you make, the more likely the insurer is to raise your premiums or cancel your policy. ●

Index

Fialkow, Gail, 216

FICO expansion score, 50

FICO score, 44, 45

 See also Credit score

Fiduciaries, 238, 242

Finances, durable power of attorney for finances, 251–252

Financial aid, for college, 209–210

Financial evacuation box, 85

Financial guardian, 247–248

Financial planners, 238

Financial planners/advisers, 237–242

Financial planning

 advisers and planners, 237–242

 education savings, 196, 209–216

 emergency reserve fund, 68–84, 219

 retirement savings, 105–107, 197–208

 See also Budgeting; Estate planning; Family spending plan

Financial Planning Association, 256

Fireproof safe, 37

Fitzgerald, Charlie, 232–233

529 college-savings plan, 95–96, 211–216

Fixed-rate mortgages, 170–171, 190, 192, 193

Flexible health spending accounts (FSAs), 129, 130–133

Florida, 262

Food

 college meal plan, 108

 spending on, 18

Forbearance

 mortgage, 187

student loans, 61–62

Foreclosure, 186–189

Forgiven loans, 181, 188

401(k) account

 loan against, 83–84, 214–215

 rebalancing, 236

 as retirement savings, 204–206

403(b) plan, 204

Franklin, Benjamin, 75

"Free checking," 78

Friends, borrowing down payment money from, 178–184

FSAs. *See* Flexible health spending accounts

"Full retirement age," Social Security, 202

FundAlarm, 224

Furnishings, for college student, 109

G

Gender stereotypes, about money, 9

Generation Y, 101

Gift cards, 33

Gifts

 charitable gifts, tax deductibility of, 157–158

 holiday spending, 33

 loan as, 182

Gift tax, 98–99

Good faith estimate, closing costs on mortgage, 191

Goodwill, donations to, 158

Government bonds, 220

Grandparents' financial gifts to children, 94–99

 contributions to child's Roth IRA, 98

Nolo
950 Parker Street
Berkeley, CA 94710-9867
www.nolo.com

- -

YOUR LEGAL COMPANION

Get the Latest in the L

1 **Nolo's Legal Updater**
We'll send you an email whenever a new edition of your book is published! Sign up at **www.nolo.com/legalupdater**.

2 **Updates at Nolo.com**
Check **www.nolo.com/update** to find recent changes in the law that affect the current edition of your book.

3 **Nolo Customer Service**
To make sure that this edition of the book is the most recent one, call us at **800-728-3555** and ask one of our friendly customer service representatives (7:00 am to 6:00 pm PST, weekdays only). Or find out at **www.nolo.com**.

4 **Complete the Registration & Comment Card ...**
... and we'll do the work for you! Just indicate your preferences below:

- - - - - - - - - - - - - - - - - - - -

Registration & Comment Card

NAME _____ DATE _____

ADDRESS _____

CITY _____ STATE _____ ZIP _____

PHONE _____ EMAIL _____

COMMENTS _____

WAS THIS BOOK EASY TO USE?   (VERY EASY)   5   4   3   2   1   (VERY DIFFICULT)

☐ Yes, you can quote me in future Nolo promotional materials. *Please include phone number a*

☐ Yes, send me **Nolo's Legal Updater** via email when a new edition of this book is available.

Yes, I want to sign up for the following email newsletters:

- ☐ **NoloBriefs** (monthly)
- ☐ **Nolo's Special Offer** (monthly)
- ☐ **Nolo's BizBriefs** (monthly)
- ☐ **Every Landlord's Quarterly** (four times a year)

☐ Yes, you can give my contact info to carefully selected partners whose products may be of interest to me.

US-MONY1

NOL

T